'In this stunning collection, a stellar lineup of television scholars explains why *Mad Men* is the most important work of "filmed entertainment" on any American screen in the past decade – including *The Sopranos*, which may have ushered in a new golden age of American television, but has been long since eclipsed by this brilliant series. And while building the case that original cable series like *Mad Men* are now the gold standard in contemporary American culture, this compendium of consistently compelling, insightful essays also indicates that the most exciting work in media studies today is being done by television scholars.'
– **Thomas Schatz**, University of Texas

'Gary Edgerton brings together leading TV scholars who think about the creators, stories, visual design, and cultural significance of AMC's break away hit. A terrific set of essays that not only sheds light on *Mad Men* but also on the role that TV plays in depicting the American dreams – and nightmares – of the Baby Boom past.'
– **Lynn Spigel**, University of Wisconsin

'Matthew Weiner's *Mad Men* is all about the hidden meanings behind sleek surfaces and evasive silences, and Gary Edgerton's collection of essays cleverly mines those depths for a rich bounty of treasure. Some of the sharpest TV-analysis minds around – Horace Newcomb, Ron Simon, David Marc, Kim Akass and Janet McCabe, David Lavery and others – tackle *Mad Men* from angles both required and refreshing. Music and props, race and sexism, costuming and lighting, poetry and literature, even the DVD extras and the TV shows these TV characters watch – all of it is covered, and uncovered, in one thoughtful readable essay after another.'
– **David Bianculli**, TVWorthWatching.com,
TV critic, NPR's *Fresh Air*

'Some of the leading names in television studies bring their analytical abilities to one of the best television shows of all time, considering *Mad Men* from industrial, and ideological and aesthetic perspectives. A winning collection – highly recommended!'
– **Roberta Pearson**, University of Nottingham

READING CONTEMPORARY TELEVISION

Series Editors: Kim Akass and Janet McCabe
janetandkim@hotmail.com

The **Reading Contemporary Television** series offers a varied, intellectually ground-breaking and often polemical response to what is happening in television today. This series is distinct in that it sets out to immediately comment upon the TV *zeitgeist* while providing an intellectual and creative platform for thinking differently and ingeniously writing about contemporary television culture. The books in the series seek to establish a critical space where new voices are heard and fresh perspectives offered. Innovation is encouraged and intellectual curiosity demanded.

Published and forthcoming:

Mad Men: *Dream Come True TV:*
  edited by Gary R. Edgerton

Makeover Television: Realities Remodelled
  edited by Dana Heller

Quality TV: American Television and Beyond
  edited by Janet McCabe and Kim Akass

The Queer Politics of Television by Samuel A. Chambers

Reading **CSI**: *Television under the Microscope*
  edited by Michael Allen

Reading **Deadwood**: *A Western to Swear By*
  edited by David Lavery

Reading **Desperate Housewives**: *Beyond the White Picket Fence*
  edited by Janet McCabe and Kim Akass

Reading **Little Britain**: *Comedy Masters on Contemporary Television*
  edited by Sharon Lockyer

Reading **Lost**: *Perspectives on a Hit Television Show*
  edited by Roberta Pearson

Reading **Sex and the City**
  edited by Kim Akass and Janet McCabe

Reading **Six Feet Under**: *TV to Die For*
  edited by Kim Akass and Janet McCabe

Reading **The L Word**: *Outing Contemporary Television*
  edited by Kim Akass and Janet McCabe, with an Introduction by Sarah Warne

Reading **The Sopranos**: *Hit TV from HBO*
  edited by David Lavery

Reading **24**: *Television Against the Clock*
  edited by Steven Peacock

Reading **Ugly Betty**: *TV's Betty Goes & Global*
  edited by Janet McCabe and Kim Akass

Regenerating **Doctor Who**:
  edited by David Mellor

Third Wave Feminism and Television: Jane Puts It in a Box
  edited by Merri Lisa Johnson

MAD MEN

Dream Come True TV

Edited by
GARY R. EDGERTON

I.B. TAURIS
LONDON · NEW YORK

Published in 2011 by I.B.Tauris & Co Ltd
6 Salem Road, London W2 4BU
175 Fifth Avenue, New York NY 10010
www.ibtauris.com

Distributed in the United States and Canada
Exclusively by Palgrave Macmillan
175 Fifth Avenue, New York NY 10010

ISBN: 978 1 84885 379 9

A full CIP record for this book is available from the British Library
A full CIP record is available from the Library of Congress

Library of Congress Catalog Card Number: available

Printed and bound in Sweden by Scandbook

Contents

Acknowledgments

I must admit I came to *Mad Men* late after the entire first season had already premiered during the summer and fall of 2007 on AMC. My oldest daughter, Katherine, bought me the downloads of season one for my iPod as a Christmas present and I caught up with the series while on transit in various airports and one long cross-country flight in particular during March 2008 in the midst of a heated presidential primary season. I mention that because of the similarities I immediately recognized between *Mad Men*'s critical nostalgia and the appeal of the Obama campaign which was at once utterly contemporary in its attitude towards many issues, especially identity politics, while also being retro-Kennedyesque in its idealism and style of presentation, especially in the cool elegance of the candidate himself. This proved to be a potent combination for both *Mad Men* and Barack Obama and it was clear to me that they – in their own very different ways – had forged an intense connection with the moment and were one with the zeitgeist. From the start, then, it was evident to me that *Mad Men* was much more about the present than the past, irrespective of the centrality of setting and historical context to the programme.

Early in the summer of 2008 I rewatched some of season one on a larger television screen and I decided that I wanted to explore the series further in a more in-depth and systematic way, so I contacted Kim Akass and Janet McCabe to see if they'd be interested in a contribution on *Mad Men* for the 'Reading Contemporary Television Series' that they co-edited for I.B.Tauris and for which I already owned and admired several volumes. Even though *Mad*

Men had only been on the air for one season, I was fairly certain that the programme was going to be significant enough culturally and aesthetically to warrant such a volume; and I gratefully thank Kim and Janet for taking a leap of faith with me in this regard and for being such insightful and supportive series editors throughout this process. As always, it is a genuine pleasure to work with them. They also put me in touch with Philippa Brewster, our main editorial contact at I.B.Tauris, who has been generous, understanding and professional in every conceivable way during the development and production of this book. I thank her and her colleagues for all the many things they've done to make *Mad Men: Dream Come True TV* a reality.

I also want to take this opportunity to thank all of the many contributors to this volume for their thoughtful essays. Since *Mad Men* was so new when I started this project, I had little to no idea which scholars were watching the show since there had been no conference panels or journal articles on the series, never mind blog entries which have since multiplied exponentially once the second season debuted in late July 2008. Be that as it may, I had my suspicions of who might be interested, and with the convenience of email, I very quickly recruited a lineup of television critics who I want to thank from the bottom of my heart for their many gracefully written and perceptive chapters. As with films and TV shows, it's all in the casting, and this group of contributors has made editing easy, enjoyable and edifying. Besides Kim and Janet, I want to personally thank Tim Anderson, Jeremy G. Butler, Mary Beth Haralovich, David Lavery, David Marc, Horace Newcomb, Sean O'Sullivan, Alison Perlman, Brian Rose, Ron Simon, William Siska, Robert Thompson, Mimi White and Maurice Yacowar. I owe an enormous debt of gratitude to them all as each author has added an indispensable dimension to the book from his or her own special perspective.

Finally, I want to express my deepest thanks to my family. My wife, Nan, and I have enjoyed innumerable hours together watching and discussing *Mad Men* since I introduced her to the series in the late summer of 2008. My daughter, Kate, remains steadfast in sending me timely articles and other useful information on the series; hearing her opinions on the series is always instructive and most appreciated as well. My youngest daughter, Mary Ellen, has contributed to this project with her good humour and as a research assistant who also digitized a number of the images that appear in this volume. Nan, Katherine and Mary Ellen's many enthusiasms and insights are a source of continuing inspiration to me each and every day. This book is dedicated to them with all my love.

Contributors

Kim Akass is Visiting Lecturer (TV Drama) at Royal Holloway, University of London. She has co-edited and contributed to *Reading Sex and the City* (I.B.Tauris, 2004), *Reading Six Feet Under: TV To Die For* (I.B.Tauris, 2005), *Reading The L Word: Outing Contemporary Television* (I.B.Tauris, 2006), *Reading Desperate Housewives: Beyond the White Picket Fence* (I.B.Tauris, 2006) and *Quality TV: Contemporary American TV and Beyond* (I.B.Tauris, 2007). She is currently researching the representation of motherhood on American TV and is one of the founding editors of the television journal *Critical Studies in Television* (Manchester University Press) as well as (with Janet McCabe) series editor of "Reading Contemporary Television" for I.B.Tauris.

Tim Anderson is Assistant Professor at Old Dominion University in the Department of Communication and Theater Arts. He has published in journals such as *Cinema Journal, American Music,* and *The Velvet Light Trap.* His book, *Making Easy Listening: Cultural Material Issues in American Recorded Music and Sound, 1948–1964,* was published by University of Minnesota Press in 2006. His latest research focuses on the practices of the new music industry in an era of networked computing and online societies.

Jeremy G. Butler is Professor in the Telecommunication and Film Department at the University of Alabama and the author of *Television Style* (Routledge, 2010) and *Television: Critical Methods and Applications* (4th Edition, Routledge, 2011). He has published on style in television and film in *Screen, Cinema Journal, Jump Cut,* the *Journal of Film and Video*, and the *Journal of Popular Film and Television*.

Gary R. Edgerton is Eminent Scholar, Professor, and Chair of the Communication and Theatre Arts Department at Old Dominion University. He has published eight other books – most recently *The Essential HBO Reader* (University Press of Kentucky, 2008) and *The Columbia History of American Television* (Columbia University Press, 2007) – more than 75 book chapters, journal articles, and encyclopedia entries on a wide assortment of media and culture topics, and is co-editor of the *Journal of Popular Film and Television* (Routledge).

Mary Beth Haralovich is Professor in the School of Media Arts at the University of Arizona in Tucson. She teaches courses in television and film history, is Director of Internships in Media Arts, and serves as head of the Producing Division of the School. Her essays on television include: 'Series Design and Popular Appeal in *Magnum, P.I.*'; 'Geo-Politics of Civil Rights in *I Spy*'; 'Social History of Domestic Space in the 1950s Suburban Family Comedy'; and 'Narrative Pleasure and Chance in the Reality Game Show, *Survivor*'. Co-editor of *Television, History, and American Culture: Feminist Critical Essays* (Duke University Press, 1999), Haralovich is a founder and Board Member of the International Conference on Television, Video, New Media, Audio and Feminism: Console-ing Passions. Among Haralovich's studies in film history are film advertising of the 1930s and 1940s; color in 1950s Sirk melodrama; Sherlock Holmes film series of the 1940s; promotion, adaptation and motherhood in *Mildred Pierce*; and the studio production of 'proletarian' woman's films in 1930s Hollywood. Her most recent publications, on promotion of 1930s films of Marlene Dietrich and Norma Shearer, are derived from her book-in-progress, *Marked Women: Local Promotion of 'Scandalous Female' Films of the 1930s*. A fireworks enthusiast, her research on "fireworks in film and television" looks into how the meanings and pleasures of fireworks are incorporated in fiction, documentary and experimental film and television.

David Lavery is Professor of English at Middle Tennessee State University. The author of over one hundred published essays, chapters, and reviews, he is the author/co-author/editor/or co-editor of seventeen published or under-contract books, including *Joss: A Creative Portrait of the Maker of the Whedonverses* (forthcoming from I.B.Tauris/St. Martin's). He is the organizer of international conferences on *Buffy the Vampire Slayer* and *The Sopranos*, a founding co-editor of the journals *Slayage: The Online International Journal of Buffy Studies* and *Critical Studies in Television*. He has lectured around the world (Australia, Turkey, the UK, Portugal, New Zealand, Ireland and Germany) on the subject of television.

Janet McCabe is Honorary Research Fellow in TV Drama at Birkbeck, University of London. She is author of *Feminist Film Studies* (Wallflower, 2004), and is co-editor of several collections on contemporary US television including *Reading Sex and the City* (I.B.Tauris, 2004) and *Quality TV: Contemporary American TV and Beyond* (I.B.Tauris, 2007). She is a co-founding editor as well as managing editor of the television journal, *Critical Studies in Television* (MUP). Along with Kim Akass, she is series editor of "Reading Contemporary Television" for I.B.Tauris. She is currently writing a book on *The West Wing* and her current research interests include policing femininities and cultural memory on television.

David Marc is the author of six books, including *Comic Visions: Television Comedy and American Culture* (2nd Edition, Wiley-Blackwell, 1997) and *Bonfire of the Humanities: Television, Subliteracy, and Long-Term Memory Loss* (Syracuse University Press, 1998), as well as more than 300 articles and reviews for such periodicals as *The Atlantic Monthly, Television Quarterly* and *The Village Voice*. He has taught at Brown University, Brandeis University, the University of Southern California and Syracuse University. *Our Movie Houses: A History of Film and Cinematic Innovation in Central New York* by Norman Keim with David Marc was named "Book of the Year" for 2008 by the Theatre Historical Society of America.

Horace Newcomb holds the Lambdin Kay Chair for the Peabody Awards and is Professor of Telecommunications at the University of Georgia, where he is also the director of the George Foster Peabody Awards Programs. He is the author of numerous works about television and editor of the *Museum of Broadcast Communications Encyclopedia of Television* (2nd Edition, Fitzroy Dearborn, 2004).

Sean O'Sullivan is Assistant Professor of English at The Ohio State University. His forthcoming book, *Mike Leigh*, will be published by the University of Illinois Press series on Contemporary Film Directors. He has published articles on Dickens and *Deadwood*; British television drama of the 80s; and narrative structures and strategies of *The Decalogue, Six Feet Under*, and *Lost*.

Allison Perlman is Assistant Professor in the Federated Department of History at the New Jersey Institute of Technology and Rutgers University-Newark. Her current research examines the intersection of media reform activism and twentieth century social movements in the United States.

Brian Rose is Professor in the Department of Communication and Media Studies at Fordham University. He is the author of *Television and the Performing Arts* (Greenwood, 1986), *Televising the Performing Arts* (Greenwood, 1992) and *Directing for Television* (Scarecrow, 1999). He is also the editor of *TV Genres* (Greenwood, 1985) and the co-editor of *Thinking Outside the Box: A Contemporary Television Genre Reader* (University Press of Kentucky, 2005, with Gary R. Edgerton).

Ron Simon is Curator of Television and Radio at The Paley Center for Media. He has presented several Bob Dylan events, including a unique screening of *Eat the Document* (1966), showing how it might have looked on network television in the late 1960s, complete with commercials. He has also consulted with George Lois in acquiring material for the permanent collection. Furthermore, Simon is an Associate Adjunct Professor at Columbia University and New York University, where he teaches courses in the history of the media. He is former Chair of the Peabody Awards jury, which gave *Mad Men* its distinguished medallion for the series' first season.

William Siska is past Chair of Theatre and Film Studies at the University of Utah, where he has taught for thirty years. He is the author of *Modernism in the Narrative Cinema* (Arno, 1980) and numerous articles and reviews about art cinema and films about the American West.

Robert Thompson is the founding Director of the Bleier Center for Television and Popular Culture at Syracuse University, where he is also the Trustee Professor at the S.I. Newhouse School of Public Communications. Professor Thompson has written pieces for *The New York Times*, *Newsday*, *The Los Angeles Daily News*, *The Christian Science Monitor*, *Electronic Media*, *Multichannel News*, *Encyclopaedia Britannica*, and many other publications. His commentaries have been heard on NPR's *Morning Edition* and *All Things Considered*, he is a frequent contributor to *The Washington Post*, and he writes a regular column for *AdWeek*. Thompson is the author or editor of six books: *Television in the Antenna Age* (Wiley-Blackwell, 2004, with David Marc), *Television's Second Golden Age* (Continuum, 1996), *Prime Time, Prime Movers* (Little, Brown, 1992, with David Marc), *Adventures on Prime Time* (Praeger, 1990), *Making Television* (Praeger, 1990, with Gary Burns) and *Television Studies* (Praeger, 1989, with Gary Burns). The general editor of an ongoing series of books about television published by Syracuse University Press, Thompson is also a past president of the national Popular Culture Association.

Mimi White is a Professor in the School of Communication at Northwestern University. She has published widely on film and television, and is co-editor of *Questions of Method in Cultural Studies* (Revised Edition, Wiley-Blackwell, 2006).

Maurice Yacowar is Professor Emeritus of English and Film Studies at The University of Calgary. His thirteen books include *The Sopranos on the Couch* (Continuum, 2006), *The Sopranos Season Seven* (lulu.com, 2007), *The Great Bratby: A Portrait of John Bratby RA* (Middlesex University Press, 2008), and the satire *Mondays with Moishe* (Lulu.com, 2009).

Foreword: From Rod Serling to Roger Sterling

Robert Thompson

Among the entertainment stories that got significant attention in the early fall of 2009 were these: *Mad Men* won its second consecutive Emmy Award for 'best drama' on 20 September and, less than two weeks later, *The Twilight Zone* (CBS, 1959–64) turned fifty years old. It is only right that these two shows stood side by side for a moment in the media spotlight, for they have a lot in common.

Mad Men creator Matt Weiner has named *The Twilight Zone* as one of his muses, and it shows. Even the opening title sequence of his series, with its drifting cut-and-paste collage style and distinctive musical motif, is evocative of its predecessor. So are many of the storylines, which gravitate towards both the uncanny (Don/Dick's double identity) and the macabre (the John Deere incident). Not to mention the fact that 'A Stop at Willoughby', a notable *Twilight Zone* episode written by series creator Rod Serling, featured an emotionally complex gray-flannelled advertising executive who, like Don Draper, commuted each day to Manhattan from his home in a distant suburb.

The first three seasons of *Mad Men* are set precisely during the years in which *The Twilight Zone* ran on CBS; the debut episode takes place in the spring of 1960, when 'A Stop at Willoughby' first aired. Even before Serling created *The Twilight Zone*, he had already settled some of the dramaturgical territory of high-voltage urban corporate intrigue, most notably in *Patterns*, a 1955 instalment of the anthology drama *Kraft Television Theatre*. Weiner has acknowledged the anthology dramas as another of his major creative influences.

The original *Twilight Zone* played on CBS from 1959 to 1964, a five-year period that might itself aptly be described as a 'twilight zone'. Straddling the transition between the sureties of the Eisenhower era and the turbulence of what would become known as the Sixties, *The Twilight Zone* was not like other television series of the day. It communicated, through parable, the disturbing nature of radical epistemological change. Nothing was what it seemed; an altered point of view could annihilate one's sense of reality. This may have been befitting to a time in which the headlines – from microchips to Motown, Castro to Cassavetes, birth control pills to fallout shelters – seemed themselves to be coming from another dimension, but it was highly irregular.

One of the things that made *The Twilight Zone* so eerie was that practically nothing else on TV was doing what it was doing. Most of the real change and anxiety of the transition from the Eisenhower Fifties through the Kennedy, Johnson, and Nixon Sixties was invisible on entertainment television. We'd grown to expect prime time to act as a sorbet, clearing the palate of all that real-world unpleasantness. If the news at eleven took us to Little Rock and Birmingham, prime time took us to Mayberry and Hooterville. If Dr. King amazed audiences because he spoke so movingly, Mr. Ed amazed Wilbur because he spoke at all. Prime-time television in the early 1960s very rarely embraced the texture and detail of the liminal times in which it was made. By doing so, at least metaphorically, *The Twilight Zone* looked ahead and seemed positively creepy.

Mad Men, on the other hand, looks backward to the same period. It retroactively reclaims a time with a representation that would have been impossible in those days before HBO, FX and AMC. *Mad Men* shows us things about the Sixties that couldn't have been shown in the entertainment TV *of* the Sixties. If *The Twilight Zone* seemed strange because it resisted the norms of the medium to present a world of uncertainty and ambiguity, *Mad Men* seems strange because it presents a readjusted vision of the Sixties that is so different from how we saw it represented the first time around. *The Twilight Zone* seemed surreal because it looked forward to an era of fundamental change; *Mad Men* seems surreal because it looks back across the intervening half-century to remind us that those changes have become our most venerable orthodoxy. Watching pregnant women smoke and executives hit on women at the water cooler on *Mad Men* seems as alien to us as watching the aliens or talking dolls did to contemporary viewers of *The Twilight Zone*.

Each of the 15 essays about *Mad Men* that follow provides new insights about this exceptional series. But that's not all. 'They're toasted' – all 15 of them.

Introduction: When Our Parents Became Us

Gary R. Edgerton

> If I made the show eight years ago, I don't know if it would have resonated.
>
> – Matthew Weiner, creator of *Mad Men* in 2008 (Wyatt)

Every few years a new television programme comes along to capture and express the zeitgeist. *Mad Men* is now that show. Since premiering in July 2007 on AMC (formerly American Movie Classics from 1984 to 2003), it has attracted wide critical acclaim and an extraordinary amount of public attention for a series that appears on what was once an also-ran basic cable network. Moreover, *Mad Men* is today syndicated in three dozen countries across North/Central/and South America, Europe, the Middle East, Asia, and Australia; its international reach is expanding all the time. In its first three seasons, *Mad Men* won four Golden Globes, thirteen Emmys, and a prestigious George Foster Peabody Award for excellence in broadcasting. The Hollywood Foreign Press Association has voted *Mad Men* the Best Television Drama of 2007, 2008, and 2009. The National Academy of Television Arts and Sciences has similarly selected *Mad Men* the Outstanding Drama Series of 2008, 2009, and 2010, being the first basic cable series ever to win this award. The British Academy of Film and Television also named it the Best International Show in 2009 and 2010. Most surprisingly, *Mad Men*'s imprint is evident throughout contemporary culture, inspiring TV commercials and print advertisements, magazine covers and feature articles, designer fashions and department store displays, and all sorts of ancillary merchandise from cigarette lighters to hip flasks to assorted media-related tie-ins such as soundtrack CDs, episode downloads, and season-long DVD sets.

The creator, executive producer, head writer, and showrunner of *Mad Men* is Matthew Weiner. He broke into television as a staff writer and later producer working on *Party Girl* (in 1996 for Fox), *The Naked Truth* (in 1997 for ABC), *Becker* (from 1999–2002 for CBS) and *Andy Richter Controls the Universe* (in 2002 for Fox), before sending his spec script, 'Smoke Gets in Your Eyes' (which eventually became *Mad Men*'s pilot episode) to David Chase, the creator and executive producer of *The Sopranos* (HBO, 1999–2007). According to Weiner, 'a week after [Chase] got it' in 2002, 'I was in New York on the show,' quickly working his way up on *The Sopranos* from staff writer to one of the executive producers during its final two seasons (NPR: *Fresh Air*, 9 August 2007). Weiner's earliest draft of 'Smoke Gets in Your Eyes' was actually written back in the spring and summer of 1999 (*Inside Media at the Paley Center for Media* – 'Smoke and Sympathy: A Toast to *Mad Men*,' 10 October 2007). During his initial years in broadcast TV, Matt Weiner grew progressively bored and frustrated with the strictures there, thus motivating him to write his *Mad Men* script and eventually send it to Chase, a television writer-producer he greatly admired. In turn, David Chase instantly recognized Weiner's talent and assumed the role of mentor to him over the next four years. On *The Sopranos*, Weiner learned that a series could have 'depth and complexity,' while 'at the same time' be 'commercially successful' (NPR: *Fresh Air*, 9 August 2007). Although the historical backdrop, genre, and themes of *Mad Men* are much different than those of *The Sopranos*, both of these serial narratives develop in a slow and deliberate fashion and resist closure. They are also emotionally complicated and populated by characters who are compelling though deeply conflicted.

Mad Men is set in the sleekly sophisticated go-go world of Madison Avenue in the early 1960s. This period drama begins during a time of socio-political and cultural transition between the Fifties and the Sixties (season one takes place in 1960; season two 1962; season three 1963; season four 1964 and 1965) – a bevy of years that is often left out of most popular remembrances of the 1960s. The cultural shorthand in this series isn't bushy-haired hippies dressed in tie-dyed regalia listening to rock 'n' roll. Instead, the cultural mores and artifacts of *Mad Men* belong more to the button-down WASPish (white Anglo-Saxon Protestant) world of Sterling Cooper, a second-tier white-shoe advertising agency run by members of the so-called lost generation (born between 1889–1907) and G.I. generation (1908–26) – Bertram Cooper, Roger Sterling, Don Draper, Duck Phillips and Lane Pryce – while a passel of younger wannabees (1927–45) – such as Peggy Olson, Pete Campbell, Ken Cosgrove, Betty Draper, and Joan Holloway, among many others – struggle to find their ways around the workplaces and homes of post-war America. *Time* coined this particular cohort the silent generation in a 5 November 1951 cover story that described those individuals who came of age at the tail end of World War II and spawned the new baby boom (1946–64) along with their older brothers and sisters. 'The most startling fact about the younger generation is its silence,' wrote the editors of *Time*, 'it wants to marry, have children, found homes . . . Today's generation, either through fear, passivity or conviction, is ready to conform' ('The Younger Generation,' *Time* 45, 50).

'The silent generation was a phenomenon of the 1950s, as characteristic as its tailfins and white bucks,' wrote William Manchester in *The Glory and the Dream* (1973), 'never had American youth been so withdrawn, cautious, unimaginative, indifferent, unadventurous – and silent.' A member of the G.I. generation himself, Manchester continued: 'They would conform to the dictates of society in their dress, speech, worship, choice of friends, length of hair, and above all, in their thought. In exchange they would receive all the rights and privileges of the good life; *viz.*, economic security' (Manchester 576, 580). This description pretty well sums up the cultural terrain of *Mad Men*. It is a world where advertising as a profession is in the ascendancy, positioned smack dab in the middle of the country's corporate elite and their sponsor-clients. They have equal access to artists and psychologists, spinning visions of the good life to consumers in cities and suburbs throughout the United States and internationally. Probably no one captured the inner workings of this post-war mass society at mid-century better than sociologist David Riesman, along with his colleagues Nathan Glazer and Reuel Denney, in their unexpected best-seller, *The Lonely Crowd* (1950), a title suggested to them by their publisher. 'In the now-familiar terminology of *The Lonely Crowd*, there are three dominant types of social character, which correspond to phases of Western, but especially American, societal development, and are correlated with demographic changes: persons who are tradition-directed, inner-directed, and other-directed' (Tallack 221).

The traditionalists (Bertram Cooper, Roger Sterling) resist change and rigorously follow time-honoured beliefs and practices; the inner-directeds (Don Draper, Peggy Olson) are far more self-made, stubbornly self-reliant, and goal-oriented, while the other-directeds (Betty Draper, Pete Campbell) tend to obsessively seek approval, prefer group over individual action, and freely sublimate their own needs and desires to the will of the crowd. Obviously, these aforementioned characters from *Mad Men* sometimes resist such easy stereotyping, but part of the achievement of the series is how certain personalities on the show embody many of the ways of thinking that were au courant in America during the 1950s and early 1960s. For instance, the mildly eccentric conservative Republican Bertram Cooper is an evident devotee of Ayn Rand's objectivism; just as Joan Holloway is the living embodiment of Helen Gurley Brown's *Sex and the Single Girl*; and Betty Draper suffers daily from what Betty Friedan called 'the problem that has no name' in *The Feminine Mystique* (13–29). Riesman and his colleagues recognized that the zeitgeist of the era 'was different somehow from life in decades past, and that, for all their outward success, many Americans were [now other-directed] leading lives of inner emptiness and desperation' (McGrath 34). They found a large and sympathetic readership for *The Lonely Crowd* in which they critiqued corporate culture and those people who are 'at home everywhere and nowhere'. Sloan Wilson's *The Man in the Gray Flannel Suit* (1955) and William Whyte's *The Organization Man* (1956) struck similar chords.

Households like the Drapers consisting of a working dad, a mainly stay-at-home mom, and one or more young children living in the suburbs separated from the traditions of an extended family had then become the majority lifestyle in the United States. 'The increase in single-family homeownership between 1946 and 1956 outstripped the increase during the entire preceding century and a half. By 1960, 62 per cent of American families owned their own homes, in contrast to 43 per cent in 1940. Eighty-five per cent of the new homes were built in the suburbs, where the nuclear family found new possibilities for privacy and togetherness' (Coontz 24). Rates

Don and Betty Draper live in a seemingly picture-perfect world. Why is their dream come true not enough? Courtesy of AMC.

of divorce and illegitimacy fell, as Elaine Tyler May reports that 'the isolation of the nuclear family sometimes helped keep couples together' (May 166). Still, 'most people understood the 1950s family to be a new invention,' contends Stephanie Coontz in *The Way We Were*. 'The Great Depression and the Second World War had reinforced extended family ties, but in ways that were experienced by most people as stultifying and oppressive.' As a contemporaneous alternative, suburban homeowners in the G.I. and silent generations currently 'hailed' the nuclear family 'as the most basic institution in society' (Coontz 24). It is the picture-perfect world of Don and Betty Draper as represented in *Mad Men*. He is a hard-living advertising executive on the fast track to success. She the Bryn Mawr graduate and former fashion model who can now luxuriate her days away as a suburban princess. They have two boys and a girl and live in Ossining, some 30 miles north of New York City in wealthy Westchester County, which also happens to be the hometown of celebrity broadcaster, Edward R. Murrow and John Cheever, the quintessential chronicler of the post-war suburban experience in America. Why then are the Drapers so unhappy? Why is their dream come true not enough?

Historian Daniel Boorstin once described the changing landscape of post-war America as a land of newly expanding 'everywhere communities' spreading out from coast-to-coast. Beginning in the late 1940s and continuing throughout the remainder of the century, the nation's cities and suburbs started developing similar kinds of interchangeable neighbourhoods, shopping malls, franchised retail outlets, and fast-food chain restaurants. 'Americans in suburbs leaned on one another as they moved rapidly about the country and up the ladder of consumption' (Boorstin 1, 290, 370–393). In their upwardly mobile quest for a good life marked by mounting levels of comfort, convenience and predictability, members of the G.I. and silent generations with their baby boomer children shared a common culture – a culture progressively defined by 'words and images' whereby 'relations with the outer world and with oneself [were] increasingly mediated by the flow of mass communication' (Riesman, Glazer, and Denney 20–21, 25). Admen like Don Draper were victims of their own successes. They 'aimed at something new – the creation of consumption communities' (Boorstin 145). Moreover, once these advertising and publicity specialists persuaded enough consumers to create and settle in thousands of 'everywhere communities' all across the country, they also bought their own dream houses and moved right in next door with their wives and children. They too took their cues from the advertising they both conceived and internalized. *Mad Men* reminds us in retrospect that the creative directors of Madison Avenue like Don Draper were the people imagining our parents' and grandparents' America – a place where many viewers of the series also grew up.

By and large, *Mad Men* traffics in presentism by unapologetically framing its characters small personal dramas through the eyes of the present. The series also offers an alternative mythology to the overly simplified and saccharine poetics surrounding the cottage industry of books, films and television programmes that bathe the 'greatest generation' in the unreflective mist of wistful nostalgia. Likewise, *Mad Men* never wallows in the feel-good revisionism of works such as *American Graffiti* (1973), *Happy Days* (ABC, 1974–84), and literally dozens of other like-minded movies and TV shows that focus on the coming-of-age of the silent generation. In contrast, the critical nostalgia of *Mad Men* comes with a much different attitude towards the past. The series uses the language of myth – the conventions of the domestic and workplace melodrama – to represent the sorts of places where friends and relatives in the not-so-distant past lived and worked. The characters in *Mad Men* – who are basically stand-ins for our parents and grandparents – are hardly representatives of a 'greatest' or silent and carefree generation. They are merely an earlier, confused and conflicted version of us, trying to make the best of a future that is unfolding before them at breakneck speed. Audiences today understand and relate to their disorientation. Where better to begin to make sense of yet another transformative moment like our own than in a narrative such as *Mad Men* where the characters are similarly caught in a kind of limbo wedged between the recent past and a shadowy uncertain future.

At the outset, *Mad Men* is set in the midst of a tightly contested 1960 presidential campaign when the country is undergoing a profound cultural shift. No one in the political arena symbolized the era's spirit of change more so than John F. Kennedy. Not surprisingly, Matt Weiner has fashioned Don Draper in the JFK mold. Each is tall, handsome and typically turned out in a custom-made dark suit with a matching skinny tie. Their demeanours are outwardly cool but sexy; old-school handsome if a bit aloof; elegant in style while projecting a kind of ironic intelligence. They both embody what David Newman and Robert Benton characterized in a feature article for *Esquire* in July 1964 as 'The New Sentimentality'. By that time, the Kennedy mystique was reaching mythic proportions in the immediate wake of his assassination on 22 November 1963, which in turn ushered in the Sixties and all the major historical and cultural currents that are usually associated with that era in America, such as the Civil Rights movement, President Lyndon B. Johnson's Great Society, the generation gap, rock 'n' roll music, the Vietnam War, student protests, women's liberation, the rise of the counter-culture and the subsequent backlash by the silent majority, among many other seismic developments. Surely these events and issues simmered for years beneath the placid exterior of post-war America before finally boiling over with a pent-up fury that took many people in the country by surprise. Indeed, this seemingly calm cultural period before the storm belongs more to the Fifties than the Sixties and fully informs the first three seasons of *Mad Men*.

Daniel Boorstin has also observed that the 'most popular' method of organizing historical periods is in yearly, decade-long, and 'hundred year packages. Historians like to bundle years in ways that make sense, provide continuity and link past to present' (Boorstin 37). More often than not, though, history is not that neat and clean. For all intents and purposes, the era known as the Sixties did not kick into high gear until after JFK was gone and America had experienced the shock of his passing. This turbulent and transformative period also extended well into the early-to-mid 1970s in the USA, culminating with Watergate and the withdrawal of the last American troops from Vietnam on 30 April 1975. One of the most distinguishing and innovative aspects of *Mad Men* so far is that the series spent 37 of the 39 episodes of its first three seasons on the front of the decade before the Kennedy assassination – a time that has been largely suppressed and long forgotten in popular culture – and with good reason. *Mad Men* exposes much of the over-the-top and out-in-the-open sexism, racism, adultery, homophobia and anti-Semitism, not to mention all the excessive smoking and drinking that sparked much of the ongoing re-evaluation of the 'Old Sentimentality' that began in the Sixties. The comparative-historical sociologist, Eleanor Townsley, refers to the Sixties in hindsight as a 'trope' that 'denotes a definitive break between "then" and "now"'. She classifies the Sixties as an '*originary point*' that identifies 'a break or major change in American history, after which nothing is the same' (Townsley 105–106). Historian Stephan Feuchtwang similarly uses the term, 'caesura', to 'refer to points of before and after that inaugurate a present and demarcate a past.' He adds that 'such caesurae are mythic: they mark the moment of creation of a relative past, the before of a given event and the after of a new present' (Feuchtwang 180).

In their modish excitement, David Newman and his collaborator Robert Benton, who later won an Oscar for their original screenplay of *Bonnie and Clyde* (1967), were describing a 'caesura' in 1964 when they heralded the emergence of a 'New Sentimentality, but nobody knows it exists.' Their article confirmed a 'changeover' that 'came in the Fifties. Eisenhower was a key figure, perhaps the last bloom of the Old Sentimentality', grounded in an absolute faith in country, church, and good common sense (25). In no particular order, Newman and Benton named Lenny Bruce, Audrey Hepburn, François Truffaut, the Beatles, Roy Lichtenstein, Jean Shrimpton and Malcolm X as representative purveyors of a 'New Sentimentality'. They are part of a 'vanguard' who lived by 'a different set of rules, of concepts, and, most importantly, of attitudes' (31). The acknowledged exemplars of this 'New Sentimentality' were still 'Mr. and Mrs. John F. Kennedy' because 'they created a style that succeeded' (25). Even in death, JFK remained a prototype for the future to many; his image was forever frozen in time at a point before the assassination, always poised above the rest as a harbinger of enlightened change. 'Jack and Jackie were impresarios of style' during the early 1960s, writes journalist and Kennedy chronicler Laurence Leamer. 'The Kennedys' achievement was to turn style into substance and to celebrate the opening up of broad new cultural and social vistas that would never again be shut down' (573–574). It is no accident, therefore, that Matt Weiner utilizes Jack and Jackie Kennedy more so than any other historical figures in shaping the parameters of his serial narrative.

In the first episode entitled 'Smoke Gets in Your Eyes', for example, senior partner Roger Sterling asks Don Draper to 'think about the product: he's young, handsome, beautiful wife, Navy hero, honestly Don, it shouldn't be hard to convince America Dick Nixon is a winner.' Once again, Sterling Cooper is on the wrong side of history. As with the candidates themselves, Jacqueline Bouvier Kennedy was the more signature beauty than Pat Nixon. She was educated, cultured, and well-to-do. Jackie symbolized the ultimate trophy wife for members of the World War II generation. In the first episode of the second season, 'For Those Who Think Young' (i.e., the 'New Sentimentality'), Jackie Kennedy is presented as the arbiter of taste for both her husband and the rest of America in CBS's *Tour of the White House*, which was seen by more than 56 million Americans when it was first telecast on 14 February 1962 (as well as by Don and Betty Draper, Sal and Kitty Romano and Joan Holloway with her doctor boyfriend in the *Mad Men* narrative). In fact, Betty evokes Jackie at the start of the episode as Don watches her descend the spiral staircase into the lobby of the Savoy to the strains of Rimsky-Korsakov's 'Song of India', where they have made a Valentine Day's date for a romantic rendezvous in a room upstairs. Don's bride, Elizabeth 'Betty' Hofstadt Draper, comes from an upper-middle class Philadelphia family, speaks fluent Italian and is an accomplished equestrienne. Betty is never more Jackie than in 'Souvenir' (3:34) when she is away on a Roman holiday with Don who is on a business trip for Conrad Hilton. She becomes a vision of haute couture with her black fringe evening dress, beehive hairdo, and dangling earrings. Like JFK before him, Don Draper enhances his own cachet by marrying well.

For his part, Don recalls an old American character who rises above his modest station in life by hard work and talent, charm and deception. Don Draper (née Dick Whitman) is the archetypal self-made man hiding his hillbilly roots so he can succeed in business and assimilate seamlessly into the WASP establishment, not unlike the familial road travelled by the Irish Catholic Kennedy clan from impoverished immigrants to the White House in only five generations. The usual Fifties and Sixties preoccupation with the toll taken by the rat race and the stifling conformity of the suburbs no longer ignites the kinds of passions they once did, as the new hot-button issues of today cluster mostly around questions of identity. 'Don is one thing on the inside and another thing on the outside', explains Matt Weiner, 'I think that's the American story' (KCRW). Weiner and his writing staff thus select three seminal episodes from the Kennedy presidency to catalyze the action and character development and bring them to a boiling point during each of the first three seasons of *Mad Men*. In season one, it's the twelfth episode, 'Nixon vs. Kennedy', where all hell breaks loose as the younger employees at Sterling Cooper let their hair down at an impromptu office party to ostensibly watch the election returns on television. The Sterling Cooper crowd is solidly behind Dick Nixon except for the office weasel, Pete Campbell, who tries unsuccessfully to blackmail his boss Don Draper for a promotion upon accidently finding out that he's really Dick Whitman. Lucky for Draper, his own boss, Bertram Cooper, responds to Campbell's accusation in typical Ayn Rand fashion by telling him: 'even if this were true, who cares? This country was built and run by men with worse stories than whatever you've imagined here.' For the time being at least, Don has dodged a bullet with his name on it. He has also followed JFK's lead by pushing his own doppelgänger named Dick as far into the background as possible.

The backdrop for the last episode of season two, 'Meditations in an Emergency', is the October 1962 Cuban Missile Crisis. Apparently faced with the prospects of the world coming to an end, many of the key characters in *Mad Men* take the opportunity to act out of character. For example, Betty finds out she's pregnant and has a fling with a stranger in a bar; Don who was AWOL in California for three weeks, returns and writes a heartfelt letter of apology and love to Betty; Pete tells Peggy he thinks she's 'perfect' and wants to be with her, prompting Peggy to reveal to Pete that 'I had your baby and gave it away'; and the much larger British advertising agency, Puttnam, Powell, and Lowe, acquires Sterling Cooper, forcing Don to play the trump card that he's not under contract as his only way left of keeping his independence. Throughout season two, Don Draper proves that his first reaction to any kind of serious trouble at home or work is to run. In this way, Don is simply a more extreme version of what the philosopher George Santayana once observed about all Americans. He noted that they 'don't solve problems, they leave them behind . . . If a situation bothers them, they leave it in the past' (Brooks 47). The triple witching hour arrives for *Mad Men* in the penultimate episode of season three, 'The Grown-Ups'. Don was finally forced to tell everything to Betty about his dual identity as Dick Whitman in 'The Gypsy and the Hobo' (3:37), catapulting the Drapers' already fragile marriage into uncharted territory between Halloween 1962 and November 22, 1963. Just like 11 September 2001, the Kennedy assassination is the 'caesura' that once again jump-starts the narrative to even greater heights of conflict and change.

John Rossant, the European editor for *BusinessWeek*, wrote on the one-year anniversary of 9/11 that 'already that crystal-clear September morning is fast becoming an historical memory, the way some of us still remember a November day in 1963 when gunning down a young American president seemed to mark the end of one age and the beginning of another. We sense that history will divide into "before September 11" and "after."' In *Covering the Body*, Barbie Zelizer likewise identified the Kennedy assassination as a shared milestone for an earlier generation, reassessing how journalists had utilized that tragic event at the time to promote their own agendas and shape collective memory. Matt Weiner also employs the Kennedy assassination – indeed the whole Kennedy presidency as well as the images of Jack and Jackie – to better understand the present and discover the future. The 'New Sentimentality' celebrated by Newman and Benton at the dawn of the Sixties, grew old by the Eighties and Nineties, and now it's 'new' again in an albeit updated and reconfigured way. Just consider that 'Don Draper was voted as the No. 1 Most Influential Man of 2009 in a poll conducted by AskMen.com. And Don's not even a real person', reports Katherine Stephen of *The Christian Science Monitor*. Yet another new and improved Kennedy reboot, Barack Obama, only ranked third in the same poll. In the end, Weiner has appropriated JFK's style in modelling Don Draper. Like Kennedy before him, Draper's dedication to work gives his life a purpose it wouldn't otherwise have. Significantly, Don and his protégé, Peggy Olson, respond to the Kennedy assassination by going to the office as the only way they can think of to cope with the tragedy.

Also like JFK, Don Draper shares in the 'New Sentimentality'; in the context of the Sixties, he like Kennedy is an outlier in his profession of choice. Don Draper literally pretends to be a part of the WASP establishment and its values, but he is a harbinger of the new emerging educated class of today, steeped in an alternative sensibility that is much more committed to meritocracy than nepotism (Roger Sterling) or social class (Pete Campbell). Don labours daily in the belly of the corporate beast, but it makes all the difference in the world that he is a creative director, not a director of accounts services (like Duck Phillips) or a chief financial officer (like Lane Pryce). Don blends the values of the Sixties counterculture with the aspirations of the ambitious, acquisitive Yuppie cultural backlash of a generation later. In short, Don Draper is a man of today. Now with Jack Kennedy gone for good from the *Mad Men* narrative, neither Don nor any of the other main characters in the series is likely to be quite the same again. Matt Weiner is free to tinker with and maybe even reinvent Don Draper/Dick Whitman anew for the Sixties, only this time sans Betty, Sterling Cooper, and whatever remains of the 'Old Sentimentality'. Whatever path *Mad Men* takes, it is already destined to be one of the signature television programmes of the late 2000s and early 2010s. Matthew Weiner has signed on for two more seasons, while expressing interest in writing and producing at least six seasons altogether (if not more), taking his characters up through the turbulent end of the 1960s and into the early 1970s (Littleton).

Overall, *Mad Men: Dream Come True TV* is divided into five parts – industry and authorship; visual and aural stylistics and influences; narrative dynamics and genealogy; sexual politics and gender roles; and cultural memory and the American Dream – to correspond with those topical areas that most define *Mad Men* and distinguish it as an innovative and influential series. For example, *Mad Men* is a singularly important show from an 'industry and authorship' perspective, not only being the first basic cable series ever to win an Emmy, but reinforcing once and for all the pre-eminence of the cable-and-satellite sector over the broadcast networks as the first place to look for original programming on American television. Part 1 therefore begins with my production history, 'The Selling of *Mad Men*', tracing the programme's genesis as a spec script in 1999 through its multiple rejections by various networks before finally being picked up by AMC and subsidized by Lionsgate TV in 2006. Chapter 2, '"If It's Too Easy, Then Usually There's Something Wrong": An Interview with *Mad Men*'s Executive Producer Scott Hornbacher' by Brian Rose, next provides some behind-the-scenes insight into the series. This interview article with Hornbacher sheds light on Matt Weiner and his whole creative team's motivations, intentions and opinions about *Mad Men*, including where the series might be headed in the future. Part 1 culminates with Chapter 3, 'Don Draper Confronts the Maddest Men of the Sixties: Bob Dylan and George Lois' by Ron Simon. Here Simon examines how *Mad Men* is informed by the creative revolution in American advertising, which began with the work of legendary adman George Lois at Doyle Dane Bernbach in 1959, as well as by the critical and irreverent rock 'n' roll counterculture that emerged several years later as epitomized by Bob Dylan.

Part 2 deals specifically with *Mad Men*'s 'Visual and Aural Stylistics and Influences'. Jeremy G. Butler starts this section with Chapter 4, '"Smoke Gets in Your Eyes": Historicizing Visual Style in *Mad Men*', which defines the distinctive visual stylistics of the programme as a hybrid between Hollywood movies of the 1950s and television's contemporaneous 'quality' dramas. Tim Anderson next assesses the cultural significance of the show's musical heritage in Chapter 5, 'Uneasy Listening: Music, Sound, and Criticizing Camelot in *Mad Men*', while Maurice Yacowar caps off Part 2 with a close textual reading that underscores a television aesthetic that is usually given short shrift in his Chapter 6, 'Suggestive Silence in Season One' of *Mad Men*. Part 3 is devoted to 'Narrative Dynamics and Genealogy'. In Chapter 7, Horace Newcomb kicks off this section with a delineation of the many ways in which television is utilized as a narrative trope in 'Learning to Live with Television in *Mad Men*'. Sean O'Sullivan then employs the first-season finale, 'The Wheel' (1:13), as well as Don Draper's central assertion in that episode that the Kodak Carousel 'isn't a space ship, it's a time machine', as a jumping off point to explore how this metaphor helps in illuminating '*Mad Men* and the Serial Condition.' In Chapter 8, O'Sullivan underscores television's inherent ability as a medium to move fluidly backwards and forwards in telling its stories. Finally, David Lavery ends Part 3 by evaluating the preoccupations, outlook and milieu of 'Frank O'Hara, Don Draper, and the Poetics of *Mad Men*' in his Chapter 9, 'The Catastrophe of My Personality', which is a celebrated line taken from O'Hara's 'Mayakovsky', the final poem in his 1957 volume entitled, *Meditations in an Emergency*.

Mimi White leads off Part 4 on 'Sexual Politics and Gender Roles' with 'Mad Women', an apt counterpoint to the privileged point of view that is implicit in the programme's title. In Chapter 10, White provides an in-depth inquiry into the show's major female characters. In a related vein, Mary Beth Haralovich investigates 'Women on the Verge of the Second Wave' in Chapter 11, revealing the tacit power relationships inherent in the layout and design of both Sterling Cooper's base of operations and Don and Betty Draper's suburban home. Kim Akass and Janet McCabe then hone in on some of the more telling patterns of workplace sexism and misogyny in Chapter 12 with their evocation of Rona Jaffe's 1958 best selling novel, '*The Best of Everything*: The Limits of Being a Working Girl in *Mad Men*', where the authors also connect these representational tendencies back to actual working conditions today. William Siska launches Part 5 by shifting the focus from women to 'Men Behaving as Boys: The Culture of *Mad Men*', where he emphasizes how the male characters in the series experience an increasing loss of innocence and an overwhelming sense of foreboding that ultimately pervades the entire series. Allison Perlman next contributes Chapter 14, 'The Strange Career of *Mad Men*: Race, Paratexts and Civil Rights Memory', in which she compares and contrasts the main narrative text of the series with its paratexts – such as DVD special features, interactive websites and interviews with cast and creative personnel – evaluating whether or not text and paratexts together offer a consistent critique of the past, especially in terms of race relations. Lastly, David Marc concludes Part 5 with Chapter 15 entitled, '*Mad Men*: A Roots Tale of the Information Age', where he characterizes *Mad Men* as a fictionalized peak into the professional and private lives of the admen and women who so strongly influenced the direction of American culture during the late 1950s and early 1960s. Taken as a whole, these fifteen essays, along with Robert Thompson's 'Foreword: From Rod Serling to Roger Sterling' and this introduction, provide the first in-depth scholarly look at *Mad Men* as a compelling and innovative serial narrative, a significant and evocative cultural product, and a widespread and influential popular phenomenon.

Works Cited

Boorstin, Daniel J. *The Americans: The Democratic Experience*, Volume 3, New York: Random House, 1973.

———. 'The luxury of retrospect,' *Life, Special Issue: The 80s*. Fall 1989: 37–43.

Brooks, David. *On Paradise Drive: How We Live Now (And Always Have) in the Future Tense*, New York: Simon & Schuster, 2004.

Brown, Helen Gurley. *Sex and the Single Girl*. New York: Random House, 1962.

Coontz, Stephanie. *The Way We Were: American Families and the Nostalgia Trap*, New York: Basic Books, 1992.

Feuchtwang, Stephan. 'Mythic moments in national and other family histories', *History Workshop Journal* 59 (Spring 2005): 179–193.

Friedan, Betty. *The Feminine Mystique*, New York: W. W. Norton, 1963.

Inside Media at the Paley Center for Media – 'Smoke and Sympathy: A Toast to *Mad Men*', 10 October 2007, Matthew Weiner and the *Mad Men* cast regulars interviewed by Brian Lowry, TV critic for *Variety*, 56 minutes.

KCRW. *The Treatment*. 4 November 2009. Matthew Weiner interviewed by Elvis Mitchell, 27 minutes.

Leamer, Laurence. *The Kennedy Men, 1901–1963: The Laws of the Father*, New York: William Morrow, 2001.

Littleton, Cynthia. '*Mad Men* creator Weiner inks deal: Lionsgate TV pact includes feature component,' *Variety*, 16 January 2009 at

http://www.variety.com/article/VR1117998730.html?categoryid=
14&cs=1. Accessed on 19 January 2009.

Manchester, William. *The Glory and the Dream: A Narrative History of
America, 1932–1972*, Boston: Little, Brown, 1973.

May, Elaine Tyler. *Homeward Bound: American Families in the Cold War
Era*, Revised and Updated Edition. New York: Basic Books, 1999.

McGrath, Charles. 'Big thinker: His book crowned an age when eggheads
had the answers.' *New York Times Magazine*, 29 December 2002: 34.

Newman, David, and Benton, Robert. 'The New Sentimentality,' *Esquire*,
July 1964: 25–31.

NPR (National Public Radio): *Fresh Air*, 9 August 2007, Matthew Weiner
interviewed by Dave Davies, 51 minutes.

O'Hara, Frank. *Meditations in an Emergency*, New York: Grove Press,
1957.

Rand, Ayn. *Atlas Shrugged*. New York: Random House, 1957.

Riesman, David, Glazer, Nathan and Denney, Reuel. The Lonely Crowd.
New Haven, CT: Yale University Press, 1950.

Rossant, John. 'Special report: A fragile world – September 11 Shattered
the Old Certainties.' *BusinessWeek*, 11 February 2002: 24.

Stephen, Katherine. '*Mad Men*'s Don Draper effect', *The Christian
Science Monitor*. 6 November 2009 at http://www.csmonitor.com/
Commentary/Opinion/2009/1106/p09s01-coop.html. Accessed on
8 November 2009.

Tallack, Douglas. *Twentieth-Century America: The Intellectual and
Cultural Context*, New York: Longman, 1991: 221.

Townsley, Eleanor. '"The Sixties" trope', *Theory, Culture & Society* 18.6
(2001): 99–123.

Whyte, William H. *The Organization Man*, New York: Simon and
Schuster, 1956.

Wilson, Sloan. *The Man in the Gray Flannel Suit*, New York: Simon and
Schuster, 1955.

Wyatt, Edward. 'Newcomers and veterans share the hardware at the
Emmy Awards', *New York Times*, 22 September 2008 at http://www
.nytimes.com/2008/09/22/arts/television/22emmys.html?_r=1&scp=1
&sq=Edward%20Wyatt,%20%E2%80%9CNewcomers%20and%20
&st=cse. Accessed on 22 September 2009.

'The younger generation', *Time*, 5 November 1951: 45, 50.

Zelizer, Barbie. *Covering the Body: The Kennedy Assassination, the Media,
and the Shaping of Collective Memory*, Chicago: University of Chicago
Press, 1992.

Part One.
Industry and Authorship

1.
The Selling of *Mad Men*:
A Production History

Gary R. Edgerton

At first blush, *Mad Men* may appear to be an overnight sensation. Since its debut on 19 July 2007, this widely acclaimed series has won one major award after another while exceeding the annual expectations of its production company, Lionsgate, and its network, AMC. For his part, creator and executive producer Matt Weiner has realized his wildest dream. Even before winning the 2008 Emmy for Outstanding Drama Series, he likened himself to Charlie at the end of *Willie Wonka and the Chocolate Factory* (1971) because he'd 'gotten everything he wanted'. At the same time, Weiner described the long and arduous eight-year process from researching and writing the first draft of his pilot script to the television premiere of *Mad Men* as being a lot like 'pushing a rock up a hill that you don't think ever has an end' (Keveney, '"Mad Men" Stands Test of Time'). *Mad Men* was born out of Matt Weiner's deep 'dissatisfaction' with the assembly-line storytelling and endless recycling of canned jokes that went along with being a staff writer on CBS's *Becker* (1998–2004), a top-twenty prime-time series during his three years of working on the programme.

'I was 35 years old', recalls Weiner, 'I had a job on a network sitcom. It was rated number nine, which means I was basically in major league baseball for my job. There's 300 people in the country that have this job ... I was like, what is wrong with me? Why am I unhappy?' (NPR: *Fresh Air*, 22 August 2008).

In February 1999, Matt Weiner started writing 'Smoke Gets in Your Eyes' (1:1) as a spec script at nights and on weekends. He was married to an attractive and successful architect (Linda Brettler);

they had three children at the time (now four); and his job was firmly situated within the mainstream television industry. He had successfully broken into the TV business and was working regularly. He was also handsomely compensated if not personally fulfilled. 'I was at this point in my life where Don is', Weiner explains (PaleyFest '08). He was left thinking what Don Draper eventually gives voice to in the second episode of *Mad Men* when he says, 'Who could not be happy with all this?' ('Ladies Room', 1:2). Matt Weiner admits he was 'driven by rage and resentment', but also inspired by the newest breakout series on HBO – *The Sopranos* (PaleyFest '08). It 'had been on the air for about six episodes', he remembers, 'and there was such depth and complexity to the show, and at the same time it was so commercially successful' (NPR: *Fresh Air*, 9 August 2007). Weiner thus wrote and rewrote 'Smoke Gets in Your Eyes' over the next year finishing it in early 2001. He then had his agent submit the script to various development departments at major production companies to see if there was any interest in optioning the screenplay. Time and again, word came back that no one was seriously interested in picking up and developing the project.

The feedback that Weiner received on 'Smoke Gets in Your Eyes' turned into a common refrain that he heard over and over again. The producers and story analysts who read the script were impressed by its quality, but they found the period nature of the piece problematic, not believing that it had enough popular appeal to sustain a weekly series, especially among the always coveted younger viewers. In addition, a number of the development executives were confused by the fact that 'Smoke Gets in Your Eyes' is a drama, since Matt Weiner's reputation up to that point was based solely on his credits as a comedy writer. As a result, the script piled up nearly two years worth of rejections. He finally had his agent send 'Smoke Gets in Your Eyes' to David Chase who called Weiner back personally. 'A week after he got it', recalls Matt Weiner, 'I was in New York on the show' (NPR: *Fresh Air*, 9 August 2007). *The Sopranos* (HBO, 1999–2007) was then at the peak of its popularity, playing a leading role in turning HBO into the most talked about, widely celebrated, and profitable networks in all of television during the early 2000s. Dozens of original programmes are tested each year by the broadcast and cable-and-satellite networks, handicapped by critics and sampled by audiences. Most of these shows fall quickly by the wayside, as an estimated 75 per cent never make it beyond their first seasons. Still, breakout series do occasionally transform a few select networks into the hottest destinations on TV – and *The Sopranos* did just that for HBO during its initial six-season run that began on 10 January 1999 and ended on 10 June 2007.

Matt Weiner joined David Chase and company in 2003 during preparation for *The Sopranos'* fifth season. In the previous fall, the series' fourth season debuted on 15 September 2002 attracting an audience of 13.4 million, which not only won its time slot, but was placed 'sixth for the entire week against all other prime-time programs, cable and broadcast', despite HBO's 'built-in numerical disadvantage'. Even though Home Box Office was based on an entirely different business model than most of the rest of the US television industry, it had beaten all of the advertiser-supported networks at their own game. More significantly, it was also asserting once and for all that 'the underlying assumptions that had driven television for six decades were no longer in effect' (Castleman and Podrazik 419). Cable-and-satellite channels were now the first place to look for breakout programming on all of TV. Clearly the momentum in the industry had shifted unmistakably and irrevocably away from the traditional broadcast networks and more towards the cable-and-satellite sector of the business with *The Sopranos* providing HBO with the kind of signature series that it needed to compete for viewers with any channel on TV. In turn, the success of the show increased 'the status of showrunners', such as David Chase, and 'transformed cable television into its own television universe, with its own rules'. Chase's experience of realizing 'his vision only by going to cable – ha[d now] become the model of how cable TV work[ed] in the post-*Sopranos* era' (Weinman 49–50).

During his four-year tenure on *The Sopranos'* creative team, Matt Weiner worked his way up from supervising producer (2003–04) to co-executive producer (2005–06) to finally executive producer (2006–07). Weiner admits in hindsight that 'everything about [*The Sopranos*] influenced me' (KCRW). 'There was such depth and complexity to the show, and at the same time it was commercially successful . . . Then of course seeing how the sausage was made' (NPR: *Fresh Air*, 9 August 2007). Weiner's experience on *The Sopranos* was his first with a one-hour drama. More importantly, he was no longer being pressured to either dumb down or sweeten up his writing as he had been during his seven-year tenure at the broadcast networks. HBO and *The Sopranos* were also spearheading an alternative narrative style for television 'in opposition to the regular networks' where 'the pacing (was slower), the storytelling (more fragmented) and the structure (organized around the lack of commercials)' (Weinman 50). Chase encouraged the entire writing team to trust their imaginations and be as realistic and honest as possible with the storyline and characters. 'David viewed himself as the audience and the people in the room', reveals Weiner, 'and if we liked and understood it, that's what we did' (NPR: *Fresh Air*, 9 August 2007). The impact on Weiner was liberating, making him 'feel less alone' (KCRW). Now an integral part of *The Sopranos*' inner circle of above-the-line talent, he was no longer alienated professionally, but 'Smoke Gets in Your Eyes' was still languishing in development hell as an unproduced spec script.

Literally weeks after Weiner joined *The Sopranos*' crew, Chase recommended the screenplay to HBO's development department suggesting that 'Smoke Gets in Your Eyes' should be the source material for the network's next original series once *The Sopranos* finished its fifth and (assumed at the time) final season. HBO's former programming chief and newly installed chairman and chief executive officer, Chris Albrecht, counter-offered that HBO 'would make *Mad Men* on the condition that Chase be executive producer'. Being a television journeyman and not yet a proven showrunner, Weiner understood and was open to this arrangement. He even invited Chase to 'direct the pilot'. Despite being 'very tempted', David Chase finally decided against coming aboard the *Mad Men* project, 'wanting to move away from weekly television'. Chase still continued to champion the script, however, as Weiner resubmitted it to HBO's development department in 2004 (Handy 283). While admitting that 'Smoke Gets in Your Eyes' was 'obviously written for HBO', Weiner also acknowledges in retrospect that 'he never got a straight explanation from the network for its pass' ('Smoke and Sympathy: A Toast to *Mad Men*'; Handy 283). Recognizing the groundswell of original programming on cable television, Weiner's agent then sent the screenplay to Showtime, the USA Network and FX later in 2004 and early 2005; in short order, all three networks also declined participation, leaving the project open for consideration by development executives at an also-ran cable channel that was looking to raise its profile by making a serious move into original programming ('Basic Cable Shows Get Emmy Nods').

American Movie Classics was founded as a pay-TV network in 1984 by Rainbow Media, a subsidiary of Cablevision, the fifth largest cable provider in the United States. The channel stalled as a subscription service since its format of providing uncut, uninterrupted pre-1950 motion pictures was not sustainable in the increasingly competitive premium cable marketplace of the mid-1980s. Rainbow Media thus transitioned American Movie Classics into a basic cable channel in 1987, making it available to cable systems nationwide. Over the next two years, the network's access to viewers skyrocketed from 7 million paying customers to 39 million basic cable households (Gomery 94). American Movie Classics' first foray into original programming during the mid-1990s mirrored a similar awakening at HBO, Showtime, FX and the USA Network. The initiative at American Movie Classics was nevertheless short-lived as it only produced two half-hour dramedies, *Remember WENN* (1996–98), which followed the personal and professional lives of the resident staff at a Pittsburgh station during the Golden Age of Radio; and *The Lot* (1999–2001), set behind the scenes at the fictional film studio, Sylver Screen Pictures, during the 1930s. Both series were designed to complement the old-time movie fare on the channel, but neither programme enjoyed much success in attracting viewers.

By October 2002, with an available audience approaching 83 million cable households, a new executive team shifted direction at the network by updating its schedule to mostly post-1970 films in order to further broaden its appeal to a larger, younger audience. In March 2003, they shortened the network's name from American Movie Classics to AMC; they also began rebranding the channel with a promotional campaign built around the slogan, 'Long Live Cool', as a way of repositioning it as a more hip and discriminating alternative cable network; and most significantly, they adopted 'what could be called the HBO formula' where AMC development executives went out of their way to recruit 'top-notch talent and giving them a wide berth' to produce programming that was edgy, sophisticated, and as innovative as anything on television (Alston). Within this context, *Mad Men* provided AMC's executives with just the kind of passion project they were looking for from a now proven writer-producer with a pedigree that included *The Sopranos*. Vice president of scripted series and miniseries, Christina Wayne, initially showed interest in developing 'Smoke Gets in Your Eyes' during the spring of 2005. She scheduled a luncheon in May with her boss Robert Sorcher, executive vice president for programming, packaging, and production, where they asked Weiner, 'what is the rest of the series?' ('A Conversation with Matthew Weiner'). Matt Weiner returned four months later with a treatment outlining the 13-episode narrative arc of *Mad Men*'s first season and they promptly greenlighted the pilot at a budget of $3 million (Schwartz).

Overall, Wayne, Sorcher and their new executive supervisor and general manager, Charles Collier, who joined AMC in early 2006, were all committed 'to combining the network's great movie library with high-end originals' as a way of enhancing their position in the cable-and-satellite sector as 'a quality player more than quantity' (Becker). 'Quality is a commercial decision', observes Weiner ('A Conversation with Matthew Weiner'). 'I know when Christina and Rob first read ['Smoke Gets in Your Eyes'] and met with me, they had a very clear agenda and a lot of it was trying to produce shows like HBO' (PaleyFest '08). Their aspiration was aesthetic as well as commercial. 'We're trying to do cinematic-television shows', adds Collier, 'series that stand side-by-side with the best movies on TV' (Brodesser-Akner). AMC next commissioned the up-and-coming transmedia commercial house, @radical.media, to produce the pilot. It was shot over four weeks in April and May 2006 at Silvercup Studios in Long Island City, Queens (which was also the home base of *The Sopranos*), along with several on-location sites in midtown Manhattan (Elliott, 'That 60's Show'). Weiner actually cast the programme during the fall while simultaneously executive producing the sixth and final season of *The Sopranos*, which HBO extended from the usual 13 to 21 episodes at the last minute. In this way, season six of *The Sopranos* is divided into two parts with the first 12 episodes premiering between 12 March and 4 June 2006, followed by the final nine episodes between 8 April and 10 June 2007. Chase was supportive of Weiner throughout this hectic work period where he often found himself wearing two executive hats at once.

As an example, Matt Weiner told David Chase after the completion of a *Sopranos* production meeting early in December 2005 that he was leaving to start the casting process for *Mad Men*. Drawing on his *Sopranos* experience, Chase advised: 'You're going to hear

['Smoke Gets in Your Eyes'] and it's going to sound really bad. And when the right person reads it, it'll sound good. Don't change it, it's good' ('Smoke and Sympathy: A Toast to *Mad Men*'). In addition, Weiner tapped several of his current *Sopranos* above-the-line colleagues to shoot the *Mad Men* pilot with Chase's blessing. They were all on hiatus after finishing part one of season six, waiting around while part two was being prepared for production. For instance, veteran director, Alan Taylor (9 *Sopranos* episodes) and cinematographer Phil Abraham (47 *Sopranos* episodes) ended up shooting the *Mad Men* pilot on 35 mm film just as they had similarly lensed *The Sopranos*. More appropriately, though, they worked with Weiner to create a totally different look for this new series establishing 'a somewhat mannered, classic visual style that is influenced more by cinema than TV.' *Mad Men*'s template is further enhanced by production designer Robert Shaw's (67 *Sopranos* episodes) sleek, modernist conception of the Sterling Cooper office complex and his more retro-treatment of the Drapers' suburban colonial home, complete with a white picket fence encircling the front yard. Both of these televisual spaces are meticulous in their set design and décor and suitably evocative of the Hollywood movies, 'photography, graphic design and architecture of the period' (Feld, Oppenheimer and Stasukevich 46). Line producer, Scott Hornbacher (43 *Sopranos* episodes), hired many of the remaining above- and below-the-line crew members numbering well over 125 personnel while also supervising them, along with managing the schedule, budget, transportation and technology needs.

As far as the actors are concerned, Weiner contends that he and his casting directors, Kim Miscia and Beth Bowling, were lucky enough to secure all of their 'first choices' for *Mad Men*'s lead characters ('Smoke and Sympathy: A Toast to *Mad Men*'). Not surprisingly, 'Don Draper was the trickiest role to cast.' Director Alan Taylor admits at first that there existed a 'reverse prejudice' towards Jon Hamm because of his striking good looks and 'old-fashioned masculinity' (Handy 337). 'I basically had to start at the very bottom', concedes Hamm, 'and worked my way up from there' (NPR: *Fresh Air*, 22 August 2008). On the outside, he appeared to be this 'icon of maleness', affirms Taylor (Handy 337). 'But he also projected this inner "lost" and "vulnerable quality"', explains Weiner (NPR: *Fresh Air*, 9 August 2007). Taylor, moreover, remembers that when Weiner and the rest of the creative team first saw Jon Hamm in full costume with his hair cut short and combed 1950s-style, they realized that it was fortuitous 'to cast sort of the perfect male in this part because what we were doing in the show was basically deconstructing that' (Handy 337). Matt Weiner did need to assure AMC's executive team that Hamm 'is the guy', since the actor had never carried a movie or television programme as the lead before (NPR: *Fresh Air*, 22 August 2008). Still, Weiner describes his relationship with the executives at AMC as a healthy and constructive give-and-take. For example, his original idea for *Mad Men*'s opening title sequence was to shoot an anonymous businessman jumping out of his high-rise office window in live action. AMC balked at the literalness of the approach, suggesting a more abstract means of presentation. As a result, Weiner moved more in the direction of animation, working with designers Mark Gardner and Steve Fuller at Imaginary Forces to create what turned out to be the 2008 Emmy winner for 'Outstanding Main Title Design'.

In just 36 seconds, *Mad Men*'s opening title sequence is full of obvious and hidden clues as to what this series is all about. The programme is a stylistic hybrid merging elements of Hollywood movies and television programmes from the late 1950s along with TV's contemporaneous 'quality' dramas of today. The debt Matt Weiner and the designers at Imaginary Forces owe to Hitchcock is immediately apparent in this sequence with its pastiche of Saul Bass's title work from *Vertigo* (the optical disorientation), *North by Northwest* (the iconography of the Manhattan skyline) and *Psycho* (the foreboding strings à la Bernard Herrmann). Yet, the most startling aspect of *Mad Men*'s title sequence is the depiction of the male protagonist falling from the top of a skyscraper. The action begins as he enters his office in black silhouette, puts down his briefcase, and watches as the furniture begins to implode, almost melting. A small rotating fan spins in an open window, but we never see how the silhouetted man ends up outside the building; we just see him in a graceful free fall for over half of the sequence tumbling past seductive images of women, a glass of whiskey, advertising slogans ('Enjoy the Best America Has to Offer'; 'It's the Gift That Never Fails'), two hands wearing wedding rings, a couple kissing, a smiling nuclear family and four old vintage photographs. The slow, languid pace of the fall almost suggests a dream where the protagonist is watching his life pass before his eyes. On a deeper level, *Mad Men*'s perspective is resolutely post-9/11. This vantage point is not just chronological; it is psychic and visceral. The falling image captures the full intensity and unease of our time. As the protagonist lands smoothly on his chair, his perspective is that of the viewers who look over his shoulder. He may strike a confident pose with a cigarette dangling from his fingers, but situated behind him, the audience knows better.

In point of fact, 'the pilot was shot exactly the same word for word' from what is in the 'Smoke Gets in Your Eyes' screenplay except for three additions: The first two resulted from 'network notes' recommending that a pair of critical plot developments be foreshadowed 'because the people at AMC knew what the story was', while the third sprung from Weiner's desire to include a small atmospheric vignette in order to enhance the verisimilitude of the setting ('Smoke and Sympathy: A Toast to *Mad Men*'). In the former case, Roger Sterling's ironic reference to a 'young, handsome . . . Navy hero' that ends up alluding to 'Dick Nixon' rather than Jack Kennedy, augurs the upcoming 1960 presidential election ('Nixon vs. Kennedy', 1:12); at the same time, it signals that most of the employees at Sterling Cooper are sleepwalking on the wrong side of history. Likewise, the quiet, intimate scene where Don Draper takes a box containing a purple heart out of his office desk drawer prefigures the dramatic plot twist that is yet to come involving the true nature of his identity dating back to his wartime experiences in Korea (again revealed in 'Nixon vs. Kennedy'). In the latter case, Weiner created a new scene where 'Don looks up at the ceiling and sees this fly in the light fixture'. Rather than denoting anything symbolic, the showrunner's 'intention was to say, "There is a fly in the light fixture and that fly is not period"' (NPR: *Fresh Air*, 9 August 2007). In other words, 'Matt wants *real*', confirms Charles Collier of AMC. For Weiner, 'it's not television; it's a world' (Handy 274).

Once the pilot was completed in the summer of 2006, @radical .media submitted 'the episode to AMC for a decision' (Elliott, 'That 60's Show'). This small independent production house had been working with the network on the possibility of attracting a lone advertiser for each individual episode of *Mad Men*. This single-sponsor strategy harks back to the earliest days of television and would have provided the series with a unique 'commercial-free format' within the participation advertising environment of AMC.

Jon Kamen, Radical CEO, admits that 'despite his background and relationships with brands, the adult themes in *Mad Men* initially proved too disconcerting for advertisers to consider wholly sponsoring the series' (Brodesser-Akner). Thus, when the executive team at AMC screened the pilot and decided to pick up and schedule the series, 'we lost control of the show', admits Kamen. 'Lacking a presenting sponsor', AMC went looking for a more formidable partner who could step in and 'finance the AMC period drama' (Brodesser-Akner). The network found its new business ally in the maverick mini-major studio, Lionsgate, a Canadian-owned producer-distributor of theatrical movies and television programming launched in 1995 by investment banker, Frank Guistra, whose ambition was to capitalize on the growing number of runaway productions from Hollywood that were regularly travelling north of the border throughout the 1990s to shoot in his hometown of Vancouver, British Columbia.

After a slow start at Lionsgate, Guistra was replaced at the top by Jon Feltheimer in 2000 and the studio relocated its headquarters to Santa Monica, California. In that year, it had its first major box office success with *American Psycho*, which established its reputation as the company that specialized in motion picture properties that were either too controversial or arty for the major film studios, a branding image reinforced over the next few years by *Monster's Ball* (2001), *Fahrenheit 9/11* (2004) and the Academy Award-winning Best Picture *Crash* (2005), among others. Lionsgate's president for television programming and production, Kevin Beggs, was recruited by Guistra back in 1998 to jump-start the TV subsidiary of the studio. With the cable-and-satellite sector's renaissance in original programming during the early 2000s, 'Lionsgate's TV production revenue grew exponentially from just $8 million in fiscal 2000 to nearly $210 million in fiscal 2008.' The 'game changer' for the studio was *Weeds*, which Lionsgate began producing for Showtime in 2005 (Moss). On the heels of this success, AMC approached Feltheimer and Beggs to see if they would be interested in partnering on *Mad Men*. Just like *Weeds*, *Mad Men* was singular in style, distinctive in voice and definitely earmarked for the niche sensibilities of cable rather than the mass appeal mindset of broadcast TV. Both series fit the profile of a 'Lionsgate show [which] is unexpected, subversive, edgy, [and] indie-feeling', insists Beggs. 'It mirrors our film brand, yet it finds a way to be commercial. And that is not an easy feat' (Moss).

Once they screened the pilot, Beggs and Feltheimer were enthusiastic about producing *Mad Men*. Drawing on Lionsgate's resources as a mini-major, they proposed 'a budget of $2.3 million per episode' when 'the average budget for a one-hour drama' at a major studio or broadcast network was '$2.8 million' (Witchel 34; La Ferla G6). The executives at AMC and Weiner thought the offer fair and workable given the studio's circumstances. They in turn agreed to join forces and preparation for *Mad Men* began just as soon as *The Sopranos* wrapped in early 2007. Weiner and his creative team moved the entire production to the West Coast as shooting began in April at Los Angeles Center Studios. Each episode was lensed in seven rather than the usual eight days and the results were astonishing considering the budgetary and scheduling limitations. *Mad Men*'s production values were as high as any series on television. According to Weiner, 'I'm of the persuasion that budget constraints are very, very good for creativity. I think people having unlimited amounts of money makes you lazy' (Handy 274). The first season of *Mad Men* premiered on 19 July and ran through 18 October 2007 on Sundays at 10 p.m. on AMC, averaging an estimated 915,000 viewers per telecast over 13 episodes. To be sure, this audience number is modest when compared against the highest-rated broadcast and cable shows, although it signalled a 27 per cent increase over AMC's usual prime-time viewership that year and *Mad Men* 'clearly outperform[ed] a standard movie AMC would put in its time slot' (Umstead; Keveney, 'Success Suits the "Mad Men" Brand', 2D). Audience size, however, was only part of the story.

'The network was looking for distinction in launching its first original series', declares Ed Carroll, CEO of Rainbow Media, 'and we took a bet that quality would win out over formulaic mass appeal. In our view, there's no doubt it paid off' (Witchel 56). 'We're looking for continuing growth', adds Charles Collier, who was promoted to president of AMC in 2008. 'We look at *Mad Men* as an asset on multiple levels, including pop-cultural relevance. Obviously it did well for the brand' (Handy 338). At first, *Mad Men* was 'more a cultural than a commercial hit', but the show's impact on AMC was immediate and transformative, replicating in a smaller way what *The Sopranos* had done for HBO eight years earlier (Umstead; Keveney, 'Success

Suits the "Mad Men" Brand', 2D). By the finale of season one on 18 October 2007, which attracted 1.4 million viewers, *Mad Men* had emerged as AMC's most identifiable product. It was now generating unprecedented word of mouth for the channel, beginning to create multiple revenue streams for all parties involved (AMC, Lionsgate and Weiner), and rebranding the network like no other programme before or since. The momentum at AMC began with the 25 June 2006 debut of the original Western miniseries, *Broken Trail*, which was nominated for 16 Emmys the following year, winning four statues including Outstanding Miniseries and Outstanding Lead Actor (Robert Duvall). The pump was thus primed for the arrival of *Mad Men*, although viewers still did not automatically look to AMC for original programming.

Interest built slowly but steadily for *Mad Men* over the next few years. This heightened profile was hardly by accident, since AMC's marketing and promotions executives were hard at work crafting a multi-year strategy even before the series premiered, never mind being picked up for a second season. 'We knew we couldn't go a traditional route in marketing this show', acknowledges AMC's senior marketing vice president, Linda Schupack. 'We felt we needed to be provocative, confident, and bold' if we were to have 'a chance to rebrand the network with an intelligent, upscale series' (Young). Her colleague, Theano Apostolou, vice president for publicity, talent relations and promotional events, 'worked to make the show part of pop culture through fashion, design, the history of advertising, and even other TV shows' (Maul). Apostolou started with a two-year strategy where the first 12 months would focus on Matthew Weiner and his *Sopranos* connection. 'In her opinion, Matt was the star of the first season in the sense that he was the one who had the heft and he was the most recognizable.' If all went well, and the series was renewed for a second season, then Linda Schupack, Theano Apostolou and their staffs, would begin 'breaking out cast members like Jon Hamm' (Maul). Like clockwork, the style and content of *Mad Men* struck a responsive chord and the behind-the-scenes marketing and promotional campaign took the series to another level. 'Intelligent TV can sometimes be the hardest to market', explains Schupack, 'relying more on critics and creative positioning'. Apostolou continues, 'We could have gone broad and lowest common denominator by putting the emphasis on the sex and scandals, but we pushed this as a writer-driven drama, which gave the series more credibility' (Young).

The critical and institutional recognitions began coming in by the end of 2007 with *Mad Men* being named to literally dozens of top-10 best TV show lists, such as *Time* magazine, where it was chosen '#1 New Show', while *The Sopranos* was selected '#1 Returning Show' (Poniewozik, 'The Ten Best TV Shows'). On 13 January 2008, *Mad Men* won two Golden Globes for Best Television Drama Series and Best Television Actor (Jon Hamm). On 2 April, it garnered a prestigious Peabody Award as an 'exemplary period dramatic series' (Holston). Then on 17 July *Mad Men* received 16 Emmy nominations, the most for any dramatic series that year. By then, AMC's Ed Carroll and Charles Collier had allocated $25 million specifically to market and advertise *Mad Men,* unleashing a tsunami of commercial tie-ins that included partnerships with companies such as American Airlines, Banana Republic, Bloomingdale's Department Stores, BMW, Brooks Brothers, Clearasil, Clorox, Heineken, Hilton, Jack Daniel's, Maidenform, and Mattel with Don and Betty Draper, Roger Sterling, and Joan Holloway Barbie dolls; publications such as *Advertising Age, Ad Week, GQ Magazine, Vanity Fair, Variety* and *Women's Wear Daily*; individual entrepreneurs such as fashion designer Michael Kors' retro-cool 2008 Runway Collection; and viral marketers such as Eight O'Clock Coffee, which created a new online avatar application 'Mad Men Yourself', a 'Which MadMan Are You' quiz game and 'Mad Men eCards' (Schwartz; Elliott, 'A Blitz That Has Don Draper Written All Over It': Elliott, '"Mad Men" Dolls in a Barbie World'; Rosen; Young; Clifford).

Mad Men was, moreover, being referenced all over the television dial. In June 2008, the series was the subject of a $8,000 question on the syndicated version of *Who Wants to Be a Millionaire* (2002-present), 'asking which business *Mad Men* is about. When a contestant asked the audience for help, 86 per cent answered correctly' (Elliott, 'Madison Avenue Likes What It Sees in the Mirror'). In an ABC telecast on 21 September 2008, *Mad Men* became the first basic cable programme in history to win the Outstanding Drama Series Emmy. A couple of weeks later in early October, there was a *Mad Men*-themed category on the syndicated quiz show *Jeopardy!* (1984-present). On 25 October Jon Hamm hosted *Saturday Night Live* (NBC, 1975-present) starring in two sketches ('Two A-Holes at an Ad Agency in the Sixties' and 'Don Draper's Guide to Picking Up Women') that parodied the series. On 2 November, *The Simpsons* (Fox, 1989-present) included a homage to *Mad Men*'s opening title sequence with Homer slowly tumbling in black silhouette down the Springfield skyline. TNT failed to replicate *Mad Men*'s success with the short-lived clone *Trust Me* (13 episodes between 26 January and 7 April 2009), an uninspired drama set in a Chicago advertising firm ('They're Not Mad Men, Just Loud Ones'). And as *Mad Men* was reaching the midway point of its third season on 27 September 2009, AMC was temporarily renamed EMC (the Emotional Movie Channel) by *Sesame Street* (PBS, 1969-present) in a new vignette starring three muppets named 'Don Draper' and his two 'sycophants', who acted mad, sad and happy as they brainstormed together to create the perfect ad for bear's honey.

Overall, Matt Weiner's narrative strategy for *Mad Men* has been to create a brand new story every year. 'The first season was about Don's identity and it was important to distinguish this personal world and this public world for all the characters', he recounts (WBUR). 'The central conflict of [season two] was Don and Betty's marriage' (Sepinwall). And 'season three to me is about chaos. It's how people respond to change. And we're in a period of great change in 1963, and right now' (WBUR). Likewise, *Mad Men*'s promotional campaigns were constructed in tandem with these storylines. 'Central to the marketing of each season', affirms AMC's Linda Schupack, 'is a key image' and branding line. With the first season's emphasis on identity, AMC's marketers decided 'to sell the enigma' with the sitting, black silhouetted image of Don Draper from behind holding a cigarette. To underscore the personal secrets and hidden motives of the main characters, they employed the catchphrase 'Where the Truth Lies'. This branding line continued through the dissolution of the Draper marriage in season two, while the central image shifted to 'a noirish shot' of Don Draper in a fedora standing alone in a blurry and indistinct crowd of people at Grand Central Station, an iconic New York location which is also a place of transit and departure. For season three's agenda of change, the image was of Don Draper sitting in his office again, only this time looking straight at the camera as he smokes a cigarette with water inexplicably rising up to his knees. The new branding line is 'The World's Gone Mad', which 'has a triple meaning' maintains Schupack: 'mad change in the early Sixties, mad

With the first season's emphasis on identity, AMC's marketers decided to 'sell the enigma.' Here is the original live action shot of Don Draper that was turned into the show's signature black silhouette. Courtesy of AMC.

The central image for season two is a noirish shot of Don Draper in a fedora standing alone in a blurry and indistinct crowd at Grand Central Station, an iconic New York location which is also a place of departure. Courtesy of AMC.

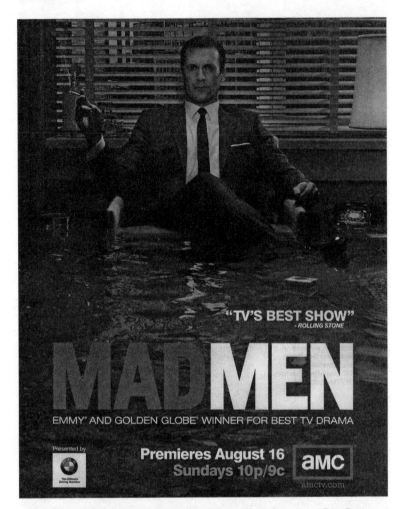

For season three's agenda of change, the central image is of Don Draper
sitting in his office again, looking straight at the camera with water
inexplicably rising up to his knees and accompanied by a new branding line,
'The World's Gone Mad.' Courtesy of AMC.

change in the world today, and the pop-cultural phenomenon – the
world's gone mad for *Mad Men*' (Schulman).

Season three debuted on 16 August and concluded on 15 November 2009. The audience size rose again from season two's average
of 1.5 million to 1.8 million viewers for each Sunday 10 p.m. telecast, although these numbers only tell half the story. If compiled

'live-plus-same-day', which means adding together the cumulative amount of unduplicated viewers for AMC's 10 p.m., 11 p.m. and 1 a.m. encores, season two actually averaged an audience of 2 million, while season three attracted nearly 3 million viewers (Umstead; Gibbons and McNamara; Reynolds). More importantly, though, is the demographic make-up of *Mad Men*'s viewership and the general readiness of the show's audience to watch TV across all of the currently available technologies. First off, '*Mad Men* draws the highest percentage (49 per cent) of viewers 25 to 54 who make $100,000-plus' of any original series on cable, 'which makes it particularly appealing to advertisers' (Keveney, 'Success Suits the "Mad Men" Brand', 2D). Secondly, 'many viewers [do] tune in to watch original episodes', but *Mad Men* also 'relies heavily on DVDs, downloads, and video-on-demand services.' In fact, 'more than 30 million viewers saw the show last year on downloads, video-on-demand services and all broadcasts, including repeat broadcasts the same night as original episodes' (Chozick). When considering this much larger, under-the-radar-sized audience for AMC's signature series, it's much easier to understand why 'it's *Mad Men* that's permeating the zeitgeist' ('"Mad Men" Makes a Splash Bigger Than Its Ratings').

'It's *Mad Men* who has the pulse of our moment', proclaimed Frank Rich in an August 2009 *New York Times* editorial, even 'though the show unfolds in an earlier America'. Celebrity fans include Meryl Streep, Sean Penn, Paul McCartney and Jerry Seinfeld (Rosen). Candidate Barack Obama was even spotted with a *Mad Men* DVD set as he boarded a plane less than two weeks before the November 2008 presidential election ('"Mad Men" Makes a Splash Bigger Than Its Ratings'). 'Success breeds success', declares AMC president Charles Collier (Guthrie). 'We branded the network recently under the heading "Story Matters Here." I don't think we'd be able to say that credibly if we weren't creating original stories' (Keveney, 'Success Suits the "Mad Men" Brand', 1D-2D). Matt Weiner and his creative team have reached back to an earlier time to rescue 'a genre from the 1950s and 1960s that has disappeared' ('Smoke and Sympathy: A Toast to *Mad Men*'). In that way, they have revivified Hollywood's post-war melodrama with its highly stylized socio-sexual preoccupation with women and men struggling against conformity and repression at home and work – only this time on prime-time TV. Not surprisingly in this regard, *Mad Men* is fully informed by women writers, 'a rarity in Hollywood television'. Even in the first season, the writing staff was comprised of three men and three women. By season three, 'seven of the nine members of the writing staff [were] women', while 'women directed five of the thirteen episodes... drawing on their experiences and perspectives to create... a world where the men are in control and the women are more complex than they seem, or than the male characters realize' (Chozick).

In retrospect, *Mad Men*'s success is an improbable story. Matt Weiner shopped his spec script around for nearly seven years before the stars aligned at AMC with its executive staff taking a chance on a quality though widely dismissed screenplay that no other network was interested in producing. Almost immediately, Weiner was transformed from a journeyman writer-producer to one of the most celebrated showrunners in all of television. For its part, AMC became 'a player in the original series game overnight', while also rebranding itself as one of the premiere destinations for drama on American television. The critical praise and cultural cachet generated by *Mad Men* also elevated 'Lionsgate's stature in the creative community, as the studio began a protracted negotiation with Weiner throughout the fall of 2008 when his initial two-year contract expired (Littleton). On 16 January 2009, Lionsgate and Weiner finally agreed on a new two-year deal for a reported $9 million salary; the studio also increased *Mad Men*'s per episode budget to $2.8 million and preserved its 48-minute running time when 'compared with 42-ish for most network dramas' (Littleton; Handy 274; Poniewozik, 'The Pauses That Refresh'). Matt Weiner now talks 'about carrying on the show for many more seasons, maybe six' (Williams). 'What I always wanted to do', he reveals, 'is take this classic American archetype [the enigmatic self-made man], with all the trappings of the late 1950s, and see how he ends up in 1970 or '72' (PBS: *The Charlie Rose Show*; Kaplan). For Weiner, 'it is all about the future', as *Mad Men* continues to raise the bar for high-end cinematic television in the United States and in over three dozen other countries all around the world at the dawning of the 2010s (Littleton).

Works Cited

Alston, Joshua. 'Get "bad," get "mad," and you'll get glad', *Newsweek*, 7 January 2008: 95.

'A Conversation with Matthew Weiner', *Writers on Writing Series 2008*. Moderated by Chris Brancato. The Writers Guild Foundation, Los Angeles, CA, 85:30 minutes.

'Basic Cable Shows Get Emmy Nods.' *All Things Considered* (National Public Radio), 17 July 2008, Matthew Weiner interviewed by Michele Norris, 4:29 minutes.

Becker, Anne. 'GM Charlie Collier raises AMC's profile', *Broadcasting & Cable*, 19 January 2008 at http://www.broadcastingcable.com/ article/99734-GM_Charlie_Collier_Raises_AMC_s_Profile.php.

Brodesser-Akner, Claude. '"Mad Men" gives wide berth to Madison Avenue', *Advertising Age*, 8 October 2007: 1.

Castleman, Harry and Podrazik, Walter J. (2003). *Watching TV: Six Decades of American Television*, Second Edition. Syracuse, NY: Syracuse University Press.

Chozick, Amy. 'The women behind "Mad Men"', *Wall Street Journal*, 7 August 2009 at http://online.wsj.com/article/SB10001424052970 2049086045743322284143366134.html.

Clifford, Stephanie. 'How does "Mad Men" find advertisers? On twitter, of course', *New York Times*, 29 July 2009 at http://mediadecoder.blogs .nytimes.com/2009/07/29/how-does-mad-men-find-advertisers-on-twitter-of-course?scp=2&sq=%E2%80%98How%20Does%20% E2%80%9CMad%20Men%E2%80%9D%20Find%20Advertisers?% 20%20&st=Search.

Elliott, Stuart. 'A blitz that has Don Draper written all over it', *New York Times*, 10 July 2009: B5.

——. 'Madison Avenue likes what it sees in the mirror', *New York Times*, 23 June 2008 at http://www.nytimes.com/2008/06/23/business/ media/23adcol.html?scp=1&sq=%E2%80%98Madison%20 Avenue%20Likes%20What%20It%20Sees%20in%20the%20Mirror &st=cse.

——. '"Mad Men" dolls in a Barbie world, but the cocktails must stay behind', *New York Times*, 9 March 2010 at http://www.nytimes.com/ 2010/03/10/business/media/10adco.html.

——. 'That 60's show: The industry and how it has changed', *New York Times*, 30 May 2006 at http://www.nytimes.com/2006/05/30/ business/media/30adco.html?sq=That 60â€™s Show: The Industry and How It Has Changed&st=cse&adxnnl=1&scp=1&adxnnlx= 1267988571-be0Zp0ImaFBMoLVZsQ9LpA.

Feld, Rob, Oppenheimer, Jean and Stasukevich, Ian. 'Cinematographers from three top series (*Mad Men*, *Desperate Housewives* and *Bones*) reveal their secrets', *American Cinematographer*, March 2008: 46–57.

Gibbons, Kent and McNamara, Mary. 'More "Mad Men" viewers make critical choice', *Multichannel News*, 3 August 2008 at http://www.multichannel.com/article/84430-More_Mad_Men_Viewers_Make_Critical_Choice.php.

Gomery, Douglas. (2004). 'American Movie Classics: US cable network.' *Museum of Broadcast Communications Encyclopedia of Television*, Volume 1, Second Edition. Ed. Horace Newcomb. New York: Fitzroy Dearborn, 93–4.

Guthrie, Marisa. 'From ad man to "Mad Men": AMC's Collier has moved smoothly from sales to programming hit series', *Broadcasting & Cable*, 21 July 2008 at http://www.broadcastingcable.com/article/99510-From_Ad_Man_to_Mad_Men_.php.

Handy, Bruce. 'Don and Betty's paradise lost', *Vanity Fair*, September 2006: 268–83, 337–9.

Holston, Noel W. 'Complete list of 2007 Peabody Award winners'. Press Release: The Peabody Awards Committee, Grady College of Journalism and Mass Communication, University of Georgia, 2 April 2008 at http://www.peabody.uga.edu/news/press_release.php?id=154.

Kaplan, Fred. 'Drama confronts a dramatic decade', *New York Times*, Sunday Arts and Leisure Section, 9 August 2009: 18.

KCRW (National Public Radio affiliate in Santa Monica, California): *The Treatment*, 4 November 2009, Matthew Weiner interviewed by Elvis Mitchell, 27:56 minutes.

Keveney, Bill. '"Mad Men" stands test of time: Matt Weiner stood by his script – for years', *USA Today*, 17 September 2008: 6D.

———. 'Success suits the "Mad Men" brand: Distinctive drama about the '60s ad game reaches out to today's style, culture', *USA Today*, 14 August 2009: 1D-2D.

La Ferla, Ruth. 'A return to that drop-dead year 1960', *New York Times*, 23 August 2007: G1, G6.

Littleton, Cynthia. 'Weiner wins pay raise', *Daily Variety*, 19 January 2009: 1.

'"Mad Men" makes a splash bigger than its ratings', *New York Times*, 23 October 2008 at http://mediadecoder.blogs.nytimes.com/2008/10/23/mad-men-makes-a-splash-bigger-than-its-ratings/?scp=1&sq=%E2%80%98%E2%80%9CMad%20Men%E2%80%9D%20Makes%20a%20Splash%20Bigger%20Than%20Its%20Ratings.%E2%80%99%20&st=cse.

Maul, Kimberly. 'AMC's Apostolou gives "Mad Men" crossover appeal', *PR Week*, 10 November 2008: 4.

Moss, Linda. 'Lionsgate roars into cable: How the team behind "Mad Men" and "Weeds" is building a next generation studio', *Multichannel*

News, 14 September 2008 at http://www.multichannel.com/article/ 134676-Film_Studio_Lionsgate_Roars_Into_Cable.php.

NPR (National Public Radio): *Fresh Air*, 9 August 2007, Matthew Weiner interviewed by Dave Davies, 45:12 minutes.

——. *Fresh Air*, 22 September 2008, Matthew Weiner interviewed by Terry Gross, 46:10 minutes.

PaleyFest '08 (The Paley Center for Media's 25th Annual William S. Paley Television Festival at the Arclight Cinemas in Hollywood, CA), 27 March 2008, Matthew Weiner and the *Mad Men* cast interviewed by Matt Rousch of *TV Guide*, 75:21 minutes.

PBS (Public Broadcasting Service): *The Charlie Rose Show*, 28 July 2008, Jon Hamm, John Slattery, and Matthew Weiner interviewed by Charlie Rose, 22:05 minutes.

Poniewozik, James. 'The pauses that refresh: Back for its third season, the sexy, smart *Mad Men* is still working its silences', *Time*, 24 August 2009: 54.

——. 'The ten best TV shows', *Time*, 24 December 2007: 75.

Reynolds, Mike. '"Mad Men's" third-season finale marks substantial viewer, demo gains', *Multichannel News*, 9 November 2009 at http:// www.multichannel.com/article/388189-_Mad_Men_s_Third_Season_ Finale_Marks_Substantial_Viewer_Demo_Gains.php.

Rich, Frank. '"Mad Men" crashes Woodstock's birthday', *New York Times*, Sunday Opinion, 16 August 2009: 8.

Rosen, Lisa. 'It's good to be "Mad": The AMC show has gone from cool to obscure to cool and all over the place, with celeb fans, iconic status and awards galore', *Los Angeles Times*, 3 June 2009: S10.

Schulman, Michael. 'Poster girls', *New Yorker*, 27 July 2009: 21.

Schwartz, Missy. '"Mad Men": Inside Summer TV's no. 1 hidden gem', *Entertainment Weekly*, 2 June 2008 at http://www.ew.com/ew/article/ 0,,20203313,00.html.

Sepinwall, Alan. '*Mad Men*: Matthew Weiner Q & A for season two', *What's Alan Watching?* 26 October 2008 at http://sepinwall .blogspot .com/2008/10/mad-men-matthew-weiner-q-for-season-two.html.

'Smoke and sympathy: A toast to *Mad Men*', *Inside Media Series*. The Paley Center for Media, Los Angeles, CA. 10 October 2007, Matthew Weiner and the *Mad Men* cast interviewed by Brian Lowry of *Variety*, 56:59 minutes.

'They're not mad men, just loud ones', *New York Times*, 25 January 2009: 8.

Umstead, R. Thomas. 'AMC's "Mad Men" connects with viewers', *Multichannel News*, 28 July 2008 at http://www.multichannel.com/ article/84831-AMC_s_Mad_Men_Connects_With_Viewers.php.

WBUR (National Public Radio affiliate in Boston, Massachusetts): *On Point with Tom Ashbrook*, 25 September 2009, Matthew Weiner interview, 45:52 minutes.

Weinman, Jamie J. 'How the Sopranos shot up TV', *Maclean's*, 9 April 2007: 48–50.

Williams, Alex. 'It's an easy sell for the cast of "Mad Men"', *New York Times*, Sunday Styles Section, 9 August 2009: S1, S7.

Witchel, Alex. '*Mad Men*'s moment: How Matthew Weiner turned early-'60s advertising culture into the smartest show on television', *New York Times Magazine*, 22 June 2008: 34–9, 56–8.

Young, Susan. 'How to hook highbrow audiences: Peabody honorees used smart marketing tactics', *Variety*, 13 June 2008 at http://www.variety.com/index.asp?layout=awardcentral&jump=features&id=peabodyawards&articleid=VR1117987486.

2.

'If It's Too Easy, Then Usually There's Something Wrong': An Interview with *Mad Men*'s Executive Producer Scott Hornbacher

Brian Rose

The challenges of producing a TV series set in the New York City of the 1960s are formidable. The usual episodic television issues of tight budgets, limited shooting schedules and coordinating a large ensemble of above- and below-the-line talent are compounded by the need to create a varied collection of costumes, props, hairstyles, studio sets and remote locations that feel authentic to the period and comfortably 'lived-in'. As executive producer Scott Hornbacher notes, producing *Mad Men* is a continuous process of creative problem solving that is both exciting and demanding.

Hornbacher is well-suited to the role. He and his fellow executive producer (and series' creator) Matthew Weiner worked together on *The Sopranos* (HBO, 1999–2007) where they learned the values of specificity and careful attention to detail from TV veteran David Chase. Prior to his experience as a co-producer and unit production manager on *The Sopranos*, Hornbacher had worked for many years in New York City, first as a location assistant, moving up to a location manager for several feature films, as well as line-producing a few low-budget features.

Working on *Mad Men* is a complex and exacting enterprise, as he discloses in the interview below. But it's also an environment of strong and supportive creative collaboration (to the degree that it led Hornbacher to try his hand at directing with Episode Nine ('Wee Small Hours') in season three. The show's finely tuned production process, and its ability to bring Matt Weiner's artistic vision so fully to life, is ultimately one of the crucial factors contributing to *Mad Men*'s success.

When Did You First Become Involved with the Pilot?

I didn't know about it until I got a call in late January/early February 2006 from Radical Media who were producing the pilot and approached me about working on the show as a producer and unit production manager (UPM). They were a non-traditional company to be involved in this, since they largely produced commercials, documentaries, and reality game shows and this was their first pilot.

It was my understanding, and this may not be 100% correct, that *Mad Men* was sort of a notoriously unproduced pilot. It was deemed to be an exceptionally good piece of writing, but I'm assuming people weren't jumping to produce it because it was a period piece, which tends to frighten the networks. AMC, which had a fledgling scripted entertainment department, specifically Christina Wayne, read the material, thought it was fantastic, and basically said, 'if we don't produce this, we shouldn't be in this business'.

AMC tried to find a studio partner for the pilot and were unable to get anyone to commit, so they in essence said let's go and make it ourselves. But their business model wouldn't let them do that, so they needed to look for an entity that would act as a studio. So Josh Weltman, who's our advertising consultant and a long-time friend of Matthew's, recommended Radical Media.

You and Matthew Weiner Worked on *The Sopranos* at the Same Time from 2004–2006. How Well Did You Know Each Other?

We didn't know each other very well, since we had different capacities. I was a co-producer and UPM, after starting out as a production manager. Matthew started out as a writer and then moved up to an executive producer of the show. He was under pressure to deliver David Chase's vision and I was under pressure to execute production in the most efficient fashion.

How Difficult Was It to Actually Produce This Pilot?

The pilot was extremely challenging. What made me feel like it was a possibility to even do it was that it had been written very specifically,

I think, with an understanding of how challenging it would be. Matt always says he doesn't understand production, but he doesn't really mean it, or he means it, but he's not right – one or the other. In the pilot, there was not a ton of locations. There were literally four exteriors – one was an overhead shot establishing the ad agency, one was a 1950s movie-style establishing shot of a medical office building that Peggy goes to for her gynecology appointment, there was the exterior of the house at night, and the exterior of the train station.

The pilot was done for $3 million and shot in ten days and we had everything going against us. We were considered to be an independently produced television movie and got smacked with 30 per cent rate premium by all of the production unions, because we didn't have the power of the studios or some kind of larger AMPTP (Alliance of Motion Picture and Television Producers) negotiated deal. Generally speaking, the other pilots shooting in New York that spring had budgets of $5–6 million and shooting schedules of 15 days.

We ended up with by and large the crew from *The Sopranos* who were on hiatus, which was great because they were already familiar with working as a unit. However, we were used to shooting on location in New Jersey and then a stage at Silvercup Studios in Queens, as opposed to on-location in Manhattan. And I was concerned that we were importing not just the skill but some of the comfortable ways of doing things on *The Sopranos* that we could not afford on the pilot. The crew was fantastic and rose to the occasion and they were very creative in problem solving.

My background was as a location manager so on some level I knew where we could shoot certain scenes, and where we could combine this with this and that with that so it would permit us to make our schedule. That, plus we worked our damnest to make the locations look exceptional and authentic to the period given our limited resources.

The hardest thing for us to do was the sequence of Don commuting home at night, because shooting on a train is hugely complex and expensive and time consuming. We kept coming up with different solutions. There was a train in Connecticut that was the correct period train, we talked about going there and shooting it in the train yard, at night, but it didn't fit in the schedule and it took us outside of the incentive zone for New York City, so it became expo-nentially more expensive. We couldn't figure out a way to make it affordable.

We were shooting on our sets at Silvercup Studios and we came up with the idea to use these banquettes that we had made for the strip club location, so we put them in a black void. And we got a piece of Plexiglas, placed it perpendicular to one of the banquettes, added some 'rain' with a Hudson sprayer and had Jon Hamm sit just behind the glass, smoking a cigarette and reading the paper. We had some extras in a second banquette across from him, had a woman cross 'in the aisle' and stumble like the motion of a train was knocking her off balance. Then we dollied into Jon's close-up and jiggled the camera emphasize the train motion. A total cheat. This was followed by a scene of him exiting a train station, which we shot in Douglaston, Queens. He was inside this little commuter train station, walking through the doors, and we were perpendicular to him outside. And we had glass in the foreground between us and him. We were using the contemporary commuter train's reflection at night in the glass, as it pulled out of the station, you couldn't tell the train was non-period since it was in reflection, it was dark and rainy. To me this is the best kind of film-making, where you're telling a very convincing lie and the audience just believes it. Nobody's ever said to me 'that shot of Don on the train is horribly cheap and stupid'.

Once the Pilot Was Completed, What Happened Next in Terms of Getting the Show on the Air?

AMC was looking for a studio since they had to have a partner to deficit finance the show. Lionsgate, who had originally passed prior to production, looked at it again and decided to do it. But this took a long time. We shot the pilot in late April, early May of 2006, finished it in June, but didn't hear until August/September that it was picked up – and then nothing happened for what seemed like forever. Lionsgate started to wind up the machine to get us up and running and then there was a big drama about where the series would be produced.

Matthew was adamant that it be in Los Angeles, which in hindsight is probably one of the only reasons we're able to produce the show effectively as a series, just because of the costumes and set dressings and volume of scenery. Turning around a show every seven days that is set in a different period, you need the depth of resources you can only find in L.A. The resources to do that exist in Los Angeles like no other place in the world. Even though you would think that New York, being a major character in the story, would be a no-brainer – why wouldn't you shoot it in New York, it would be much easier to not have to cheat L.A. for New York – but going outside in New York is probably as difficult as it would be here. Everything's wrong wherever you go on the street; it's not period anymore either, unless you remove and erase all of the modernity. So being in L.A. didn't present any more problems than shooting in New York and it eliminated a lot of problems in terms of access to goods, resources and services that we needed.

Matthew was in the process of finishing up the extended 'dance mix' episodes of season six of *The Sopranos* which weren't completed until January 2007, and once that was done we made a trip out to Los Angeles and started meeting casting people, costume designers and production designers, and I started looking for production facilities. In February 2007 we closed the deal to film at Los Angeles Center Studios and moved in. Matt was already in the process of hiring a writing staff and we were able to get the show in production by mid-April of 2007.

As a Producer on the Series, How Did You Meet the Challenges of Period Production? What Changes Did This Mandate in Your Typical Operations?

I knew that we would build more sets. And we knew collectively that we needed to be in proximity to locations that we could shoot that would work for the period. Matt grew up in Los Angeles since he was 11 or 12 and his wife is an architect, and he would walk around lamenting that every time he turned around some amazing landmark had been torn down. He had a pretty good sense of what appropriate locations still existed in the older parts of L.A., which are predominately downtown and Hollywood, which meant we had to be in proximity to those two areas. L.A. Center Studios is a complex built around the defunct UniCal Oil headquarters, which is very much in the architectural style of the Sterling Cooper Offices – mid-century modern, clean lines – so we shoot the lobby of the office there. Originally, we were going to recreate the offices in one of the unused floors of the tower, where a number of other television shows have filmed. Eventually I realized that we were going to be in the Sterling Cooper set so much and that we would be limited by being in a location, in terms of time of day and efficiently moving to and from other sets, and we decided it made much more sense to build our own set on the stages. This was a big shift late in the pre-production for season one, but it was a huge critical decision and a good one. I think it would have been a big mistake in terms of both production efficiency and creative flexibility to have shot in a practical location, even on our back lot.

Do You Remember the Kind of Discussions You and Matthew Had Concerning the Kind of Vision the Series Was Going to Have and How This Would be Implemented?

We did establish something in the pilot. I think everybody on the show now would say that we improved on and I think that's largely due to the fact that we were able to build the sets and have more time and resources to figure things out.

Even though we were basic cable and not able to pay people particularly attractive salaries, we wanted to attract a very high caliber of people to work on the series. We felt the pilot was pretty great, and would serve as its own sales pitch for what we were trying to do creatively. We wanted to import all the good things about producing *The Sopranos* to our show – such as a certain level of professionalism and attention to detail and being specific. Even though *The Sopranos* was a non-period show, there were lots of really specific props and really specific cars, sets and locations. The audience feels that attention to detail and I think they kind of fetishize it and get off on it.

Did That Attention to Detail Come Right from David Chase?

He was very specific about things. I think that was a big part of setting *The Sopranos* apart from others. I learned those lessons there. Ilene Landress always said that when she first met with David about the pilot he talked to her about doing the show the way people make independent films. I've never had this conversation with him but I can only assume that's driven by his history as a writer/producer for network television, where there is often a constant battle 'you can't do this' and 'you can't do that because it costs too much'.

You Mention Costs. Did You Anticipate That Your Attention to Period Detail and Specificity Would Present Budgetary Problems?

Oh yeah, but if you are fortunate enough to be making something good there are always budgetary issues. If it's too easy, then there's usually something wrong. That's just the way it is. Storytelling is a creative process and if you are pushing the envelope there is always tension with the business side of the process.

I worked very hard with AMC during the post-production phase of the pilot to come up with a budget to do the show in New York vs. Los Angeles. Matthew was pretty adamant that it had to be in Los Angeles. I kept saying that this budget is premised on making a show every week that is exactly what we did on the pilot, not some version where we never leave the offices of Sterling Cooper. My initial number knocked their socks off, which on some level I did on purpose. And then they said it has to come down this much, and it did. And when Lionsgate got involved, it was reduced another 20% or so. But it was a long process of fighting for the number to be what it was going to be. I always think of it as 'oh, Matt and I fought for that', but he says 'that was your battle that I stayed out of it'.

One of the reasons I think that he made me an executive producer is he considers me to be his creative partner and calls me that, and I think that's born out of the fact that I am always trying to support his creative process, as opposed to just getting the show done on a certain timeline and on a certain budget, which isn't to say that I'm not excruciatingly aware of cost and schedule and efficiency and all that. I think that we're highly efficient and have lots of procedure and policy in place on our show.

How Do You Two Function as a Team of Executive Producers? Is It Essentially That He Writes the Script, Tells You What He Wants, and It's Your Job to Implement It?

That's basically the job – they give it to you and you execute it. We collaborated, of course, on hiring all of the creative below-the-line people and we collaborated on hiring the directors.

In terms of the process, when Matthew starts putting together what he thinks the season will be, first he'll start talking to me about ideas. And of course I'm cataloguing – ok, we're going to have to build that, we're going to have to find that on location and that's going to be a challenge.

Will He Give You the Entire Arc of all of the Season's 13 Episodes as a Way to Provide an Overall Production Picture?

That would be nice. What happens is he will start to give me bits and pieces, meaning we'll talk about it as he starts to flesh out the season. He may tell me a larger thematic thing or one specific plot development or a character thing or even 'I think we're going to need so and so's apartment'. It's interesting – some story ideas go from a three-episode story arc to a 'B'-story in an episode to a scene in an episode to a line of dialogue. It just happens. Good ideas they tend to hang onto in the writers' room, but they are forced to prioritize and sometimes they realize they don't have room for things.

There's a 12-week writers' pre-production, and there is a revelatory process that happens over the course of those 12 weeks. They're sitting in that room and there's a giant bulletin board and down the left hand side is a column with all the character names and across the top is a row of all the episode numbers. And then they write one or two-word ideas on index cards, and say 'that's Don in Episode Three' and pin it up. They map out these events and then they take those and starting from Episode One they start to break story and develop the specific plot and character things that are going to happen in that episode. And they beat it out. And usually they're anywhere from 23 to 28 beats that ends up being a five-page document that becomes the outline for the script.

At What Point Do You Become Involved? Are You Sitting in on These Meetings?

I have plenty of other business aspects I'm involved in during this time. But what happens is Matt will ask me into the room and pitch me something 'can we do this?' And usually I'm like, 'well, I don't know, it depends on what else you're doing' or 'that sounds great, why don't you just write it and we'll figure it out' Or 'can we do it like this instead'. By week four or five, they have an outline for the first episode, which he shares with me. And then I know what sets will work in that show. I continue to get outlines, the set lists, the characters lists, and I start sharing that information with everybody. And then I'll start going back to Matt to say 'this is what I'm thinking about doing based on what you've told me' or I'll just say 'this is the solution. Does that make sense to you? Is that something you're really going to do?' We've designed sets in pre-production that we've ultimately never built because by the time we got close enough to production that specific idea has fallen by the wayside or changed to take place in an existing set.

Four or five weeks before we start shooting, I might have outlines for four or five episodes and set lists. And based on that, we'll do certain guest casting and recurring deals. I try to aggressively scout locations with the location manager and the production designer and then eventually the director of photography way before any of the directors start. We try to say, when we shoot that scene in the outline, this is a good location. About 60 to 70 per cent of the time the locations we choose in pre-production will end up sticking. For example, we are prepping Episode Three and have a location that was picked seven weeks ago. This is not the normal process when people are producing contemporary shows. They don't have to worry about the specificity of finding period correct locations. They have the location department go and scout a bunch of options the week before the episode shoots. But for us, there aren't a bunch of options. There's like one option and often it is an elaborate process of eliminating choices because of the amount of work it will take in set design, paint, construction, set dressing, removals and sometimes visual effects to make a location viable.

We needed a riding stable for season two. There are a variety of equestrian centers and horseback riding places in the local Los Angeles area, but we had to pick the one that was easiest to deal with in terms of the existing architecture of the buildings, the type of trees that were around (we were looking for deciduous), the local topography. We knew we were going to have to do a lot of modifications, both physical and visual effects. We always have limited choices, because it's a period show. There's an incredible specificity to the location scouting. On a contemporary show, if you're just looking for the lobby of an office building there are more choices. There's a demand for a deeper authenticity on a period show or maybe we just demand it.

How Much Lead Time Do You Usually Get Once You're Handed the Finished Script?

The true pre-production for each episode is seven days. You're supposed to get a script seven days before shooting, so what you then have to figure out is what additional sets or locations, casting and all other elements do we need to pull together in that time. Often it comes down to 'we can only accomplish this' or 'if you want it to be this specific, we can only do it in this limited way, but if we try a creative option, you can have more flexibility.' We try to present solutions.

What's the Typical Production Schedule for an Episode?

We produce the show on a seven day cycle – of which we're in the studio five days and we're out on location for two days. We have a pattern budget that reflects five days in and two days out, but we generally try to go out on location one day or a day-and-a-half. We may shoot a restaurant on location for half a day, and then move back to the stage, or go to an exterior in Pasadena, and then move back to the stage for the second half of the day.

What Episode Proved to be the Most Challenging in Terms of Production?

It's hard to catalog. But 'The Jet Set,' (2:24) was one of the most expensive episodes we've ever produced. As I mentioned before, we're supposed to shoot the show in seven days. That said, we almost always have a 'second unit', which is a euphemism for an eighth day that's shot with another crew and the director from the episode that is just finishing. 'The Jet Set' was so expensive and part of the way we got it done was to do it in exactly seven days. There was not any post-production photography or any second unit shots period. The house we filmed for Palm Springs was in Chatsworth and was on top of a hill. It was very expensive not just because the fee was high, but also because of logistics. We had a ton of night work there and we could only bring trucks in and out between the hours of 7 a.m. and 10 p.m. All the equipment had to shuttle up the hill in smaller secondary trucks called stakebeds and because of the time restrictions a separate group of crew and drivers had to come in on Saturday and take vehicles and equipment out. On top of that we had to find the period L.A. hotel where Pete and Don stay, which had to have a period pool, a period bar and a period main entrance with a driveway we could control. We ended shooting it all at the Altadena Country Club instead of a hotel because we just couldn't find all of those things together in an actual hotel. The country club, fortunately, was pristine enough and not filled with the wrong kind of glass doors, signage fixtures, etc. The umbrellas and chaise lounges all had to be custom-made and it was a huge, huge undertaking on our seven-day prep.

That was one of those instances we were almost making an entirely different show, we were out of our normal paradigm. We had to cast all those Euro-trash jet setters, who not only had to have a specific European authenticity, but also had to act. We were looking for period Los Angeles and period Palm Springs as opposed to our normal east coast settings. Our characters were out of their usual environment, and everything had to be redefined. Matt was very influenced by the photographs of Slim Aarons, who followed and photographed jet setters during this period, so we had a very specific reference. Essentially, we had to reconceive the entire look of the show for that episode in terms of hair, make-up, costumes, vehicles, color, design and even cinematography. It was like making a 48-minute movie and it was a lot to do in the confines of an episodic series. It was way outside of our normal box which is also what made it fun and rewarding.

Do You Find These Problems Exciting or Just Another Part of the Constant Headaches Associated with Production?

If I didn't find them exciting I probably shouldn't be a producer. I think by and large film and television production is just creative problem solving. That's true for actors, directors, writers and everyone who is a part of the process. It's prioritizing, problem solving, and making choices. We're pretty good at making decisions and choices and *Mad Men* is probably one of the most collaborative environments I've ever experienced in my film and television career. I think this goes back to Matt and me working on *The Sopranos*. The specificity we learned from working there and the quality of work we were doing there, we wanted to import to the producing of *Mad Men*. We looked to hire creative people with exceptional credits whom you would not necessarily find working on a basic cable show, because they have a lot of options and a lot of opportunities. Janie Bryant [costume designer] had done *Deadwood* (HBO, 2004–06); Dan Bishop [production designer] had done *Carnivàle* (HBO, 2003–05); Phil Abraham had shot *The Sopranos*. Our pitch to them was 'you don't know what *Mad Men* is. We're proud of the pilot we produced. You don't know what we're going to do with it, but we want to create a place where people who do creative work on your level are appreciated. We don't want to just crank it out. We want to really see your skills come to play as a character in the show'. I think that's what's appealing to the Janie Bryants, and Dan Bishops and Chris Manleys [cinematographer] of the world that we have working here. It's been our philosophy of how to make the show.

The work is hard and there is tension and we fight about stuff because everyone is always trying to push for the best they can do things creatively.

Has It Ever Happened That Matthew or the Writers Have Proposed Something and You've Had to Say It's Just not Possible to Execute?

It hasn't happened a lot. One of the episodes in the first season had a scene on a golf course, which meant we had to find a physical location that would double for Westchester 1960. It was a somewhat expositional scene, and we already had challenges in the episode. Financially and schedule-wise the location just didn't fit, so that scene was given up.

We've taken scenes that were set in one place and rewritten them to be in another. In one of the early episodes of season one, there was a scene where Roger and Don were supposed to drink at a bar after work. There were difficulties finding a bar on location that fit that particular schedule and the added cost of going on location. I asked if they could be having a drink in Don's office after hours. Matt agreed that they could and rewrote the scene. In the end he said that he even liked it better. It ended up being kind of incredible – it was the first time we saw the Sterling Cooper set at night looking out those windows and it looked really great. We've used it two or three times since, Don and Roger go to have a drink and an intimate conversation after hours.

Do You Think That Matthew's Years in Television and Work as an Executive Producer Have Now Led Him to Anticipate Production Problems in Advance So That He Doesn't Write Scenes That Will Pose Difficulties?

I think on some gut level he knows when things are going to be hard, but he also says, things like 'who knew it would be cheaper to build a barn than shoot a barn on location?' There are certain times when there isn't necessarily a clear logic to why some things are more difficult or expensive if done in a practical way. And I think that's where there's sometimes a disconnect for him. He's very astute about production issues, though he would tell you he's not. Usually what happens is when he's breaking a story or outlining and they come up with something and he's worried about it, he'll talk to me about it. And generally speaking, I'll usually say just write it and we'll figure it out. And we do. It's a partnership and we trust each other.

Other Than the Extraordinary Work That Your Production Designer and Costume Designer Do, Is There Anyone on the Show Who Was a Contemporary of This 1960s New York Environment Who Can Look at Things and Instantly Say, 'that's not quite right'?

This season and last season we had Bob Levinson who was a senior agent at ICM and used to work as an ad agency art director in New York during this period. This year we also had Frank Pierson, the writer of *Cool Hand Luke* (1967) and *Dog Day Afternoon* (1975), as a consulting writer/producer, who is obviously vintage to the era.

But what happens overall is that we research stuff pretty painstakingly. The writers' office now has worked out that the script coordinator and an army of interns do research on subjects, places, current events, politics, etc. as the writers are outlining the episodes. Matthew will say, 'I need to know more about that and how it was really done' and they start digging.

Cinematography Is One of the Show's Most Distinctive Features. How Was It Conceived from the Beginning?

There were a lot of discussions when we were making the pilot about how is the show going to be photographed. Somebody suggested we shoot it in black and white, and Matt was adamantly against that, I think rightfully so. His whole idea was that things were very contemporary then, and we're not trying to kitsch-ify the show because it is set in that period. Again *The Sopranos* served as an example of a very artfully photographed show that we wanted to emulate. Occasionally, there were fancy cinematic shots, but for the most part it was just a straightforward traditional kind of film-making. I think there was a consensus that what we were putting in front of the camera should be beautiful to look at and that what the people were saying was good and the characters were worth watching. Often in current television there seems to be a desire to make the photography 'exciting', which to me can be emblematic of a lack of confidence in the underlying material, the writing. I guess the feeling is that the audience will watch it if the camera is moving all the time, energetic and underscoring the drama. I think on *Mad Men* we want to let things unfold which comes from Matthew's original vision of the show.

Matt was always very much interested in trying to make the show feel like it was shot on location in New York. *Sweet Smell of Success* (1957) has great exteriors in it because it was shot on the streets of New York, as opposed to many films of the early 1960s which were shot in Hollywood and are very artificial. He was very interested in Chabrol's *Les Bonnes Femmes* (1960), which was shot in Paris on location. You could see what clothes looked like and what the cars looked like. In most Hollywood films you're looking at a stylized version; when you look at period magazines you're looking at a stylized version. You're not necessarily seeing what people really looked like. Those are ideas that Matthew has been discussing since the beginning. At the beginning of season two we watched John Cassavetes' *Shadows* (1959), which was shot with a 16 mm. camera on location with what looks like a single light bulb. Matt is always attracted to the grittiness in those films. It turns out it's almost impossible for our people to do that. The environment our characters inhabit in advertising, their lifestyle and clothing, it's very hard to find gritty. We've had a number of opportunities like the gambling club in 'Six Month Leave' (2:21) and we have a couple of sets this year, but the characters aren't often in seamy, gritty, low rent places. It's something he is attracted to, but it's not necessarily inherent in the scenes at the Draper house or at the Sterling Cooper offices. However, darkness isn't something we're afraid of photographically. Matthew enjoys letting things really fall off.

What Types of Problems Have You Encountered in Dealing with AMC and Lionsgate?

The people that work at studios and networks are always under the pressure of somebody looking over their shoulder about the economics even when the show is critically acclaimed like *Mad Men*. Their vision of things becomes more and more global. So that ultimately if somebody is looking at quarterly profits and wonders 'how much money did we spend on *Mad Men* this quarter and what were our gross earnings this quarter?' they might end up saying 'somebody ought to talk to the television department.' And then the television department might say, 'hey, you guys aren't coming up with the right solution.' It goes downhill from there. Lionsgate and AMC have been great collaborators, but they are by nature about commerce and we are inherently about the creative process. There is always a certain amount of tension in that relationship. They have given Matthew and the show, in general, unprecedented creative freedom.

Has the Pressure from Above Lessened as the Show Has Become More Successful?

As a natural part of the process, making successive years of the show, there's more balance between what we think the show costs and what the studio thinks the show costs. They're actually more in alignment because everyone on all sides has learned what it really takes to produce the show. I guess in any good business situation that happens. There's a lot of trust. They give us an immense amount of their trust and we endeavor not to let them down on the product. You hope and dream for a certain amount of autonomy, and yet at the same time you want a safety net and support – they provide a lot of structure for us. Sometimes they have a new and different perspective that is helpful just because they are outside the process a little. Sometimes we need that objectivity. It's a marriage of commerce and art. There's a certain amount of inherent conflict. Everyone's agenda is to make the show as creatively good as possible, but theirs is also tempered by a very real need to try and make a profit. The tension is necessary. I think limitations in a way force you to make creative solutions and I believe Matthew would agree.

How Do You Think the Production Style of the Show Has Changed from Season to Season?

I think it's gotten more refined. In season one, for example, the show was, I think, written slightly simpler. There were fewer scenes and fewer characters, which on some level makes sense because all these characters were new to the audience, Matthew and the writing staff. We had less money. The machine wasn't quite as well oiled yet and we could do less in a day. I think that our photographic style was slightly more self-conscious.

Now the show feels denser. There are more scenes. There's a wider array of characters and more layers. You can't have, for example, Don and Pete having the same conflict all the time. Photographically, the show has gotten more confident and a little simpler, not that we don't do anything elaborate. In terms of production, our capacity has increased in terms of the amount of work we can accomplish, but there's more work to accomplish because the scripts are denser. It's kind of unbelievable to me, that we're able to pull off the show every week given the level of detail, being period and all the preparation that goes into that.

What Do You Think Accounts for the Critical and Popular Success of the Series?

First and foremost, the characters are engaging. There is a mysterious quality to the show. It's not a straightforward drama about an advertising agency. There's a rich back story and internal life to the characters. It's complex, things aren't neatly tied up all the time and there's a challenge to not always knowing what's going to unfold.

Plus, audiences are fascinated with this moment in American history and culture. There's something incredibly attractive about it and it's very alluring to both men and women because there's all this visual iconography that comes from the time. I'm 45, so I was not born yet in the world of *Mad Men*. But everything about the show in the early 1960s permeated my childhood. And there's a spectrum of people who are older than me that actually lived through all of this. And there are younger people who look at it all like total science fiction.

3.
Don Draper Confronts the Maddest Men of the Sixties: Bob Dylan and George Lois

Ron Simon

Oh, Jokerman, you know what he wants.
Oh, Jokerman, you don't show any response.
— Bob Dylan, 'Jokerman', a song from *Infidels* (1983)

The fictional work of *Mad Men* is haunted by two of the Sixties' maddest men, Bob Dylan and George Lois, both of whom defined and defied the era with incomparable bursts of artistic energy and rebellious outrage. Creator Matt Weiner is certainly conscious of Dylan and Lois's creative contributions and has made subtle references to each throughout the first three seasons. He understands that the iconic duo shifted the cultural landscape for a generation, and his fictional Don Draper and the ad agency Sterling Cooper must respond to those changes for any credible authenticity. One of the small, but profound, pleasures in watching *Mad Men* is to witness how Weiner summons up Dylan and Lois to comment upon his ongoing narrative and his characters in professional and personal turmoil.

One of the deepest antinomies in the *Mad Men* universe is the clash between entrenched norms and emerging post-war values. The show's narrative reflects the now clichéd symbolism of Dylan's signature song 'The Times They Are A-Changin'. In an online interview Weiner summed up prosaically what his series delves into poetically: 'It's the beginning of the baby boom and it's completely driven by young people – and by old people's desire to embrace young people.

Bob Dylan is twenty years old and everyone thinks he's the wisest person in the world'.[1] While this statement is factually inaccurate – Dylan at twenty had barely penetrated the consciousness of anyone beyond Greenwich Village – it is the one of the operating principles of the series: Draper and his colleagues must come to grips with a cultural upheaval. Or, in Dylan's words, 'you better start swimmin' or you'll sink like a stone'.

Weiner set the first season of *Mad Men* in 1960, a pivotal year for George Lois, the enfant terrible of the ad world. He was advertising's street fighting man, one of the main architects of the design earthquake of the Sixties. Lois learned his trade at the ad colossus Doyle Dane Bernbach, whose leader William Bernbach called for a 'creative revolution' in 1949. With his fiery Bronx dialect, Lois embodied that insurgency in his art and character. In 1960 he launched his first company, Papert Koenig Lois with fellow DDB renegades. Lois had the creative guts that mystified the more staid members of the advertising field, whose members included Don Draper and his staff.

At DDB, Lois learned how to sell 'big-idea' thinking, juxtaposing crisp, clean visuals with strong, emphatic text. Lois and his colleagues dreamed up the defining ad of the era: a tiny visual of the Volkswagen beetle is juxtaposed with the words 'Think Small'. The image and words leave plenty of blank space, like a minimalist painting by Frank Stella with a hint of Andy Warhol pop. The campaign defied the received wisdom about ads and how to sell a product. The Volkswagen onslaught rocked the entire advertising world, most notably the fictional agency of Sterling Cooper. Eventually, the 'Think Small' promotion would become the gold standard of the industry, hailed by *Advertising Age* in 1999 as the top campaign of the century.

The follow-up to the 'Think Small' ad was a larger picture of the Volkswagen with a startling word underneath – Lemon: the foreign car looked like that fruit, but described with the one word that connotes a faulty auto. That self-deprecating beetle ad was an opening image of the third episode, catching Don's derisive eye as he was riding the train. When he arrived at the office, his fellow executives are as totally flummoxed as Don by the campaign, in Dylan's words, criticizing what they didn't understand. Certainly, the group was behind the times, with such negative comments as

'I don't know what I hate about it the most, the ad or the car'. No wonder even its workers pegged Sterling Cooper as a 'third-tier' agency.

Lois summarized his Madison Avenue-shaking philosophy for the American Institute of Graphic Arts: 'Everything I did was looking for the Big Idea, but you're not going to get an idea thinking visually in most cases. You have to think in words, then add the visual. Then you can make one plus one equal three'.[2] Lois was creating advertising that verged on art, blurring the lines between commerce and self-expression.

If Don Draper is bewildered at his competitor's work, he is bothered at play as well during the first season. His bohemian paramour Midge Daniels confounds him by her lack of drive and concern for materialism. His conception of success is challenged on every visit to her pad, which serves as an office, salon, and love nest. Midge's world is part beatnik, part social consciousness informed by Dylan and his gang. In the DVD commentary for the first season Weiner incorrectly states that Dylan arrived in New York in 1960, which would have tied nicely into his time frame. Actually, Dylan hitches a ride to Manhattan in January 1961. The folk scene was very vital then, but Dylan would take it to another level over the next two years. But like Draper, Dylan assumed a new identity in his career, changing his name from Zimmerman.

In the sixth episode of the first season, Weiner envisions the cataclysmic impact of Dylan. After a disagreement about responsibility, the button-down Draper and the carefree Midge venture into the Gaslight Café, a key nightclub incubating a new sensibility in Greenwich Village. Midge's other lover, the avant-garde Roy Hazelitt, accompanies them, all the while mocking the falsity of Don's existence. Midge attempts to defend Don, who looks totally out of place in this smoky joint, with the words 'you gotta serve somebody', a indirect reference to Bob's born again transformation in the late seventies. The Dylanesque quotation is a curious flash forward in time, which serves as an introduction to the performer on Gaslight stage. His presence and stirring song interrupts the trio's debate and propels the episode to a conclusion.

In the DVD commentary of the episode, director Andrew Bernstein cites Dylan as a major influence on the costuming of their lead singer Ian, who is backed up by two musicians. Certainly, the performer's cap and tan sheepskin coat are taken directly from the cover of Dylan's first album. Although Dylan's initial effort, comprised mostly of traditional songs, was a commercial failure, the pose and clothes of Dylan attracted attention. (Dylan would change his style for his second album, *The Freewheelin' Bob Dylan*, released in 1963 with that much duplicated shot with girlfriend Suze Rotolo walking down a Village street.) Weiner and his music director David Carbonara, selected a traditional song to close this episode, 'Babylon', which also gives the episode its title. The song is a multi-part round, whose lyrics were based on Psalm 137, and was probably composed in the early nineteenth century. Weiner first heard 'Babylon' on Don McLean's *American Pie* album released in 1971. He and Carbonara did not alter the old English arrangement, with Carbonara himself singing lead, but the biblical lyrics suggest the Gospel flavor of late Fifties Odetta, a major influence on all folkies of the Sixties, especially Dylan and McLean, who began singing on the East Coast in 1964.

Psalm 137 speaks of exile, the singer in a foreign land separated from his God and country. Certainly, Don and others in the montage, like Roger with his girlfriend and Betty with her children, are struggling for wholeness in their lives. Music in *Mad Men* underlines the character's plight, occasionally offering some sort of salvation. For example, Father Gill expressed his hidden longings strumming the Peter, Paul and Mary standard, 'Early in the Morning', which closed the eighth episode of the second season. Ironically, it was the man of cloth that directly embraces the tremors of the folk counterculture in Weiner's storyline.

The final episode of the first season, 'The Wheel', delves into Don's professional and private spheres. Don is seen at his corporate best, winning the account for Kodak's new slide projector. His pitch is purely nostalgic and sentimental, labeling the carousel a time machine taking 'us to a place where we ache to go again'. Don projects pictures of his own happy family, masking the desperation of the present, where he and his wife will not spend Thanksgiving together. He is miles away from the groundbreaking artistic breakthrough that Lois helped to engineer. In his own words, Lois was the 'guy who worked a little differently. Edgier. More punch-in-the-mouth'. Don's personal problems affected his view of the design revolution around him. He hungers to retreat personally and publicly, adrift in his life and times.

At the close of the final episode Don returns to an empty home, imaging the embrace of a loving family. Don's life is an empty shell game and he has become the huckster that hipster Roy mocked. Don slumps on the stairway and Weiner closes the season with the nasal voice of Dylan in one of his defining performances, 'Don't Think Twice, It's All Right'. Dylan debuted the song at the Gaslight in 1962 and was released on the *Freewheelin'* LP in March 1963. Obviously, 'Don't Think Twice' does not fit the time frame of *Mad Men*'s first season, to the dismay of many viewers and bloggers. But the lyrics captured the spirit of the season, suggesting where the series is headed, in time and narrative.

Whether Weiner knew the genesis of 'Don't Think Twice' or not, it certainly reflects the crises of his characters. Dylan wrote the song after his girlfriend Suze left him for Europe. It was a song of personal encouragement in the face of loss. Or, as Dylan ruminated, the lyrics are 'as if you are talking to yourself'. Weiner suggested in the DVD commentary it was really Betty's lament with the song 'an emotionally powerful statement about how lovers separate'. The wife has had enough, taking the kids to her parents for the holiday. But if we take into account the self-pity in the creation of the song, it belongs equally to Don, bemoaning his own loss.

The first episode of the second season, 'For Those Who Think Young', frames generational clash as a dominant theme of episodes to come. Don is asked by the management to hire younger talent to create fresh advertising with a Pepsi generation spirit. Don is resistant, complaining, 'young people don't know anything'. He is almost the archetypal Mr. Jones from Dylan's 'Ballad of a Thin Man' ('something is happening and you don't know what it is, do you Mr. Jones?'). He reluctantly hires a young duo, who epitomized the latest in agency collaborations: the copywriter and art director partnership. As the pair, both ironically named Smith, leave the office, Don states that he sees the 'fingerprints of Julian Koenig' all over their work. Koenig was a collaborator who worked closely with Lois at DDB. The duo would form a boutique firm with another former Bernbacher, Frank Papert. Like many creative teams, Koenig and Lois in later years would argue about credit over many ads.

The new creative twosome, the American Smitty and the foreign-born Kurt, form an alliance with the upstart Peggy, against the older men who consider the agency their province. They devise a coffee commercial with the new calypso sound permeating the cafes. The tune was adapted from Serge Gainsbourg, a Dylan-like artistic provocateur who shook up the French scene. In the eleventh episode of the second season, 'The Jet Set' (2:24), cultural territory is further demarcated. To delineate the trio from the other creatives, Weiner uses an appreciation of Dylan as the new calling card. During a meeting in which the older guys reference *Playboy* and Loretta Young, the trio stakes their claim to the emerging youth culture. Interrupting the old school banter, Smitty announces his partner does not have a TV and saw Bob Dylan at Carnegie Hall. Peggy immediately injects: 'I heard him on the radio'. New culture has trumped the old guard.

Peggy sidles up to Kurt after the meeting and asks 'does he sound like the album?' Kurt explains, 'he plays it himself', and Peggy, obviously charmed by Kurt's accent, injects, 'he must be something to see.' He then invites her to see Dylan that evening. The exchange raised so many questions for perspicuous fans. Obviously, Weiner and his cohorts were returning to their stated metaphor of Dylan incarnating youth. But did Dylan actually penetrate everyone's consciousness by September 1962? We know the date by the Kennedy speech on integration that comes later in the programme. Dylan did perform at Carnegie Chapter Hall, a small auditorium next to the shrine, on 19 November 1961. It was one of the singer's first mainstream ventures outside the Village and about fifty people attended. Dylan's first album was released several months before Peggy's conversation, but was conceived a commercial failure. That effort created little word of mouth outside the folk circle; Peggy would have really had to have been into the scene to know about Dylan's music. Peggy might have heard Dylan on radio, but she would have to have been an FM aficionado. Dylan's songs were not yet part of AM's Top Forty, although he performed on small FM stations a few times.[3]

The dialogue about Dylan's performance style rings false. During those early years, Dylan mostly performed solo, just voice and guitar. The debut album was raw, but did not totally capture Dylan's mystique in concert. A truer answer from Kurt would have invoked Dylan's underlying humour; in fact, many critics and friends described this early Dylan as Chaplinesque. One of his first admirers, Robert Shelton of the *New York Times*, described Dylan performing one of his shaggy-dog songs: 'He bobbed and swayed, played with his black corduroy Huck Finn cap, made faces, winced, and joked his way through the ridiculous narrative.'[4] In the early days Bob was always part jester, not a wooden idol of conscience.

We are never quite sure whether Kurt and Peggy actually saw 'the Bob Dylan'.[5] When his coworkers ask him about his upcoming date, Kurt reveals that he is a homosexual. Peggy is haunted by the news, questioning her choice of men. As they are about to leave from Peggy's Brooklyn apartment for the concert, Kurt assuages her confusion, giving her an up to date hair styling. According to Kurt, she is 'old style', and her Zelda Gilroy-like locks are transformed, yielding a modern woman à la Jackie Kennedy. Weiner quietly underscores that this new youth culture is as much about image as substance.

In episode six of the third season, 'Guy Walks into an Advertising Agency' (3:32), Weiner again uses a Dylan song to close the show. Here Don's world is entirely in flux. Professionally, the British owners of Sterling Cooper send in a young hotshot named Guy to oversee the creative department, but he meets a tragicomic demise. Personally, Don must comfort the anxieties of his daughter Sally. Whatever happens after this episode, nothing will ever be the same, especially for Don, who will have to rethink all aspects of his life. Weiner chooses one of the two original numbers, 'Song to Woody', from Dylan's first album, to settle the confusion of the episode. Dylan first came to New York to meet his muse Woody Guthrie, suffering from Huntington's disease. Guthrie's condition unnerved the young singer, who decided he now must get on with his life. In this soothing waltz with a tune borrowed from Guthrie, Dylan defiantly knows he must seek his own voice: 'I'm a leaving tomorrow. But I could leave today.' Ironically, this was the song that fits the time frame of the previous seasons, now Weiner goes back to the past to explain the present.

The third season of *Mad Men* represented a rapidly fading order, where the 'present now will later be past'. Don's professional and private lives will need to adapt to the disruptions of the coming years. Many bloggers picked up on the Dylanesque feel of the third season. In fact, Lindy King of www.examiner.com stated 'season three *is* a Bob Dylan song.' Unlike the languid first two years, which she labels 'Frank Sinatra years', the third season was 'where allusion and nothingness are the big picture'. She then selected song lyrics of Dylan that fit not only characters, but the style of the overall narrative. For Don Draper she quoted from 'It's All Over Now, Baby Blue': 'Forget the dead you've left /they will not follow you' (King). Certainly Matt Weiner with his numerous Dylan references has encouraged such a reading of his series.

At the end of the season, Draper and his colleagues are setting up their renegade agency, not unlike Lois's break from the dominant DDB. Up to that point, Lois sensed dishonesty in the programme:

> When I hear *Mad Men*, it's the most irritating thing in the world to me. When you think of the '60s, you think about people like me who changed the advertising and design worlds. The creative revolution was the name of the game. This show gives you the impression it was all three-martini lunches.[6]

But Lois later admitted that he was like a mobster looking at *The Sopranos*. He knows his world too intimately.

Lois's career arc suggests options for Draper if he desires to be more relevant to the zeitgeist. The adman wanted to shake up society with his craft, often exploring other avenues than overt advertising. His covers for *Esquire* defined the decade's tumult with witty, bold imagery, much like Dylan's hallucinatory lyrics on *Highway 61 Revisited* (1965) and *Blonde on Blonde* (1966). Whether it was Muhammad Ali portrayed as a suffering St. Stephen or Andy Warhol drowning in a Campbell's soup can, Lois's work embraces a willingness to shock his audience, what he called 'stun 'em and cause outrage.'

In 1965, Lois created a cover for *Esquire*'s college issue that fused the faces of four icons into one face: Dylan, Malcolm X, Fidel Castro and John F. Kennedy. Provocatively, the composite face was put into a rifle sight. For Lois, the creativity and innovation of the times that these 'heroes' represented were intermingled with death and loss. Later, he would remark about the cover, with a nod to Virgil's *Aeneid,* only Dylan remained to 'sing of that violent revolting age'.

Esquire's *September 1965 Cover Designed by George Lois for Its 'Back to College' Issue. Courtesy of Hearst Publishing.*

Lois actually worked with Dylan several times, and these interactions of the two maddest men propose other possibilities for Don, once he questions his corporate existence. Lois and Dylan would first cross paths in the mid-seventies, brought together in a movement to free wrongly convicted boxer Rubin 'Hurricane' Carter. Lois recruited Dylan to become active in the fight for a retrial, resulting in creation of the anthem 'Hurricane', a return to the duo's socially conscious years.

Later, in the early eighties, Dylan tested evangelical Christianity while Lois helped to convert America's young to music video. He designed the 'I Want My MTV' campaign, which helped establish the cable service as a major player in the music business. They would collaborate on the video for one of Dylan's most haunting and evocative songs, 'Jokerman'. This partnership started with the words, just as it had in Lois's advertising days. Dylan would play the copywriter to Lois's art director. Lois superimposed Dylan's fiery lyrics over a wide-ranging portfolio of iconographic imagery, a technique he jokingly labeled 'poetry right in your fuckin' face'.

In its six stanzas the video conjures complex and often contradictory images of creation and destruction in a voyage to some sort of self-discovery. The couplet that defines Dylan's trajectory also has become an emblem for Don Draper: 'Shedding off one more layer of skin, keeping one step ahead of the persecutor within'. Draper is slowly coming to a realization of himself as an individual and advertising guy. Perhaps, he will see above the corporate fray and recognize how Dylan and Lois are transforming the external and internal landscapes. Certainly, Weiner has acknowledged their impact, often conjuring up the pair as mad muses in constructing his narrative.

Works Cited

King, Lindy. '*Mad Men* to Dylan: Something is happening here, but you don't know what it is', 4 September 2009 at http://www.examiner .com/x-13070-Mad-Men-Examiner~y2009m9d4-Mad-Men-to-Dylan-Something-is-happening-he.

Notes

1 AMCtv.com has conducted a series of interviews with creator Matt Weiner that yield a surprising number of observations not discussed elsewhere. See Clayton Neuman, 'Q&A-Creator Matthew Weiner (Part I)', 31 October 2008 at http://blogs.amctv.com/mad-men/exclusive-inter/2008/10/26-week/. Accessed on 30 October 2009.

2 Much of George Lois's colourful philosophy can be found in his medalist section on the AIGA (formerly the American Institute of Graphic Arts) website. See Andrea Codrington, 'George of the Jungle', at http://www.aiga.org/content.cfm/medalist-georgelois. Accessed on 30 October 2009.

3 Bob Dylan's notable radio debut occurred on 29 July 1961 when he appeared on a special hootenanny marathon to inaugurate a small radio station, WRVR-FM, operated by the Riverside Church on the Upper West Side of Manhattan.

4 Robert Shelton gave the first major review of Bob Dylan in the *New York Times* on 29 September 1961. He subsequently published a major biography on Dylan's career, especially the formative years. See Robert Shelton, *No Direction Home: The Life and Music of Bob Dylan* (New York: Birch Tree Books, 1986), 106.

5 Actually Peggy and Kurt could have seen Bob Dylan during this time period at Carnegie Hall. On 22 September 1962 Dylan sang at a hootenanny sponsored by *Sing Out*! Pete Seeger, who also performed with such guests as the New World Singers and the Lilly Brothers,

introduced Dylan. This event connected the new with the older tradition of folk music.

6 George Lois has spoken on numerous occasions to the press and me about his displeasure of the portrayals on *Mad Men*. This quote comes from an interview with Alex Witchel, '*Mad Men* Has Its Moment', *New York Times Magazine*, 22 June 2008 at http://www.nytimes.com/ 2008/06/22/magazine/22madmen-t.html?_r=1&sq=george%20lois% 20mad%20men%20alex%20witchel&st=cse&scp=1&pagewanted= all. Accessed on 30 October 2009.

Part Two.
Visual and Aural Stylistics and Influences

4.

'Smoke Gets in Your Eyes': Historicizing Visual Style in *Mad Men*

Jeremy G. Butler

Mad Men foregrounds television style and revels in multilayered historical intertextuality. Its incarnation of 1960s props, costume, set design, and so on, enacts a shrewd critique of the period's values, one that has little patience with nostalgia. Uncomfortable discourses of the era's misogyny, homophobia, anti-Semitism, racism, and class prejudice crowd out the Panglossian vision of this time period that has been proffered by programmes such as the characteristically titled *Happy Days* (ABC, 1974–84). This chapter explores the historical texts that intersect in *Mad Men*, suggesting ways that visual style has been called upon to signify the historical.

In interviews and by allusions within the programme itself, Matthew Weiner and his creative team have begun my work for me, highlighting some of the visual texts upon which the programme draws – films such as *The Bachelor Party* (1957) and *The Apartment* (1960), plays that became films such as *Bye Bye Birdie* (play: 1960; film: 1963) and *How to Succeed in Business Without Really Trying* (play: 1961; film: 1967), and television programmes such as *The Dick Van Dyke Show* (CBS, 1961–66) and *The Twilight Zone* (CBS, 1959–64) (Waldman, Bosley 40, Taylor). But I wish to get beyond the historical texts as they have been filtered through Weiner's sensibilities in order to avoid viewing *Mad Men* as a mere 'pastiche of the stereotypical past', in Fredric Jameson's words (66–68). Part of this process has been to perform close textual analyses of films and television programmes from 1960, the year in which the first season is set. (The top moneymaking films for the year are listed in Table 1 and the top-rated television programmes are displayed in Table 2.)[1] Clearly, the most pertinent of these 1960 cultural texts is *The Apartment*, which is a virtual blueprint for *Mad Men* in terms of its representation of corporate culture at the beginning of the decade – a point made by Joan Holloway (Christina Hendricks) when she discusses the film with Roger Sterling (John Slattery) in the 'Long Weekend' episode (1:10). To understand the stylistic schemas that were predominant at the time, however, we need to look beyond a single film.[2] Examining closely the twenty most popular films and television shows of the time helps us begin to understand how *Mad Men* adopts and adapts those historical schemas.

Mad Men celebrates in its historical specificity and entreats us to examine its historical accuracy. Its pilot episode, 'Smoke Gets in Your Eyes' (1:1), includes a zoom-in on a calendar in a doctor's office, very specifically establishing the month as March and the year as 1960. And many of the subsequent episodes are set on particular dates – for example, those of Medgar Evers' murder, the Cuban Missile Crisis and the assassination of President John F. Kennedy. Weiner's attention to period detail has been called 'maniacal' (Handy). Numerous stories have circulated in the press about his stringent demands for period accuracy and costume designer Janie Bryant's and set dresser Amy Wells' dogged scouring of thrift and antique stores for true 1960s artifacts (Lomrantz, Hyde and Streiber). *Mad Men*'s visual design brilliantly implements historical signifiers. It speaks the visual language of the era, drawing on what Sue Harper calls 'deeply rooted cultural topoi' (Harper 3). The first evidence of this visual literacy may be found in the programme's mise en scène.

Historical Mise en scène: A Profusion of Bodies and Objects in a Saturated Frame

If we take mise en scène to refer to the patterning of elements before the camera (actors, sets, lighting and costume), then the principal challenge for films about major historical figures is a proliferation of bodies. As Jean-Louis Comolli points out, historical films re-present in sound and image a person that may already have an established visual heritage (44). The viewers of the film, *Frost/Nixon* (2008), likely have a firm sense of what Richard Nixon looked and sounded like. They may even have seen the televised interviews upon which the film is based. Thus, when they see Frank Langella reanimate the figure of Nixon, 'There are at least two bodies in competition, one body too much,' as Comolli would put it (44). The body-before-them of Langella conflicts with the historical body of Nixon as previously seen and heard in other media texts. This excess of body signifiers can throw a historical television programme or film into crisis – demanding an even greater suspension of disbelief than normally required. *Mad Men* copes with this through a variety of textual strategies. First, like most historical romances, *Mad Men* inscribes historical costume, make-up and hair design upon wholly fictitious characters. Even the actors chosen, with the exception of Robert Morse, had no strong presence within the popular consciousness. Viewers had no previous image of Don Draper to conflict with Jon Hamm's rendition of him. And Hamm had only undistinguished appearances in guest-starring roles before being cast in *Mad Men*. Thus, any previous image of Hamm was not a strong one. Even more significant than the casting, however, is *Mad Men*'s emblematic use of 1960s objects and clothing.

One struggles to find the appropriate metaphor for the 1960s objects and clothing that saturate *Mad Men*'s mise en scène. Are they archeological artifacts of the last century, Freudian fetish objects, commodities ('things') with 'cultural biographies' and 'social lives', or talismans conferring supernatural diegetic power on Matthew Weiner?[3] Or, à la Comolli, are they inanimate bodies too much, conflicting with our collective cultural memory of objects from the past? James Roy MacBean's essay, 'Rossellini's Materialist Mise-en-Scène of *La Prise de Pouvoir par Louis XIV*', can help us understand the function of objects in *Mad Men* (MacBean). MacBean argues that, in materialist mise en scène, '*things* – the material objects of seventeenth-century France – are not mere props and backdrops for the drama, but share equal billing, as it were, with the human figures' (21). Louis XIV controlled his court through a fetishization of material objects – wigs, clothing, jewelry, and so on. Political power was invested in such objects. But it's not just Louis XIV who is making symbolic use of objects. According to MacBean, 'Rarely, if ever, has a work of art [that is, Rossellini's film] been so solidly rooted in *things*; and rarely, if ever, has an artist explored so vividly and yet so profoundly the role of things in the making of history' (21). In *Mad Men* as in *The Rise of Louis XIV* (as the film is

Figure 1. The Drapers' kitchen contains myriad 1960s objects.

known in the USA), the profound nature of things, *la nature profonde des choses*, exists on two levels. Within the diegesis, Don Draper is the supreme master of the marketing of commodities, ruling over 'Creative' through his uncanny comprehension of appearance and how to sell it. He, like Louis XIV, understands how to manipulate appearance for maximum effect – selling Lucky Strike cigarettes in twentieth-century America in much the same way that Louis XIV acquired power in seventeenth-century court. But Don is not the only skilful manipulator of objects, clothing and hairstyle here. Weiner and his crew, like Rossellini, have made shrewd use of things to signify '1960s-ness' and meditate, as Bruce Handy has put it, on the 'deceptive allure of surface' (Handy).

Mad Men mixes genuine 1960s artifacts with fraudulent, manufactured ones. For an extremely mundane example of the latter, take the March 1960 calendar in the pilot. If one looks (very) closely at it, one will see that its February dates (the previous month) are off. However, we viewers still believe the illusion of period reality because an overwhelming wealth of authentic details populate every inch of the frame – drowning out any anachronistic noise. The Drapers' kitchen (Figure 1), the Sterling Cooper break room, and other overstuffed spaces lend credence to C. S. Tashiro's contention that 'the most consistent means to achieve a convincing image of history is through the saturated frame' (68). He explains further: 'to achieve

Figure 2. A chariot race in Ben-Hur *presents large-scale history and tests the limits of the widescreen frame.*

the saturated frame, historical mise en scène concentrates on two extremes of space. At one end, exotic apprehensible details provide confirmation of the production's ability to corral the precious. At the other, large-scale set pieces staged on streets and landscapes create images that by their scale mask the necessarily partial representation' (Tashiro 69). *Mad Men* contains none of the large-scale chariot-race stadiums (*Ben-Hur*, Figure 2) or immense battle scenes (*Solomon and Sheba*) that mark the historical films of 1960, but it does saturate its small-scale frames with 'exotic apprehensible details.' Betty Draper's (January Jones) dressing gown and the kitchen's utensils, coffee pot, tea kettle, dry-goods boxes, bric-a-brac on shelves, re-frigerator magnets, and ashtray (for the disposing of the ubiquitous cigarettes) urge us to acquiesce to its signification of the past. These objects may qualify as what John Caughie calls 'material details re-plete with history' (215). 1960 speaks to us through these details. They construct a picture for us of domesticity, work and leisure at that time.

There is pleasure to be experienced in these details, too. Caughie contends, 'The pleasures are, indeed, pleasure in detail, our engagement held not by the drive of narrative but by the ob-servation of everyday manners and the ornamental' (215). In his view, 'British television [historical] drama...seems to me to have evolved as a drama of incident and character' rather than of what David Bordwell defines as goal-oriented narrative (221). In Sue Harper's consideration of the British costume film, she makes a similar point, suggesting that Gainsborough Studios' 'languages of costume and art direction displayed the past as a series of intense, illuminated moments, resonant with sensual meaning,' but sometimes thereby sacrificing narrative drive (132). As other chapters in this book are examining narrative I will not pursue this line of narrative-versus-ornamentation beyond the comment that *Mad Men*'s narrative drive is often quite enervated, its storylines oblique and open-ended. Could it be because we take greater pleasure in *Mad Men*'s mise en scène than in its narrative development or closure or in the characters' attainment of goals?

Set Design: The Oppressive Rectangularity of the Fluorescent Light

In moving from *Mad Men*'s distinctive objects to the sets they inhabit, we might be tempted to incorporate Thomas Elsaesser's characterization of the bourgeois home in the 1950s woman's picture. He notes the 'sublimation of dramatic conflict into décor, colour, gesture and composition of frame' in the domestic spaces of directors Douglas Sirk, Vincente Minnelli and Nicholas Ray (52).[4] Certainly, the Drapers' home echoes Cary Scott's (Jane Wyman) in Sirk's *All That Heaven Allows*, which was released in and is set in 1955. And in Sirkian fashion, there are some ways in which Betty is entombed within her house, but *Mad Men*'s visual design – particularly its set design and props – do not entrap Betty the way that Sirk's mise en scène does Cary. Despite Cary's eventual rebellion against middle-class mores and her reunion with her working-class lover, it's hard to imagine her going to the extreme of taking up a pellet gun and, with cigarette dangling from her lips, firing at her neighbour's pigeons, as Betty does in 'Shoot' (1:9). Betty exerts more control over her mise en scène than Cary ever did. Moreover, *Mad Men*'s directors give us no shots of Betty forlornly gazing out the window or encased within the reflection of a television screen – as we see in *All That Heaven Allows*. *Mad Men*'s visual representation of suburbia certainly contains its share of sublimated conflict, but it is in its representation of the mise en scène of the work that the programme most archly captures the turmoil – both latent and manifest – in 1960s life.

The most striking element of *Mad Men*'s large, elaborate Sterling Cooper set is its ceiling – an oppressive grid of fluorescent lights. Billy Wilder recognized this lighting fixture's oppressiveness when he

Figure 3. In The Apartment, *C. C. Baxter is visually trapped by the lighting grid.*

conceived the visual design of *The Apartment*. It's not just row after row of identical desks that entraps aspiring businessman C. C. Baxter (Jack Lemmon). It's also the array of fluorescent lights receding into the far distance, positioning C. C. as a rat in a maze designed to crush non-conformity, individuality and the human spirit (Figure 3). The mise en scène of the twentieth-century office as a dehumanizing grid may be traced back 32 years to King Vidor's 1928 release, *The Crowd*. Vidor's camera moves in from a high-angle wide shot of a worker hive (Figure 4) to a medium shot of 'John Sims 137', as it says on his dehumanizing name plate. John is just one of a very large crowd, but he yearns in vain to escape that anonymity. *Mad Men* continues this tradition of the workplace as a scene of naked ambition, rigid conformity, despair, alienation and ennui. The mise en scène of Sterling Cooper's offices clearly delineates its power structure. Peggy Olson (Elisabeth Moss), a secretary in the first season, is positioned outside executive Don's office, a faceless 'new girl'. Her location is vulnerable. The mid-level office Lotharios, the 'junior-account boys', move past her desk with impunity, casually harassing her. To have an office, a large, preferably corner, office, is an obvious symbol of power.

In *The Crowd*, we see how a high-angle shot of a grid full of identical desks can diminish a character, making him look small and insignificant. But *Mad Man*'s directors have developed a preference for the low-angle shot, allowing them, much like Wilder, to pull a ceiling arrayed with fluorescent lights into the frame. Director of photography Phil Abraham explains, 'Normally, you think of a low

61

Figure 4. Row-upon-row of desks diminish the visual presence of The Crowd's *protagonist.*

angle on someone as a kind of heroic vision, and there's an element of that, but when you shoot everything that way, you don't necessarily feel it' (Feld, Oppenheimer, and Stasukevich). Revealing ceilings in television programmes is no small feat. Daily programmes that need to be shot extremely quickly, such as soap operas, and weekly programmes with audiences, such as multiple-camera sitcoms, typically hang lights where ceilings would be and consequently those genres rarely show ceilings.[5] In contrast, Weiner commissioned an elaborate lighting plan that puts 'practicals' – functioning fluorescent lights – into the ceiling to illuminate the *Mad Men* set.[6] Much has been made of the sleek, late-Fifties/modernist look of the show and fluorescent lights are a key component of that look. Introduced to the public during the 1939 New York World's Fair, they spread throughout factories during World War II and then became a defining feature of the office workplace in the 1950s. In 1960, they would symbolize modernist style.

Mad Men's characters have different, emblematic relationships with the lighting grid. Powerful Don moves beneath it without

Figure 5. Joan's voluptuous figure stands out against the lighting grid in a low-angle shot.

hesitation, the master of any space he enters. The voluptuous Joan is also quite mobile. When she towers over Peggy, chastising her for complaining about the relentless harassment, her curves stand out against the grid of the ceiling, emphasizing how her masquerade of femininity is the source of her power (Figure 5).[7] Peggy, however, in the early episodes, is stuck at her desk. In one of the programme's first ceiling shots, in the pilot, she and the other, nameless secretaries are framed by the lights above them. Joan's berating Peggy is followed by a shot of Peggy from an extreme low angle, the camera moving to reveal her face from behind the emblematic, but slightly anachronistic, IBM Selectric typewriter.[8] Her obvious dysphoria and humiliation are emphasized with a series of shots in which men lasciviously eye Peggy at her desk. The metaphoric glass ceiling that contains the women of *Mad Men* is incarnated in a literal one of acoustic tiles and fluorescent lights. It is only once Peggy escapes her desk, moving into an office after she becomes a copywriter, that the ceiling no longer bears down upon her.

A Period-Correct Visual Vocabulary?

Thus far I have mainly considered the people, clothing and objects that saturate the *Mad Men* frame and I have begun to allude to the work of the camera in my comments on the use of low angles to highlight aspects of set design. In this section, I will address camera style more directly and offer some thoughts about what might be called the historical film frame – that is, the state of cinematic and television screens in 1960–63. It is clear that *Mad Men* re-presents 1960s objects and interior spaces to the viewer in order to evoke a bygone time. It is less clear how the frame itself might be historicized. We can begin our investigation with published accounts of the *Mad Men* cinematographers' approaches to its visual style. In an interview with cinematographer Christopher Manley, who joined the crew in 2008, he repeatedly stresses production choices that were made in order to align the programme with standard craft practices of the 1960s, or, in other words, to keep the 'visual vocabulary' of the show period correct (Bosley 41). He says that the programme eschews a Steadicam as being too 1970s and he specifies the colour of light created for the programme: 'Matt [Weiner] is steeped in the late '50s–early '60s, and keeping the light clean and white is more reminiscent of the movies of that era when [cinematographers] tried to balance everything all the time' (Bosley 43). Notably, Manley does not allude to the *television* style of that era, but, instead, he refers solely to the style of theatrical films. Original *Mad Men* cinematographer, Phil Abraham, is more direct: '*Mad Men* has a somewhat mannered, classic visual style that is influenced more by cinema than TV' (Feld, Oppenheimer, and Stasukevich). The dismissal of 1960 television's visual style is not surprising. A glance at the top-rated narrative programmes from 1959–60 (Table 2) reveals no programmes that display a visual style that could be called 'mannered'. Rather, their zero-degree style relies on high-key lighting (even for most nighttime scenes), a preponderance of medium close-ups (neither too close nor too far away), little variation in camera height or angle, no extremely shallow or extremely deep focus, and black-and-white format – all presented in the 1.33:1 aspect ratio that would dominate television until the present time.[9] *Mad Men* may draw some elements of set and costume design from *The Dick Van Dyke Show* and *The Twilight Zone*, as Weiner implies, but otherwise there is little evidence of 1960 television style in *Mad Men*.

How well, then, does *Mad Men* match the cinematography of theatrical releases that were popular in 1960 (Table 1)? First, to be specific, *Mad Men* is shot on 35 mm, Kodak colour film.[10] Within

Table 1. Top-Earning US Film Releases During 1960

Title	Rentals During 1960 ($millions)	Release Date	ASL	Aspect Ratio
1. *Ben-Hur*	17.3	18-Nov-59	8.6	2.76 : 1 (65mm)
2. *Psycho*	8.5	16-Jun-60	6.6	1.85 : 1
3. *Operation Petticoat*	6.8	5-Dec-59	8.8	1.85 : 1
4. *Suddenly, Last Summer*	5.5	22-Dec-59	9.2	1.85 : 1
5. *On the Beach*	5.3	17-Dec-59	21.5	1.66 : 1
6. *Solomon and Sheba*	5.25	25-Dec-59	7.6	2.20 : 1 (70mm)
7. *The Apartment*	5.1	15-Jun-60	16.3	2.35 : 1
8. *Please Don't Eat the Daisies*	5	31-Mar-60	15.9	2.35 : 1
9. *From the Terrace*	5	15-Jul-60	9.6	2.35 : 1
10. *Ocean's Eleven*	4.9	10-Aug-60	12.6	2.35 : 1

the popular imagination, all old films are in black-and-white, but of the films listed in Table 1, only four out of ten are black-and-white. By 1960, colour was no longer reserved for high-budget, large-scale productions. Kodak's introduction of a relatively inexpensive, single-strip Eastman Color film stock in 1950 resulted in colour film becoming the norm over the course of the decade.[11] Thus, by 1960, even conventional comedies such as *Please Don't Eat the Daisies* would routinely be shot in colour. The choice of black-and-white for *Psycho*, *On the Beach*, *The Apartment*, and *Suddenly, Last Summer* was presumably more aesthetic than budgetary. Each is a 'serious' film dealing with downbeat subject matter (even *The Apartment*'s humour is dark and cynical). Thus, to shoot *Mad Men* in black-and-white would align it more with earlier craft practices than 1960, but it could also have more strongly linked it with its principal stylistic antecedent, *The Apartment*. At this point in television history, however, black-and-white is virtually taboo for narrative television programmes and is essentially reserved for flashbacks, commercials, music videos, and title sequences.

Table 2. Top-Rated Television Programs: October 1959–April 1960

Program	Rating	Median ASL	Series Dates
1. *Gunsmoke*	40.3	10.5	1955–1975
2. *Wagon Train*	38.4	8.25	1957–1965
3. *Have Gun – Will Travel*	34.7	6.9	1957–1963
4. *The Danny Thomas Show*	31.1		1953–1965
5. *The Red Skelton Show*	30.8		1951–1971
6. *Father Knows Best*	29.7		1954–1960
7. *77 Sunset Strip*	29.7		1958–1964
8. *The Price Is Right*	29.2		1956–1965
9. *Wanted: Dead or Alive*	28.7	8.3	1958–1961
10. *Perry Mason*	28.3	8	1957–1966

The choice of colour is time-appropriate, but *Mad Men*'s aspect ratio raises key stylistic issues. Its aspect ratio fits the standard for US-video widescreen – that is, 16:9 or 1.78:1. All but one of the top ten 1960 films are wider than this 1.78 ratio. *Mad Men*'s frame is wider than 1960's television standard of 1.33:1, but narrower than 1960's *theatrical* widescreen – whether masked (1.85:1) or anamorphic (2.35 or 2.40). The 1950s were filled with widescreen experimentation – beginning with Cinerama in 1952 – as a technique for luring viewers from their television sets. Interestingly, the widest of the widescreen films were often historical films. Tashiro notes,

> When designers were faced with filling this new, large frame, the art-historical precedent of the mural provided compositional conventions that could be employed on a large scale. Since the subjects of murals are also frequently historical and political, there was a double precedent for associating the political past with wide, horizontal images. As a result, not just History Film but history itself became equated with widescreen visualization. (120)

The biggest moneymaking film of 1960 confirms this. *Ben-Hur* was shot in a 65 mm process that resulted in an elongated 2.76:1 ratio (Figure 2), although few theatres were equipped to show it in that format. And another popular historical epic from 1960, *Solomon and Sheba*, was also shot in a special, 70 mm widescreen process.

However, this sense of 'history' is a very limiting one, presuming it to be a narrative of large-scale events, such as the *Ben-Hur* sea battle. *Mad Men*'s version of history, in contrast, emphasizes the intimate details of an era. And besides, by 1960, widescreen visualization was clearly not solely limited to historical films. The other anamorphic films of 1960 were predominantly not historical epics: *The Apartment, Please Don't Eat the Daisies, From the Terrace* and *Ocean's Eleven*. They illustrate that almost any story could be told in anamorphic widescreen.

The width of *Mad Men*'s widescreen might not match that of 1960's 35mm anamorphic widescreen but its resolution does. After being shot on 35 mm film, AMC distributes *Mad Men* though various channels in high-definition video, but many major US cable and satellite services choose not to carry AMC's high-definition, widescreen signal. Consequently, when viewers who do not have access to AMC HD watch *Mad Men* on a high-definition monitor its image is reduced and *windowboxed*. Windowboxing is a recent technique used to present HD video on standard-definition channels, when they are being viewed on HD monitors. The result is black bars on all four sides of the frame, which can be particularly frustrating in long shots (Figure 6). Many of these viewers obtain the high-definition *Mad Men* version through on-demand services and Blu-ray discs instead of watching it windowboxed. In HD, *Mad Men* truly achieves its historical potential for the saturated frame. All of the many details within the frame become available for inspection. My examination of the fraudulent calendar is only made possible by the high-definition image. In that case, it turns up a minor instance of time-period fakery, but most objects within the *Mad Men* frame reward close scrutiny.

The Rhythm of History

Mad Men's producer, directors, cinematographers, costume designer, and set dresser have all boasted of the programme's accurate use of period style, but few comments have surfaced from its editors. Does the programme match the historical rhythm of 1960 cutting style? Working from average shot length (ASL) data for the first season, it is evident that, no, it does not. (ASL data, when available, have been included in Tables 1 and 2.)[12] *Mad Men*'s first-season episodes

Figure 6. A window-boxed frame diminishes the viewer's experience of significant visual details.

have a median ASL of 5.2 seconds – up to four times faster than the ASLs of 1960s films and television programmes.

It is perhaps unremarkable that *Mad Men* is cut faster than television programmes or films from 1960. After all, we all know that the speed of television/film editing has accelerated over the decades. But looking at early 1960s ASLs and contrasting them with late 2000s ASLs does illustrate two significant points. First, there will always be limits to the simulation of a previous era's visual vocabulary. Ten- or twenty-second ASLs and black-and-white film stock will likely never return to commercial, network, narrative television in the USA – even in programmes trying to evoke the past. Second, the ASLs of these top-ten films illustrate that the pace of film/television editing need not always increase. In fact, the ASLs of many of 1960s most popular films were markedly slower than those of previous years. Factors such as composition in depth, deep focus, widescreen framing, among others, can mitigate against faster cutting speeds, because they have the potential to offer saturated frames to viewers, frames that demand more time to comprehend. Perhaps the recent implementation in television of high-definition resolution and relatively widescreen images will lead to such saturated frames in that medium. Cutting rates may decelerate and I'll be forced to recant my prediction about ASLs remaining below 10 seconds. Of course, smaller, low-resolution screens in mobile devices such as the iPod are simultaneously competing with large screens that encourage detail. Television is being pulled in two opposing directions and no one knows what the final result will be.

The Resonance of Sensual Meanings and Pleasures

A close reading of *Mad Men* reveals that its historical specificity is most strongly re-presented in its mise en scène, which resonates with many sensual meanings and pleasures. It is here that historical texts most clearly intersect the contemporary text. It is here also that *Mad Men*'s intertextuality is its densest. However, the cinematography that records this mise en scène and the editing that determines how long we'll be allowed to view each image have a more complicated connection to 1960 stylistics. Viewers who take the time and spend the money to experience *Mad Men* in high definition may revel in the historically saturated frame before them. Those who watch it in letterboxed or windowboxed format on AMC will have a slightly attenuated experience, but still the props and set design will clearly signal 'the Sixties' to them, too. Regardless of how one views *Mad Men*, one will still experience an editing pace significantly faster than that of 1960 films. Weiner and his cast and crew have not, after all, recreated a 1960 film. Would we really want them to? They have emulated 1960 film style in a way that does not displace history.[13] Rather, *Mad Men*'s style showcases historical specificity and urges us to engage with it.

Works Cited

Bordwell, David. *On the History of Film Style*. Cambridge: Harvard University Press, 1997.

Bosley, Rachael K. 'Pitch perfect', *American Cinematographer*, 30 October 2009, 30–43.

Caughie, John. *Television Drama: Realism, Modernism and British Culture*. Oxford: Oxford University Press, 2000.

Comolli, Jean-Louis. 'Historical Fiction – A Body Too Much,' *Screen* 19.2 (Summer 1978): 41–54.

Elsaesser, Thomas. 'Tales of Sound and Fury: Observations on the Family Melodrama'. Gledhill, Christine, ed. *Home Is Where the Heart*

Is: Studies in Melodrama and Woman's Film. London: British Film
Institute, 1987.

Feld, Rob, Oppenheimer, Jean and Stasukevich, Ian. 'Cinematographers
from three top series (*Mad Men, Desperate Housewives* and *Bones*)
reveal their secrets', *American Cinematographer*, March 2008 at
http://www.theasc.com/magazine_dynamic/March2008/Television/
page1.php. Accessed on 11 November 2009.

Handy, Bruce. 'Don and Betty's Paradise Lost', *Vanity Fair*, September
2009 at http://www.vanityfair.com/culture/features/2009/09/mad-
men200909. Accessed on 11 November 2009.

Harper, Sue. *Picturing the Past: The Rise and Fall of the British Costume
Film*. London: British Film Institute, 1994.

Hyde, Douglas. 'Astonishing Detail in a Time Gone "Mad,"' *CNN*,
9 October 2009 at http://www.cnn.com/2009/SHOWBIZ/TV/10/26/
mad.men.set/index.html. Accessed on 11 November 2009.

Jameson, Frederic. 'Postmodernism, or, the Cultural Logic of Late
Capitalism', *New Left Review* 146 (July–August 1984): 53–92.

Lomrantz, Tracey. '12 Questions For *Mad Men* Costume Designer Janie
Bryant', *Glamour*, January 26, 2009 at http://www.glamour.com/
fashion/blogs/slaves-to-fashion/2009/01/tk-questions-for-mad-men-
costu.html. Accessed on 11 November 2009.

MacBean, James Roy. 'Rossellini's materialist mise en scène of *La Prise de
Pouvoir par Louis XIV*', *Film Quarterly* 25.2 (Winter, 1971–72): 20–29.

Streiber, Art. '*Mad Men*', *Entertainment Weekly*, 9 October 2009: 62–7.

Tashiro, C.S. *Pretty Pictures: Production Design and the History Film*.
Austin: University of Texas Press, 1998.

Taylor, Mark. 'The past isn't what it used to be: The troubled homes of
Mad Men', *Jump Cut* 51 (spring 2009) at http://www.ejumpcut.org/
currentissue/mad-men/index.html. Accessed on 11 November 2009.

Waldman, Allison. 'Matt Weiner of *Mad Men*: The TV squad interview',
TV Squad, 8 August 2008 at http://www.tvsquad.com/2008/08/08/
matt-weiner-of-mad-men-the-tv-squad-interview/. Accessed on 11
November 2009.

Notes

1   The film data are based on rental fees earned during the 1960 calendar
year, as reported by *Variety* and listed in Cobbett S. Steinberg, *Film Facts*
(New York: Facts on File, 1980) 23–4. The TV Nielsen data are reported
in Tim Brooks and Earle Marsh, *The Complete Directory to Prime Time
Network and Cable TV Shows*, 8th ed. (New York: Ballantine, 2003)
1458.

2 Please visit the companion Website: *www.tvcrit.com/madmen*. Also for more on stylistic schemas, see Bordwell 152.

3 For more on the 'social life of things' see Arjun Appadurai, ed., *The Social Life of Things: Commodities in Cultural Perspective* (Cambridge: Cambridge University Press, 1988).

4 Along with Elsaesser, Tashiro is also drawn to this argument.

5 For a discussion of how single-camera programs such as *Miami Vice* (NBC, 1984–89), *Scrubs* (NBC, 2001–08; ABC 2009-present), and *ER* (NBC, 1994–2009) use ceilings to distinguish themselves from multiple-camera sitcoms and soap operas, see Jeremy G. Butler, *Television Style* (New York: Routledge, 2009).

6 For the actual lighting plot, see Feld, Oppenheimer and Stasukevich.

7 For more on 'masquerade' in gender studies, see Victor Burgin, James Donald, and Cora Kaplan, eds., *Formations of Fantasy* (New York: Methuen, 1986) and Mary Ann Doane, *Femmes Fatales: Feminism, Film Theory, Psychoanalysis* (New York: Routledge, 1991).

8 Slightly anachronistic because the IBM Selectric I was not released until July 1961.

9 For more on zero-degree style see John Thornton Caldwell, *Televisuality: Style, Crisis, and Authority in American Television* (New Brunswick: Rutgers University Press, 1995) 56; and Butler, *Television Style*, 26–69.

10 The specific film stocks are Kodak Vision2 250D 5205 and Vision3 500T 5219. Bosley, 43.

11 Kodak first introduced a single-strip colour film in 1950 (Eastman Color 5247) and then refined its process in 1952 with the hugely popular Eastman Color 5248 film stock. 'Chronology of motion picture films: 1940 to 1959', Kodak, at http://motion.kodak.com/US/en/motion/Products/Chronology_Of_Film/chrono2.htm. Accessed on 9 November 2009.

12 Additional statistics are available on Shot Logger: http://www.shotlogger.org.

13 Jameson argues, 'The history of aesthetic styles displaces "real" history', in Jameson, 67.

5.
Uneasy Listening: Music, Sound, and Criticizing Camelot in *Mad Men*
Tim Anderson

> Music on *Mad Men* is never an accident. The philosophy of the sound was pointed: do as much to enhance the feeling of the period while offering an artistic commentary to the themes of each show.
>
> (Matt Weiner quoted in 'On DVD: *Mad Men*, season one')

> It's as if Weiner is reminding us: If you think pre-Kennedy assassination America was all innocence and simplicity, look and think again.
>
> (Matthew Gilbert – 'Truth in Advertising')

In *Mad Men* popular music exists in a world before rock was the dominant genre. It is a world of popular records considered by many present-day audiences to be light and fanciful, anything but critical. It is a world where dance fads and comedy records comingle in an AM-oriented set of musical experiences. Most importantly, in the world *Mad Men* records act as exegetical agents that simultaneously support and forward the critical dialogue and commentary that comprises the series. Working together, Matt Weiner and Alexandra Patsavas, *Mad Men*'s music supervisor, deploy a distinctive world of recordings that fulfil two missions. First, Patsavas and Weiner choose recordings that audiences immediately recognize as suitable and relevant to the programme's early 1960s setting. In this sense, the use of recordings is unexceptional and, for many viewers, they may be heard as little more than historically accurate audio dressing. However, Weiner and Patsavas' use of recordings often operate as critical interlocutors that act as a counterpoint to the on-screen imagery. The result is these seemingly 'appropriate' recordings are used to generate both incongruities and commentary that further challenge and complicate our collective memory of early 1960s America as a time of innocence and contentment.

The issue of 'appropriateness' is of paramount importance for quality music supervision, however 'appropriate' is a flexible term that includes both aesthetic and fiduciary issues. Along with those obligations that he or she meets with producers and directors to best achieve the programme's aesthetic aims, the music supervisor is the above-the-line liaison responsible for the many complex legal and budgetary issues surrounding rights acquisition and clearance. As the music industry has moved further away from the sale of physical goods, it has embraced licensing opportunities to compensate for lost revenue sources. The result is that the potential value of the music supervisor has increased significantly in the last ten years. Alexandra Patsavas is one of the more accomplished supervisors of the decade and in 2006 she was named an 'Entertainment Marketer of the Year' by *Advertising Age* (Trakin). With a substantial history of high-quality work involving programmes such as *The OC* (Fox, 2003–07), *Gossip Girl* (CW, 2007-present), *Grey's Anatomy* (ABC, 2005-present) and *Chuck* (NBC, 2007-present), her company's services, Chop Shop Records and Music Supervision, are considered among the most prized and sought after by film and television producers who use music as an essential part of their aesthetic and narrative worlds. The term 'world' is key. According to Patsavas, 'Anytime you get a music supervision gig, you begin to delve into the world, especially if it takes place in another era. It's an exciting research project' ('AMC-Blogs-Mad Men-Q&A-Alexandra Patsavas – Music Supervisor'). *Mad Men*'s world is a televised setting of the early 1960s where each detail, no matter how small, matters. In the words of the programme's prop master, Scott Buckwald, 'When you look in the past, everybody knows the broad strokes. It's the little slices of life that make the difference' (quoted in Schwartz).

It is through these 'little slices' where Patsavas and Weiner do their best to systematically open up the period to make these murmurs of discontent audible. Out of the 57 unique recordings that AMC lists as appearing on *Mad Men*'s first three seasons, if one includes RJD2's 'Beautiful Mine (Instrumental Version)', the music for the programme's 'Falling Man' title sequence, only four of these could be labeled contemporary: Amy Winehouse's 'You Know I'm No Good' (first season promos), The Cardigans, 'The Great Divide' (Episode 2, season one) and The Decemberists, 'The Infanta' (Episode 6, season two).[1] Of the remaining 53 listed, only two others, Bob Dylan's 'Don't Think Twice, It's All Right' and Don McLean's 'Babylon' cannot claim to be historically accurate.[2] Of the 51 remaining, the recordings come from a variety of popular genres, including 'country & western', instrumental pop, popular vocals, folk, 'rockabilly', 'rock 'n' roll', 'rhythm and blues', classical and comedy. This variety is reflective of particular late 1950s and early 1960s radio aesthetic of AM top-forty radio where recordings from various genres were expected to mix from region to region, station to station and playlist to playlist. However, *Mad Men*'s audio potpourri is the result of an aesthetic aim to find recordings that act as more than a complementary force. As pointed textual foils, these pop recordings generate a critical frisson as they confront both *Mad Men*'s on-screen world and our own understanding of these cultural artifacts.

Auditing America's Camelot for Tones of Discontent from an Idealized Past

To present-day audiences, the names Percy Faith, Jack Jones, Perry Como, Ann-Margret, Julie London and Brenda Lee are rarely viewed as discontented cultural critics. The same audience member may rightly envision a show set in the early 1960s that includes three songs about 'The Twist' in its first two seasons as one that celebrated the period as a happier, more innocent period. Perhaps the same listener who views a soundtrack that includes Luiz Bonfa, Miles Davis and Bud Powell would expect a programme that glorifies the period's sophistication. Indeed, finding recordings that paint the period as 'light', 'happy' or 'chic' could be considered an appropriate, but ultimately uninteresting use of this musical heritage. However, Weiner and Patsavas employ all of the above-mentioned artists in a fashion that deliberately defies our understanding of these recordings to inflect and contest our collective understanding of the period.

Mad Men's pilot episode, 'Smoke Gets in Your Eyes', not only takes its title from the Jerome Kern and Otto Harbach standard but also exists as an explicit example of how pop music is used in the series to create moments of incongruity and critical commentary. The opening shot is a visual explanation of 'Mad Men' and its origins from Madison Avenue as a term of self-mocking endearment. Accompanying the shot is Don Cherry's 'Band of Gold', which we hear as a supra-diegetic presence. The doo-wop influenced record delivers the bridge that leads into the opening scene, provides its rhythm, and offers a set of puns that will inform our introduction to Don Draper. The initial break beat motivates a hard cut to a shot that simultaneously pushes forward into narrative space and trucks from right to left. Revealing a smoke-filled room of after-office executives, their dates and service in white jackets, we hear Don Cherry sing that his 'life has one design, a simple little band of gold, to prove that you are mine', and, through a series of shots, witness Draper nervously writing words about smoking on the back of a napkin. As the lyric ends, the volume of the song is lowered into the background of the mix as if it was a diegetic presence and an elderly, African-American male server engages Draper. Draper asks for a light and talks to the server about his loyalty to Old Gold cigarettes. The scene quickly moves through brief displays of racism, Draper's charm, and an adman's search for what smoking means to smokers. The scene ends with the record being pushed forward into the mix with the lyrics 'just want a little band of gold, to prove that you are mine' audibly rising to the top as we are given a point-of-view shot that is motivated by Draper's glance and pans from left to right to present white, upper-middle-class patrons all joyfully smoking and drinking at the bar. The scene ends as the song comes to an end with a crescendo and a hard cut to Draper knocking on the apartment door of the first woman with whom he interacts in the episode, Midge Daniels.

The remainder of 'Smoke Gets in Your Eyes' introduces us to the ensemble of characters that constitute Sterling Cooper and the numerous anxieties that inform Don Draper's creative work. Draper's most significant challenge in the episode is to find a suitable strategy by which to persuade smokers to change brands and adopt Lucky Strike. Associating the lyrics of 'Band of Gold' with 'Old Gold' and Draper's concentration on cigarettes dislodges the dominant reading of the song from one of a desire for matrimony to a focus on increasing market share. Indeed, Draper's lack of a wedding band, his night with Midge, his flirtations with Rachel Menken and his dismissal of love as a concept that 'was invented by guys like me to sell nylons' forefront his loneliness and isolation. It is this lonely quality that Menken identifies in Draper. Alluding to her own position as a Jewish businesswoman, she notes that she knows what it is like 'to feel out of place, to feel disconnected' and points out that 'there is something about you that tells me you know [this feeling] too.' Highlighting Draper's isolation is one of the primary narrative thrusts of the episode. Thus, when Draper comes home and we are finally introduced to his wife and children at the end of the episode, we are given a shocking revelation about our protagonist. An exercise in contrasts, the episode that begins with Draper, alone, in a public space of intoxication ends with him in a bedroom where his wife, Betty, watches him attend to his sleeping children. And just as the episode begins with a song, the episode ends bracketed by Vic Damone's rendition of 'On the Street Where You Live'. A song about longing for a potential love is infused with a melancholy that comes from witnessing our protagonist's previous 45 minutes of wanderlust. In the words of Drake Lelane, the 'strong music choice' winds its way through the 'surprise reveal' to offer a sentiment 'that makes it feel like Draper adores his family, but is really just visiting them, and his real home is back in the city' (Lelane 'Music on Mad Men: Classic Tunes Set the Scene for This Old Boys Club').

It is easy to understand why any advertising executive, his wife or anyone who worked in Manhattan in 1960 would view any song from *My Fair Lady* as an appropriate musical choice for the time. *My Fair Lady* was in the middle of what would be a run of well over 2,700 New York performances in New York City and several hit original soundtrack recordings, with the original cast recording as part of what *Variety* in 1962 labeled a 'mass cultural phenomenon' that included *South Pacific* and *The Music Man* (Anderson, pp. 113–14). Damone's recording of the song was also popular, reaching the number four position on the US Billboard charts in 1959 and number one in the UK two years later. However, what makes it such a strong choice is how such a seemingly light record brings such a sense of unhappiness. Both 'Band of Gold' and 'On the Street Where You Live' are placed in opposition to the on-screen images to create the disaffection that permeated the period. Pop records are not the only items used to create dissonance in *Mad Men*. Popular narratives such as *The Twilight Zone* (CBS, 1959–64) and Katherine

Anne Porter's popular 1962 novel, *Ship of Fools*, find their way into *Mad Men*'s narrative and provide a 'tremendous irony' that is in concert with the period. Furthermore, as Weiner himself points out, the show includes references to these and other irony-laden texts that were 'gigantic commercial success[es], which means that [they were] on people's minds. I wanted to make it part of that world that people were consuming' (Benson).

Details of popular disaffection and dissonance populate the world of *Mad Men* not simply to amplify the personal and professional dimensions of the show's characters, but the entire period. Sterling Cooper succeeds by exploiting discontent as Draper's ability to viscerally understand dissatisfaction and trauma is one of the firm's primary assets. As Adam Cohen notes, in the offices of Sterling Cooper we witness efforts 'to persuade Americans to buy more cigarettes', racism ('black people are largely invisible'), and 'the oppression of women is so raw that the agency's strong and self-possessed office manager, Joan Holloway, was raped at the office by her fiancé' (Cohen). To listen to this version of the early 1960s is to listen to a specifically pointed counternarrative, an 'anti-Camelot version of the era'. Gary R. Edgerton describes *Mad Men* as a form of 'critical nostalgia', 'an antidote to the overly simplified and saccharine poetics surrounding the cottage industry of books, films and television programmes that has emerged since the late 1990s mythologizing the World War II generation' (Edgerton). Challenging the many fantasies that we have of the 1950s and 1960s about the workplace, gender roles and the economic expectations of the late Fifties and early Sixties as simpler, 'happy days' is a fundamental goal for Weiner's narrative aims. As Weiner asserts, this period included, 'a lot of counterculture [and] subversion in the sense that people were not taking the American dream for granted' (Hansen).

The popularity of this dissatisfaction is extended to the realm of comedy. Arguably the most popular forum for discontent was 'sick comedy', a movement that began in the late 1950s and included, among others, Mort Sahl, Lenny Bruce, Charles Addams, the comedy team of Nichols and May, Jonathan Winters, Tom Lehrer, *Mad Magazine* and Shelley Berman.[3] While Berman and Sahl would find no place in decidedly Anglo confines of Sterling Cooper, Bob Newhart does. His debut long play record, *The Button Down Mind of Bob Newhart*, makes two brief appearances in 'New Amsterdam' (1:4), each of which involves Pete Campbell and his co-workers. The first appearance includes the group visibly listening to Newhart's 'Driving Instructor' routine until Campbell's wife, Trudy, who makes a surprise arrival, interrupts them. Trudy apologizes and tells Peter that she knows that, 'you all work so hard'. Trudy's claim is undercut by the preceding image of the junior executives behind closed doors, smoking, listening, laughing and discussing how Newhart, 'used to be an accountant'. While less than a minute of the routine is heard, the point is made: the relatively posh existence that these ad executives enjoy hardly constitutes 'hard work'.

The album makes its second appearance little more than 30 minutes into the episode after Campbell is initially let go by Draper for pitching unauthorized copy to a Bethlehem Steel client. Barging into his office, Campbell witnesses his colleagues, again, inside and listening to the same routine. After tossing them out in anger, we witness the album fly out the door, land next to his secretary, who, after glancing at the sleeve, nonchalantly goes back to work. As a prop, *The Button Down Mind* asserts a substantial popular significance. The 1960 release was the first comedy album to reach the number one position on Billboard's charts and is credited with saving the Warner Bros. record label (Manilla). One year later *The Button Down Mind* won the 1961 Grammy Award for album of the year and Newhart received the Grammy for the best new artist category. More pertinent to *Mad Men*, approximately one half of the album's material is a critique of marketing and advertising. Arguably the most famous of the album's routines is the lead track, 'Abe Lincoln vs. Madison Avenue', where Newhart invokes Vance Packard's 1957 condemnation of 'motivation research' from his non-fiction book, *The Hidden Persuaders*.[4] Although Newhart's criticism of advertising is not on full display in the episode, the presence of the record, like Newhart's comedy, acts as an acceptable if somewhat cloying critique. Like Sterling Cooper, *The Button Down Mind of Bob Newhart* is white-collar, urbane, and middlebrow.

The use of such props and records, according to Alessandra Stanley, helps provide, 'one long flashback, an artfully imagined historic reenactment of an era when America was a soaring superpower feeling its first shivers of mortality' (Stanley). The importance of these shivers cannot be understated. Resuscitating palpable sensations of irony and cynicism that were part of the period is an attempt to recast Camelot as less than idyllic and contest any notion that these were better, more innocent days of America's past. Daniel Marcus argues that representing the Fifties and Sixties in popular culture, in particular television, has been an important contest for America's collective memory

> since the advent of Ronald Reagan to national political power in 1980. Reagan called for a rejection of the legacies of the social and cultural movements of the 1960s and a return to practices and values said to have been disrupted by these movements. (Marcus, p. 9)

Drawing from John Nerone, Marcus notes that 'group memories must compete and coexist with other groups' senses of the past; in the quest for social power memories act as the archive of the past for the society as a whole' (Marcus, p. 19). The substantial dissatisfaction with the 'American Dream' that reverberates throughout *Mad Men*'s use of records asserts a particularly political tone that carries with it echoes of times past. Because audio recordings are time-based media they present listeners with a specific claim to represent past moments. The result is that in the context of any period piece, the explicit mobilization of period recordings within the soundscape or mise en scène, offers audiences promise that they are receiving at least one kind of authentic representation of the past. The reason for this is simple: unlike every other element, there is an assumption that a recording cannot be as easily manufactured as a clothing pattern or furniture design. Unlike the material prop, the temporal contingencies that mold any original recording's textures are simply too ephemeral to be effectively restaged. Thus, the tones of disenchantment that cut through the first three seasons of *Mad Men* provide America's Camelot with a particularly uncanny effect because they originate from a specific narrative world where their sources derive 'from popular music of the time, and more specifically music that the characters in this show would know' (quoted in Johans).

The systematic production of critical incongruities from seemingly innocuous sources is best demonstrated by *Mad Men*'s employment of Percy Faith's 1960 recording, 'Theme from a Summer Place', in 'The New Girl' (2:18). One of the most popular releases of its time, Faith's record charted at number one on the Billboard singles chart, remained in that position for nine consecutive weeks and, according to Joseph Lanza, 'never left the charts during the whole year of 1960' (Lanza, p. 92). Over time the record has become synonymous with the most cliché and hopelessly square representations of virginal, romantic love. Its appearance and placement underscores Bobbie Barrett and Don Draper's adulterous relationship. In the second scene of the episode, Don and Bobbie are at a restaurant celebrating the sale of Bobbie's husband's pilot, *Grin and Barrett,* and chance upon one of Don's previous mistresses, Rachel Katz née Menken and her husband. After the brief but intense encounter, Bobbie and Don drive to her house in Long Island so that, in the words of Bobbie, they can make love on the sand 'with the surf pounding behind us'. After the allusion to *From Here to Eternity* we witness the next scene where Bobbie and Don listen to 'Theme from a Summer Place' play from the radio in his car. As Bobbie tries to kiss him, Don drunkenly loses control of the car and crashes the vehicle (Getzinger). Connecting the refined orchestration of Percy Faith's 'Theme from a Summer Place' to such a brazen, dangerous moment of adultery and alcohol abuse defies the common understanding of this song as an innocent piece of easy listening. However, it is this very incongruity that lies at the heart of the composition, a theme that is associated with the failed romances and alcoholism that populate both the popular 1958 novel (Wilson) and its 1959 film adaptation (Daves). Indeed, the affair in *A Summer Place* is positioned as an 'acceptable' solution to two former, teenage lovers who are separated by differences in social stature and marry unsatisfactory partners. In short, 'Theme from a Summer Place' is not simply a significant romantic hit, but one laced with disenchantment: moreover, its position within the *Mad Men*'s narrative goes to great lengths to remind us of this sentiment.

Of Contrapuntal Endings and Critical Codas

Not every *Mad Men* episode ends with pop music, but enough do that critic and writer Gustavo Turner identifies the following *Mad Men* trope: ending an episode by deploying 'an interesting period track – often obscure – that serves as counterpoint or commentary to the week's episode' (Turner). Often these end pieces are quite complementary and provide lyrics that appropriately reflect the mood of the episode. Yet even in these cases, the recording brings with it a tone that provides one final critical dimension to the episode: *Punctus contra punctum*: the structure to shake out nascent meanings and allowing them to come to fruition. For example, at the end of 'Seven Twenty Three' (3:33) Tennessee Ernie Ford's 'Sixteen Tons' mocks Don Draper just as his boss, Cooper, mocks him after he effectively forces Draper to finally sign the contract with the firm that he has steadfastly avoided (Scherler Mayer). Less acerbic, 'Indian Summer' (1:11) ends with a shot of Peggy Olson in her bedroom using 'The Relaxcisor', a device that is marketed to women as a weight loss gadget; Peggy initially rejects the gadget after she tests it and she finds the sensations it generates embarrassing. As the shot concludes with a slow right-to-left tracking shot away from Peggy in bed using the gadget for what are clearly sexual purposes, Julie London's bright and jaunty version of 'Fly Me to the Moon' is mixed in a non-diegetic fashion. The result is a lighthearted, cheeky undertone that imbues both the scene and Peggy's struggle with her Catholic upbringing and her sexual desires (Hunter).

In some cases, themes that seem to lurk in the background effectively surface as songs act as codas that allow particularly protofeminist dimensions to flourish. Jack Jones' 'Lollipops and Roses' that arrives at the end of 'The Benefactor' (2:16) to accentuate Betty's position as Don's beautiful, innocent and charming prop of a wife. Unbeknownst to Betty who sits at a dinner table simply to appear charming, Don employs strong-arm tactics and threatens Bobbie Barrett to force an apology from her husband, Jimmy, to retain Utz as a Sterling Cooper client. Her saccharine obliviousness is part of Don and Betty's relationship and a dynamic that is powerfully reemphasized in the final scene of the episode by Jack Jones' ballad that praises the merits of paternal infantilization. Leaning blissfully against Don, Betty declares what a 'great team' they make as he drives the couple home from their engagement and Jack Jones's baritone sings from the radio, 'Tell her you care each time you speak. Make it her birthday each day of the week. Bring her nice things, sugar and spice things, roses and lollipops and lollipops and roses' (Glatter).

As Draper uses and abuses his wife, he and his colleagues likewise use and abuse the women in their working circles. Thus, the melancholy that overwhelms the women of the Sterling Cooper's secretarial staff as they digest Marilyn Monroe's death in 'Six Month Leave' (2:22) emanates from their collective understanding of the numerous romantic and professional disappointments that they have experienced at the hands of the many men in her life. As a story-line, Monroe's death is simply a historical backdrop upon which the narrative takes place. However, by ending the episode with Monroe's breathy and sullen recording of 'I'm Through with Love', her des-peration is pushed to the forefront of the episode. While it is played over the closing credits, the record appears immediately after Mona Sterling confronts Draper in his office about Roger, her husband, and informs her that he is leaving their marriage of 25 years for Draper's young secretary. As a result, Monroe's record acts as a tonic that asserts both her personal and professional disappointment and exhaustion. Exhaustion is a sentiment that not only informs Mona's exasperation, but also Betty and Don's initial separation. Monroe's record also acts as a retrospective commentary on those in the office who are also 'through with love' and opt for a dispassionate oppor-tunism as they exploit Freddy Rumson's alcoholism as a means to push him out the door and themselves up the corporate ladder.

Because *Mad Men* straddles events such as Marilyn Monroe's passing and the Cuban missile crisis, this use of period record-ings as ending comments allows them a final word that can wrest forth uncanny emotional resonances. Such is the case with Presi-dent Kennedy's assassination in 'The Grown-Ups' (3:38). Appearing in season three's penultimate episode, the event catalyzes Don and Betty's second significant separation, one that will lead to divorce, as well as the eventual dissolution of Sterling Cooper. In short, Kennedy's assassination signals the end of a specific incarnation of the programme. In this context the insertion of Skeeter Davis' pop crossover hit from 1963 about love lost, 'The End of the World', at the end of the episode reinforces the terminal possibilities of Betty Draper's declaration that she no longer loves Don, but the loss of *Mad Men*'s world as we know it (Schroeder). 'The End of the World' may be melodramatic and relatively obscure, but it effectively casts the Kennedy assassination as a liminal event, one that precipitates the complete overhaul of the programme.[5] *Mad Men* directly ad-dresses an audience that exists in its own specific historical moment of change and argues that it must listen closely to voices from this earlier period to find ourselves and understand just how much we have changed for the better since this immense national tragedy. For while many consider these years to be among America's greatest moments, the sense of disappointment, disillusion and exhaustion was just as palpable – if not more so – than it is today. In *Mad Men* we are afforded an opportunity to listen closely, make this connection, and attend to our own memories, our own critical nostalgia for a less-than-splendid Camelot, and hear the despair and discontent that percolated through the period.

Works Cited

'AMC-Blogs-Mad Men-Q&A-Alexandra Patsavas – Music Supervisor' (2008) at http://blogs.amctv.com/mad-men/2008/08/interview-with-alex-patsavas.php#more. Accessed on 23 October 2009.

Anderson, Tim J. *Making Easy Listening: Material Culture and post-war Recording*. Minneapolis, MN: University of Minnesota Press, 2006.

Anon. 'Nightclubs: The Sickniks.' *Time*, 13 July 1959 at http://www.time .com/time/magazine/article/0,9171,869153,00.html. Accessed on 16 October 2009.

A Summer Place. A romantic drama film based on the novel of the same name by Sloan Wilson. Dir. Daves, Delmer. 1959.

Benson, Jim. 'Jim Benson's TV Time Machine – Interview with Mad Men Creator Matthew Weiner', 2008. *Jim Benson's TV Time Machine*. Ed. Jim Benson. Interview, 29 November 2009 at http://www .tvtimemachine.com/radio_show_madmen.htm. Accessed on 29 November 2009.

Cohen, Adam. '"Mad Men" and the thrill of other people's misery in sour times', *The New York Times*, 16 October 2009 at http://www .nytimes.com/2009/10/17/opinion/17sat4.html. Accessed on 16 October 2009.

Edgerton, Gary R. 'Falling Man and Mad Men (1:54)', *in media res: a mediacommons project* at 20 April 2009 at http://mediacommons .futureofthebook.org/imr/2009/04/14/falling-man-and-mad-men-154. Accessed on 23 October 2009.

Gilbert, Matthew. 'Truth in advertising: Dark secrets, understated performances make acclaimed "Mad Men" riveting.' *The Boston Globe*. 25 July 2008 at http://www.boston.com/ae/tv/articles/2008/ 07/25/truth_in_advertising/. Accessed on 16 October 2009.

Hansen, Liane. 'Creating a New Work History: "Mad Men"'. National Public Radio. 2 September 2007 at http://www.npr.org/templates/ story/story.php?storyId=14124179&ps=rs. Accessed on 22 September 2009.

Johans, Jen. 'Music Review: Mad Men – Music from the Series, Vol. 1.' *Blogcritics* 2008 at http://blogcritics.org/music/article/music-review-mad-men-music-from/. Accessed on 23 October 2009.

Lanza, Joseph. *Elevator Music: A Surreal History of Muzak, Easy-Listening, and Other Moodsong.* Revised and Expanded Edition, ed. Ann Arbor, MI: University of Michigan Press, 2004.

Lelane, Drake. 'Music on Mad Men: Classic Tunes Set the Scene for This Old Boys Club', *film.com* (2007) at http://www.film.com/features/story/music-mad-men-classic-tunes/15667705. Accessed on 23 October 2009.

———, 'On DVD: Mad Men, Season 1: A Zippo-Shaped Time Machine', *film.com* (2008) at http://www.film.com/tv/mad-men/story/dvd-mad-men-season-1/21654086. Accessed on 1 November 2009.

Manilla, Ben. '"Button-Down Mind" Changed Modern Comedy', 2007. National Public Radio. 23 December 2007 at http://www.npr.org/templates/story/story.php?storyId=17561805. Accessed on 3 November 2009.

Marcus, Daniel. *Happy Days and Wonder Years: The Fifties and the Sixties in Contemporary Cultural Politics.* New Brunswick, NJ: Rutgers University Press, 2004.

Schwartz, Bruce. '"Mad Men" sells the '60s with authenticity', *USA Today*, 22 August 2007 at http://www.usatoday.com/life/television/news/2007-08-22-mad-men-props_N.htm. Accessed on 16 October 2009.

Sepinwall, Alan. 'Mad Men: Creator Matthew Weiner's thoughts on the season premiere', *The Star-Ledger*, 16 August 2009 at http://www.nj.com/entertainment/tv/index.ssf/2009/08/mad_men_creator_matthew_weiner.html. Accessed on 29 November 2009.

Stanley, Alessandra. '"Mad Men" strains to stay as button-down as ever', *The New York Times*. 13August 2009 at http://www.nytimes.com/2009/08/14/arts/television/14mad.html. Accessed on 16 October 2009.

Trakin, Roy. 'Alexandra Patsavas, music supervisor; Indie-Music fans are all ears for uncanny touch of Patsavas with soundtracks almost as popular as hit show', *Advertising Age*, 15 May 2006: S-9.

Turner, Gustavo. 'Apocalypse then: "Mad Men" scores with some vintage Skeeter Davis', *L.A. Weekly*, 3 November 2009 at http://blogs.laweekly.com/westcoastsound/video-clip/mad-men-jfk-assassination-epis/. Accessed on 16 October 2009.

Wilson, Sloan. *A Summer Place*, New York: Simon & Schuster, 1958.

Notes

1 I am operating with the AMC blog entries as a guideline, one that is quite representative rather than exacting, for the sake of brevity. There are multiple examples where popular recordings and songs are deployed in *Mad Men* without inclusion in these listings and, indeed, I refer to at least one prominent example not listed in the 57 recordings in this essay, Skeeter Davis' 'The End of the World'.

2 By using Dylan's 'Don't Think Twice, It's All Right' as the final piece of music in the final episode of season one, *Mad Men* chose to use a record that would not be released until 1962, in spite of its setting in 1960. In the case of Don McLean's 'Babylon', the recording used in the sixth episode of the first season is made by the program's cast, however, the arrangement is the same one that McLean composes and releases eleven years later than the 1960 setting on his popular 1971 *American Pie* album.

3 Noting its appeal, *Time* reported that the album, *Inside Shelley Berman* had been 'near the top of the LP bestseller list for two months, a remarkable feat for a nonmusical disk.' According to *Time*, the growth and popularity of this genre was representative of larger social change, wherein 'sociologists, both professional and amateur, see in the sick comedians a symptom of the 20th century's own sickness'. Says one: 'It's like the last days of Rome – all this horror and mayhem in humor.' Anon., 'Nightclubs: The Sickniks,' *Time*, 13 July 1959 at http://www.time.com/time/magazine/article/0,9171,869153,00.html.

4 Specifically, Newhart cites Packard's claim that the dangers 'of the public relations man or the advertising man was that they were creating images' and, thereby, manipulate the public to vote for cults of personality rather than policies. Throughout the next seven minutes Newhart plays the role of an ad agent who is on the telephone consulting an Abraham Lincoln that the audience never hears. The resulting one-sided conversation is a slow but blistering review of how a Madison Avenue executive would construct much of the iconic imagery surrounding Lincoln, specifically those of the Gettysburg Address.

5 Speaking of season three's depiction of 1963, Weiner points out, 'This year is not quite like that. Everything happens in the same three-month period, and we may not be setting things in all of those months. But I'm really interested, after doing this show for a while... is in looking at how little history actually does impact our lives.' See Alan Sepinwall, '*Mad Men*: Creator Matthew Weiner's Thoughts on the Season Premiere', *The Star-Ledger*, 16 August 2009 at http://www.nj.com/entertainment/tv/index.ssf/2009/08/mad_men_creator_matthew_weiner.html.

6.
Suggestive Silence in Season One
Maurice Yacowar

In a second-season episode of *Mad Men* Don Draper takes wife Betty and children Sally and Billy on a picnic. After the frolic they leave their garbage on the green field. On that the camera lingers for several silent seconds.

There are three levels of dramatic irony here. One, the happy scene is undercut by what we know are the tensions within each parent and between them. Two, the picnic lives out the picnic Coke ad for which Betty posed in 'Shoot' (1:9), when a rival company used her career as bait to hook Don. When he declined she was dumped. Her real picnic recalls her family first pretence when she told Don it was her decision not to resume her career. As her life imitates her ad she's still posing.

The third irony reveals the drama's essential strategy. From our twenty-first-century perspective the family's litter despoils the landscape, but that was of no concern in the mid-twentieth-century setting. Then rubble was not a cause. Matthew Weiner draws on our current awareness to read a meaning that is not articulated within the scene, not in the characters' consciousness, not even in the larger narrative. Here is the twist. If our awareness makes us feel superior to the characters we fall into Weiner's trap. For it is his advertising men's sense of superiority – for their modernity, wit, sophistication, success and affluence – that renders them hollow. These suggestive silences draw on our privileged knowledge and pull us into Weiner's satire.

Of course, in any period fiction the time in which the action is *set* occupies only the level of plot. The major themes reflect the time the work is *made*. Why else look back? The best work also holds true for whenever they are *viewed*. So Cooper's recommendation of Ayn Rand's philosophy of self-interest in 'The Hobo Code' (1:8) gained now satiric weight during the 2008–09 financial collapse, when Alan Greenspan said Rand inspired his (disastrous) economic philosophy. Greenspan simply validated Weiner's vision of capitalist greed.

In *Mad Men* whatever says 'This was them then' connotes 'This is us now', mutatis mutandis. The characters' smugness is undermined by our knowing more than they do, but that targets our certainty. Those foolish mortals are us, fifty years ago but us. Fifty years hence our present values and conventions may prove as foolish to the next enlightened age as these are to ours. When our advantage in cultural perspective tempts us to feel superior, the satire of 1950s complacency turns upon ours.

It's hard to find an episode in which some character's complacency is not satirized. For example, in 'Flight 1' (2:15) when an American Airlines crash numbs the Sterling Cooper office, Pete Campbell initiates the pack's black humour. There were enough golfers aboard, he quips, to turn the Bay plaid. Then he learns his father died in the crash. His complacency is shattered, though he recovers to use his loss to win the AA ad contract. In another reversal, his dislike for his father makes his irreverent humour his most honest response.

My present purpose is to show how such unarticulated meaning undermines the characters' delusion of superiority – then tests ours. After a close study of the first episode we will trot through the first season, which entrenched this strategy. Often what's explicit is of less import than what's implicit. Even when the heard melodies are sweet those unheard are acrid.

*   *   *

The silence begins in the title. The 'Mad' in *Mad Men* excludes, renders silent, the rest of the term 'Madison Avenue', which in the 1950s signified the Brave New World of advertising that Vance Packard exposed in *The Hidden Persuaders*. As Madison shrinks into Mad the persuader hides again. As well, 'Mad' conflates madness or anger with the lurking 'ad'. That is to say, the title quietly introduces advertising as maddening in both senses of the term, provoking anger and irrationality, to practitioners and victims alike. The 'Men' excludes the women in the title, as the drama will expose the patriarchal industry and the period's sexist conventions.

The title sequence implicitly introduces the drama's themes in abstract visuals. A man of dark heft – i.e., an intensely black Gray Flannel Suit – steps into a stylized office space. When this insubstantial world dissolves, he plummets past towers of ad images – beautiful women, a beautiful family – including the slogans 'Enjoy the Best America Has to Offer' and 'It's the Gift that Never Fails'. The implicit import is that in American consumerism the gift – whether the adman's talent or his subject bounty – is far from the best the nation could offer. That culture constantly fails its proponents. After the falling man appears to land on us, the last shot leaves us watching from behind him. We assume Don Draper's perspective.

The lie continues in 'I never wanted wealth untold', in Don Cherry's 'Band of Gold', the song over the first scene. Like this denial of greed, the wedding band and its values will be betrayed throughout this episode. In the smoke-filled bar Don's chat with the suppressed black waiter about his Old Golds (another band) establishes the drama's period. It's back when everyone was smoking two packs a day and real men discounted their mortal danger as a *Reader's Digest* rumour. The signification of the scene depends upon its implicit distance from our current knowledge and values. The smokers' complacency, the black waiter's reticence, the dismissal of women and their magazines, provoke our present perspective. The episode's title, 'Smoke Gets in Your Eyes' (1:1), cites another 1950s hit song, but we don't hear it. What's in our eyes is not the characters' smoke but the illusion of our distance from it, in time as in space. We're neither in that room nor stuck in that time, but we're implicated.

Contrary to the devotion in 'Band of Gold', the second scene takes Draper to his mistress. Midge is another ad artist whose walls betray her compromised ambition to be an Abstract Expressionist painter. Her drawings for Grandmother's Day cards pretend to family values but she refuses to make commitments and breakfast.

The next morning Peggy Olson suffers the three ad-men's open sexism in the elevator, an augur of what she will endure as she rises from secretary to junior copywriter. When Joan introduces the complex 'new technology', the punch line is the full-screen revelation of – an electric typewriter. In implicitly comparing that machine to our office electronics Weiner trumps Joan's words with the silent pertinence of our times. So, too, our awareness of sexual harassment colours the men's behaviour and the contrast between brazen Joan and virginal Peggy. When the switchboard women echo Pete's praise of Peggy's legs, the girls align with the male authority; to both Peggy must 'always be supplicant'.

The men's commanding stature is confirmed by the low-angle shooting in Draper's office scene with his ostensible superior Roger Sterling. This becomes a racial superiority when the men need to find a Jewish employee, to court a Jewish department store account. In race as in gender the workplace is a meat market: 'Want me to run down to the deli and grab somebody?' Of course, Draper will overcome his prejudice for his later affair with Rachel Menken. In the office scene the shot angle says, 'These are big men' but our ironic distance reads their venality.

The close-up on Draper's pre-meeting Alka Seltzer suggests another unarticulated theme, the extension of the characters' fictions into their lives. Like Betty's picnic, Don lives an advertising cliché. 'Plunk plunk fizz fizz' rang the old hangover relief ad. Draper lives the persuasive fictions on which he makes his living. His glance at a military medal will be explained when we learn he adopted a dead soldier's identity to remake himself, i.e., to be the kind of product he flogs. The lies he sells become the lies he lives and ultimately the lie he is. In a more positive remaking, he does a quick chest expansion, which prompts Salvatore Romano to compare him to Gidget in a bikini. Romano will deny his homosexuality with beefcake drawings and macho posturing. Like Draper, Romano lives a public fiction, aka a lie.

In this stud pretence Romano dismisses Mrs. Guttman as 'Our man in research' and disdains Freud's Death Wish theory: 'We're supposed to believe that people are living one way, and secretly thinking the exact opposite? That's ridiculous.' That's him. When Dr. Guttman proposes selling cigarettes as the spirit of American independence and danger, Romano facetiously proposes 'a skull and crossbones on the label – I love it'. We know that the health warnings on cigarette packages will take that very form. The spoken jokes are undercut by the silent history, not just of the characters' lives – that's basic dramatic irony – but by what we know of social history. Even in this episode, though Draper rejects Freud's theory he uses it to explain his success: 'Fear stimulates my imagination'.

In another undercutting of that Band of Gold, though Pete Campbell is getting married in two days, he addresses Peggy so sexually that Draper apologizes for him: 'He left his manners at the fraternity house.' But in his private lecture Draper doesn't condemn sexual harassment on principle – our view – but as a hindrance to Pete's popularity and promotion. Draper's rejection of Pete's handshake – 'Let's take it a little slower. I wouldn't like to wake up pregnant' – foreshadows Pete's impregnating of Peggy and confirms the male advantage.

By our values Peggy's doctor is undercut by his smoking and his intimacy with Joan. Dr. Emerson says he won't judge the unmarried woman for requesting a contraceptive, then cites the 'strumpet' and 'town pump'. The shots of him with the rubber gloves and cold metal forceps suggest a harsh sexism. As he looks like cigarette ad doctors he repeats the ad men's insensitivity: 'The fact is, even in our modern times easy women don't find husbands [clank].' Of course, his 'modern' is our 'historic', though old attitudes persist.

In the cigarette ad meeting the men's coughing fit may be due either to the purple haze or to one client's remark, 'Might as well be living in Russia', given the government's meddling. From this hardly 'thin air' Draper saves the account with his brainwave. By declaring Lucky Strike the cigarette that is 'toasted', Draper distinguishes the brand from all its rivals, which are equally 'toasted'. To him, saying something is distinctive makes it so.

Sterling offers Draper the presidential campaign of a sure winner – a young, handsome naval hero. But it's Richard Nixon. The twist circles back to the scene's opening Red Scare joke. The irony deepens when we remember how the Nixon (and then Bush II) administrations undermined the American ideal touted throughout the cigarette discussion.

At Pete's stag the stripper in a tight pink gown evokes Marilyn Monroe. She is an image of an image, so no amount of peeling will disclose her. As Pete exploited Peggy's naiveté to get the Guttman report from Draper's wastebasket, he leaves his stag not for his fiancée's but Peggy's home. We may not find his drunken lure very winning – 'I'm getting married on Sunday . . . You must think I'm a creep . . . I had to see you' – but as we saw in her rebuffed approach to Draper, Peggy will play by the men's rules.

Between Pete's stag and his seduction of Peggy, Draper has a conciliatory drink with Rachel Menken. His smoothness contrasts with Pete's rejected assault on the party girl, but Draper is just as calculating and self-serving. Rachel finds it 'refreshing' to have *heard* the Jewish stereotype she had only assumed people *thought*. That is, for her as for us the spoken is undercut by what is left implicit. After extolling the values of marriage – that Band of Gold again – Draper claims her love ideal was invented by admen to sell nylons. But his cynicism crumbles before her Old World warmth and honesty. Rachel reads Draper's confidence as the weakness of the disconnected, the out of place. His recoil ('You want another drink?') is understood only when we learn that he *is* disconnected, having assumed someone else's identity. Again, the explicit moment is transcended by the implicit future, what we will learn of his past. Draper lives 'like there is no tomorrow, because there isn't one.' But there was one and his drama's bite lies in our perspective from it.

Weiner cuts from Peggy's flannel seduction to Draper's trip home and our first sight of his wife, Betty. In counterpoint to the opening 'Band of Gold' here Don is characterized by the wordless 'Sheik of Araby'. Visiting the sleeping children, Draper seems the attentive father, husband and *mentsch* that the entire episode has belied. The last shot pans from the Draper house into darkness, to Vic Damone's 1956 hit 'On the Street Where You Live'. That's from *My Fair Lady* where another male authority marketed a woman by remaking her image.

Of course, the episode typically has several stretches of silence, as around the contemplative Draper, and in bridge scenes, like Peggy's arrival at the doctor's. These explicit silences set off our alternative silence, when what is said or shown is contradicted by our ironic distance. At least the first season's essential device will be undercutting the spoken or the shown with the implied.

* * *

The title of 1:2, 'Ladies Room', pivots on three scenes in these women's refuges. The first shows two executive wives' self-centredness and Mrs. Sterling's evasion of Mrs. Draper's intimacy. In the others Peggy finds her weeping co-worker Bridget. Unlike the broken women – and the man whose suicide delayed the train – the ad men base their camaraderie on their power over words and silence.

In the restaurant Sterling tells Don about his daughter's psycho-analysis, but in the office he denies it. What the men say is. As Don won't tell Betty anything about himself, she can't express her unhappiness, hence her insomnia and numbed fingers. Don claims modesty but his affair proves he wants a secret life, even though he knows Betty needs to feel closer. Wondering what women want informs his Right Guard ad and leads to Betty's therapy. Her male therapist also wields the power of speech and silence, for he says nothing to her but blabs to her husband. This betrayal offends us even more now that therapy is no longer a fad, Sterling's 'just this year's candy-pink stove'.

Betty scolds Sally for dropping the dry-cleaning, not for what alarms us – breathing in the plastic bag. The unspoken suffocation threat spreads from that image to the women harassed at work, the men whose roles preclude sensitivity, and all the compulsive drinkers and smokers who like Betty find refuge in growing numb. Mean-while the culture institutionalizes its humiliations in Art Linkletter's popular TV show, *People Are Funny*.

In 1:3, 'Marriage of Figaro', Don's study of a Volkswagen self-satire is interrupted by an army mate who calls him Dick Whitman. As the Met opera plays in the background at his daughter Sally's birthday party, operatic tensions underlie the conversations at the party as at work. The marriages range from Pete's new one to Helen Bishop, the neighbourhood's new single mom. The dialogue has to be decoded, as Helen translates Carlton's chivalric offer. Rachel's gift of shining knight cufflinks expresses her romantic hope for Don, which ends when he says he's married. He seems the Ideal Husband as he puts together Sally's playhouse (in which the children will replay their parents' tensions), but he abandons the party. The closing song explains his gift dog as a sentimental afterthought: 'P.S. I Love You'. When one man slaps another's child for knocking over a drink, the boy's father threatens more punishment then sends for his mother to clean up the mess. An unarticulated insecurity underlies the men's flex of power.

As the title 'New Amsterdam' (1:4) points to New York's history, Pete's mother's pedigree precludes his firing. Her father is buried at the Church of the Intercession (!). By selling the Bethlehem Steel executive his 'Backbone of America' slogan, Pete reasserts his own backbone after his father's rejection and his generous father-in-law's pressure ('Where's the nursery?'). When Cooper reverses Pete's firing, he tells Don 'You handle the words', but the silent clench of Don's left big toe expresses more feeling than his compliant words. To save Draper's face, Sterling tells Pete that Draper fought for Pete's second chance. But the affirmation of Draper's strength – he is Pete's 'commanding officer. You live and die in his shadow, understood?' – recalls the 'imaginary wound', the false identity he assumed in the war.

The title of 1:5, '5G', seems one step up/back from the 4H club award to which Draper compares his new honour. That rural past revives when his younger brother Adam appears. In hotel room 5G Don claims his life goes only forward but here the past rebounds. The old photo of Don and Adam recalls that of Cooper with young Sterling in the previous episode. In another revival Pete sends Trudy to her first lover to promote his short story. As Don hides his past, his business and his mistress from his wife, he conceives the private executive bank account. The wives' dependency and Betty's girlishness derive from their sense that their husbands' offices are another country, where they don't speak the language. Don's furtive withdrawal from his desk before going to 5G suggests the old soldier might draw a gun. But now the man's weapon is a wad of bills and an order.

Like the opening toast, the secrets pop up in 1:6, 'Babylon' – where the Jewish exile began. The metaphor of exile pervades. From Sterling's troubled daughter we cut to his furtive affair with Joan. Don's Mother's Day fall recalls the pains of his prelapsarian childhood. An exile in her marriage, Betty can articulate her desire for Don but not confidence in him. 'You were caught cheating' tumbles out as her giddy joke, sadly true. In the office lipstick test the sexes' separate worlds, divided by the one-way glass, confirm the men's power. Don feels an exile in Midge's bohemia and needs Rachel to explain Israel. 'More of an idea than a place', it's a Utopia, which she translates from the Greek as 'the good place' and 'the place that cannot be'. That is how Don and Rachel will view each other, Peggy her ascension to copywriter. The last song about Babylon exiles covers lonely Rachel in her tie section, Betty putting lipstick on Sally like a squire armouring his knight, Sterling zipping up Joan, and Don silently estranged from Midge. In the last shot exiles Sterling and Joan stand outside their tryst hotel like strangers, she with her caged bird and he lighting up the killer pleasure he sells.

The central metaphor in 1:7, 'Red in the Face', is adulterated innocence. Sterling adds vodka to his ulcer milk and compares redheads' lips to 'a drop of strawberry jam in a glass of milk.' The 'sweet and perfect' Betty slaps Helen in front of the 'Prod' (produce sign), for criticizing her gift to young Glen. Don charges Betty with Dr. Wayne's note of childishness. But at dinner Betty seems the gracious adult compared to Sterling's aggressive sense of entitlement and Don's defensive vanity. Pete's swagger over his rifle gives his wife ammo against his claim that *she's* childish, but it sends Peggy to the cherry Danish aroused.

At the bar Sterling admires 'the look of pure youth' in the potential pickups, but their eye for Don confirms Sterling's aging. The 23-story climb resurrects his oyster and martini lunch. From our perspective the constant smoking and drinking (which only Cooper rejects) is a sign and cause of weakness, not their power. We're bothered that the pregnant Francine smokes and drinks. While the adman's 'Har dee har har' and the garish chip'n'dip seem *au courant,* we find them kitsch. Sterling's remark that Nixon 'practically shot [a rival] in the face to win' now aligns him with Vice President Cheney's hunting misadventure, as Kennedy's alleged inexperience evokes Barack Obama.

In 1:8 our understanding of homosexuality reads Romano's rejection of Elliot as a tragic self-denial. His alternative courtship by the switchboard operator reduces Romano to the squalid conventions of office romance, as represented by Pete's morning rape of Peggy – his rifle against the wall – and his evening disdain for her Twist. Pete dislikes Peggy's independence as he resents Trudy for insisting he return the rifle and supervise their move into the new flat he didn't want. Don applies rape to ad strategy: when 'seduction is over and force is being requested'.

The title, 'The Hobo Code', derives from Don's memory of a New York hobo who didn't treat Don like a – in his Christian stepmother's view – 'whore-child'. Yet his stepmother is more generous than his father, who reneges on paying the hobo for work. As the hobo left his mortgaged life for the open road, Don gets stoned with Midge's beatniks. Freedom is illusory, as even these women have to listen to their men preen. With the new Polaroid Land camera Don discovers his mistress loves the beatnik. Working with posed images enables Don to read a natural one, as he learned the hobos' signs to each other. The Depression roads, Greenwich Village, Madison Avenue, friendships, marriages and affairs, all have their own illusions of freedom and their own codes. With the police outside the hippies can't leave but the stoner in the gray suit and hat can. In the indifferent universe the strong man is the one who shows the right signs.

His father's abuse of the hobo prompts Don to promise never to lie to his son. But the last shot – Donald Draper's name on his door – is the lie he tells everyone. The closing country song, 'That Old Time Religion', implicitly contrasts to such new-time religions as Ayn Rand, nihilism beatnik or corporate, and the changing technologies of image making, from the hobo's chalk signs through the Polaroid to today's digital.

After losing Midge through his photo, in 'Shoot' (1:9), Don sees a bigger ad agency offer to revive Betty's modelling career to lure him. The salaries – $35–45,000 for Don, Suzy Parker the leading model at $100,000 – remind us that one period's large is another's small. In an echo of Romano's sellout, Hobart's apparently gay brother-in-law runs the Coke account. The stiffness of Betty's picnic ad contrasts to the flying pigeons, at which Betty shoots BBs when she resumes her role as mother.

In 1:10, 'Long Weekend', with the wives away for Labor Day the men run free in Manhattan. The episode presents two questionable judgments: Pete criticizes Peggy's procedure and Betty rejects her dad's girlfriend. Both dress personal biases as morals. But there is no explicit criticism when Sterling and Draper hustle twin models. Sterling compliments his girl's 'translucent skin', then Don reads his boss's mortality in skin thin as paper. Sterling expresses his lust as a vampire's hunger for such young flesh. Today the men seem foolish, the twins exploited, and Joan's roommate – whose love Joan deflects – a touching victim of unconventional ardour.

In Joan's saddest dignity, she joins Cooper to inform their clients of Sterling's coronary. She is allowed no sign Sterling is her lover. Her erasure by the elevator doors recalls her sobering lesson from Shirley Maclaine's exploited elevator girl in Billy Wilder's *The Apartment*. (1960). The Sterling Cooper void of cubicles echoes the film's office set. Fred MacMurray portrayed Sterling's philandering exec, with Jack Lemmon's shnook a contrast to vile Pete. Wilder offered no equivalent to Cooper, who is as eccentric immorality – i.e., sometimes he is somewhat moral – as he is about his office ban on shoes.

Our response to Draper here is more difficult. Sterling's reluctant 'bait' is not the worm his boss is. Even as he plays faithful husband he respects his twin. But while the trauma drives Sterling to weep his love for his wife, Draper tells Betty she shouldn't come home, then takes his grief to Rachel. Though she knows his urgency is 'just an excuse for bad behaviour', she embraces him. If Don holds back until she asks him, we know his strategy: 'seduction is over and force is being requested' (1:8).

Draper's new adultery is complex. Rachel seems the first person of moral substance that the adult Draper has met. Her Old Testament culture suggests a heft missing in his world of lies and fictions. So he senses that she sees through him, that she instinctively understands him, that she may offer a truth like the earlier Wandering Outsider, the hobo. Draper tells Rachel the childhood truth he has denied Betty, making this affair more open than his marriage. Another exercise in male authority proceeds in the background. In the Democrats' attack ad, President Eisenhower undermines his vice-president's claim to be more experienced than Kennedy. As 'the president is a product' so is Don.

Cooper loses his moral advantage in 'Indian Summer' (1:11) when he brings Sterling back prematurely to reassure the cigarette client. When Joan covers his pallor, there is sincerity if not courtliness in Sterling's 'You are the finest piece of ass I ever had.' From our distance we are also touched by the awkwardness (and belligerence) of Peggy's blind date, the admen's vulture concerns for Sterling, Don's 'protective' care for Betty even as he deepens his affair with Rachel, and the 40-cent charge Adam incurs to mail Don his family snaps before hanging himself. With our sophistication we know why – more than Betty's *Family Circle* if less than her washing machine – Peggy's vibrator will, in the closing song, fly her to the moon.

In 'Nixon vs. Kennedy' (1:12), the real Don Draper's death proves 'smoking kills'. The soldiers survive a sniper attack but a dropped lighter blows up a fuel tank. Pete's blackmail attempt sends Don back to Rachel. The strength and purpose he draws from her recall Sterling's vampire leech off his model. But Rachel sees Don's proposal to run away as his cowardice not passion. Her refusal parallels Midge's declining his Paris offer, which ended that affair too. From Rachel, Don gets his line to confront Pete: 'You haven't thought this through'. But from the weeping, indignant Peggy, Don gets the backbone to take Pete's blackmail to Cooper.

Cooper advises Don, 'Fire him if you want. But keep an eye on him. One never knows how loyalty is born.' Though Draper sees how Pete rewarded his loyalty for supposedly saving his job before, our knowing Draper's past explains why he doesn't fire him. A bad secret is more safely kept close than sent to a rival.

The promise of President Kennedy's contracts for Sterling Cooper replays Draper's fluidity of character. As the election results may pivot on an Illinois recount they recall Bush vs. Gore in Florida. We have also retained the advertising/politics nexus that has no more principle than a football contest. In the next episode 1:13, Pete's father-in-law ties the election to the NFL closing game results. This episode closes with Nixon's concession speech on a small snowy black-and-white TV set – a world away from our technology but not from us.

The season conclusion, 'The Wheel', spins a range of romantic problems: Rachel has fled to Paris; writer Harry will quit smoking if his wife takes him back; Pete is nagged for a grandchild; and a $18(!) phone bill exposes Carlton's infidelity. In Don's phone bill Betty uncovers her therapist's betrayal, which she exploits to warn Don about his affairs and remoteness.

Draper closes the season on a climax of emotional commitment – at work. Unlike Pete's exploitation of his father's death (2:15), Draper only implicitly draws on his brother's suicide to 'give legs' to Kodak's 'wheel', i.e., to humanize a machine. He draws on Rachel's Greek Utopia for nostalgia, Greek for 'the pain from an old wound'. He makes the slide projector a time machine 'that takes us to a place where we ache to go again'. His pitch persuades him to spend Thanksgiving with his family, but he arrives too late. His fantasy scene proves the power of his imagination.

Weiner cuts this sentimentality with a double irony. Don promotes Peggy to Junior Copywriter with the Clearasil account Pete proudly landed from his father-in-law. Then Peggy learns she is pregnant. Weiner intercuts her delivery of Pete's son with the pressure on Pete to impregnate Trudy. The last shot tracks away from Don sad in his empty house, as Bob Dylan sings of 'the break of dawn'/Don, in 'It's All Right, Ma, I'm Only Bleedin'.

To young exec Harry Crane, the Lascaux handprints are the artist reaching across time to us, through the stone, saying 'I was here'. As Matthew Weiner returns us to those simpler times, the 1950s and 1960s, he expects our awareness to define the characters' vanities and insecurities which tempts us into their delusion of superiority. The series is Weiner's time machine that takes us back to where we ostensibly were but really still are. His carousel swings us too, like children, round and round, back and forth, but always here, now as then vain victims of our own wit, words, power and delusions.

Part Three.
Narrative Dynamics and Genealogy

7.
Learning to Live with Television in *Mad Men*

Horace Newcomb

In *Make Room for TV*, her groundbreaking sociocultural history of the arrival of television, Lynn Spigel chronicles many of the ways in which users of the medium understood its place in their lives. Most significantly, she explores changes, perhaps what might even be referred to as transformations, in domestic life. Gendered practices, the meanings of 'family', shifts in home design and uses of space are all examined through lenses as varied as magazine advertisements and cartoons, instructional essays and television programming itself. Summing up the point of the project, Spigel says:

> I have been interested in showing how the multiple, and often con-
> flicting, middle-class ideals of post-war America gave way to contra-
> dictory responses to television in popular culture. Although popular
> representations cannot definitively demonstrate how people actually
> used television in their own homes, they do begin to reveal the discur-
> sive conventions that were formed for thinking about a new medium
> during the period of its installation. They begin to disclose the social
> construction of television as it is rooted in a mode of thought based
> on white middle-class concepts of gender, class, and generational
> difference. Ideals of décor and suburban life-styles, as well as the
> gendered and age-related divisions of families in the home, served
> as a backdrop for the development of television as a cultural form.
> (Spigel, 186)

In this essay I approach some of the same topics, but from somewhat different perspectives. Set in a period that overlaps, to some degree, the years explored in Spigel's study, *Mad Men* depicts television in many sites and puts the device to many uses. The sites and uses vary in significance in specific episodes and also within the three seasons of the overarching narrative. Significantly, that larger narrative exceeds the specific account, the 'story' of a set of fictional characters engaged in practices and interpersonal enactments. *Mad Men* is also a narrative of a specific time in America, an account of events small and large, personal and public, domestic and professional. At times the series constructs an account almost academic in its complex representation of a society and a culture in a process of transformation. While it is likely that all we may ever know with certainty of all societies and cultures is that transformation is always present, it is also true that at some 'moments' the processes are more evident than others, some institutions more open to question, some tendencies more profoundly significant, and that even some technologies push more strongly into the process, into the emerging 'new'. At some moments in this greater account of cultural history and social change television seems peripheral in this fictional world. At others, however, it is placed powerfully at the centre.

As it appears in the series, television is emblematic of and deeply embedded in the construction of the America created in the series. In perhaps the most salient feature of the medium in the period in which it is grounded, *Mad Men* repeatedly reminds us that it was necessary to learn how to use television, how to live with it, apply it and understand it. While Spigel's account of 'making room' for TV captures broad patterns of cultural and social change, the 'education' presented in *Mad Men* is microcosmic. Here, learning what television meant – or would come to mean – was not always easy, for those meanings exceed 'watching programs' and 'making commercials'. The modes of thought 'based on white middle-class concepts of gender, class, and generational difference' the '[i]deals of décor and suburban life-styles', the 'gendered and age-related divisions of families in the home', are examined in details bound with the emotional investment we make in fictional characters and their stories. Though few moments in the series may actually focus on television, the extended narrative makes clear that, as Spigel goes on to say,

> The popular discourses remind us that television's utopian promise was fraught with doubt. Even more importantly, they begin to reveal the complicated processes through which conventions of television viewing in the home environment and conventions of television's representational styles were formed in the early period. (Spigel, 187)

The lessons learned, the habits and conventions established, the new professional strategies developed, altered the many varieties of experience represented in the series. We see lessons and habits in homes, but it is perhaps even more significant that we see the creation and manipulation of assumptions *about* the home, about gender, about age and lifestyle, as these sites and discourses are interpreted by the advertisers who would be central in defining meanings and uses of the medium.

Given that television sets appear so early and regularly in *Mad Men*, that programmes and events are both seen and overheard, and that titles and other references are common, not every instance of television can be noted. To capture some of the process of learning to live with television, then, I examine the presence and significance of television in three arenas – the individual/personal/domestic, the professional/corporate, and the cultural/social. A key aspect of the series, however, is the elaborate, at times delicate mingling of these sites. The distinctions are clearly artificial and at times some of the ways in which they overlap and relate to one another must be noted, for those examples provide the richest indications of television's significance.

Sally, Bobby, Go Watch Television

Television is pervasive throughout *Mad Men*, in homes, hotel rooms, hospital rooms and restaurants. Its uses among characters range from diversion to what would in short order be referred to as obsession, addiction or, in more neutral academic terms, 'heavy viewing'. As indicated in the section heading above, it was also a continuing factor in the Draper household, a system of reward and punishment for children. Often present as background audio as well as in flickering video images, the medium is available in scenes focused on topics and actions having little or nothing to do with TV in any specific sense. References to shows abound – *The Twilight Zone* (CBS, 1959–64), *Bonanza* (NBC, 1959–73), *The Danny Thomas Show* (ABC, 1953–57; CBS, 1957–65; ABC, 1970–71). Commercials for household products and other items provide the texture of a flourishing consumer society as well as the professional concern of Sterling Cooper.

Among the more significant aspects of television's presence is that programmes act at times as counterpoint within scenes that expand and reveal complex character relationships. In 'For Those Who Think Young' (2:14), for example, a high-profile cultural television event, *Tour of the White House* with Mrs. John Fitzgerald Kennedy, appears in a series of scenes. It's Valentine's Day, 1963, and Don Draper has prepared a special evening for Betty. She meets him at the Savoy Hotel and as she arrives she appears to him as a vision of glamour and sensuality. He surprises her with a room already reserved, but she anticipated this and has brought along her contraceptive device. When they attempt to make love he cannot perform. She suggests food and as she orders an elaborate meal, he switches on the television. He quickly passes the White House special, but she tells him to keep the programme on. They cuddle in silence as Jackie Kennedy provides her running commentary on furniture and decorations. In the next sequence Salvatore and his wife also watch. 'Where's her husband?' Sal asks. The narrative moves to Joan and her physician boyfriend, making out with the TV on. She asks to watch the special. He says no and pushes her down onto the sofa. As he nuzzles her neck, she angles her face and watches the programme. Finally, we cut to Pete Campbell. He sits alone, drinking. He watches a cartoon instead of the White House extravaganza.

Much more is going on in the brief overview of television viewing. Don certainly has no problems having sex with other women, but as this episode begins he first appears in his doctor's office. It's nothing more than a physical exam, but his blood pressure is 160/100. He tells (lies to) the doctor that he smokes two packs of cigarettes and downs five drinks a day. The doctor writes a prescription – resperine for the blood pressure, phenobarbatol to help Don relax. Betty, despite her glamorous entrance, her seductive lingerie and her birth control prep, is clearly frustrated. After telling Don not to worry about his performance and saying they have 'all night', she lies beside him, smoking, and says, 'I just wish you would tell me what to do'. Sal's search for JFK is one more obvious clue to his own sexual orientation. Joan's aggressively eager boyfriend, soon to be her husband, is inebriated with her sexuality and has no use for television when he's on top of her. Pete has earlier been immersed in yet another tense discussion with Trudy regarding her insistent desire for children. Perhaps the cartoon viewing and his earlier behaviour suggest that one child already occupies their household and that he would not welcome another.

In still other cases the presence of television and television viewing provide an eerie counterpoint to other events. In 'New Amsterdam' (1:4), Helen Bishop, the neighbourhood's only divorcee, asks Betty to serve as an emergency babysitter for her son, Glen, who first appeared in the series at Sally's birthday party. Glen appears to have, to say the least, some behavioural difficulties. In this episode, before Helen leaves for the evening (to work for the Kennedy campaign), she tells Glen he must go to bed 'after The Real McCoys are over'. Before bedtime, however, he opens the door to the bathroom to watch Betty as she urinates. Astonished and outraged, Betty berates him for this behaviour. Later, however, as they watch westerns together, she accedes to his bizarre request for a lock of her hair.

An equally disturbing sequence occurs in 'A Night to Remember' (2:21). While preparing for an important dinner party, Betty notices a wobbly leg on one of her dining room chairs. As Sally and Bobby watch television and simultaneously pay increasing attention to their mother, Betty proceeds to destroy the chair, slamming it into the floor until it lies in pieces. The children stare silently as Betty quietly gathers the sticks and leaves the room.

In such contexts, the presence of television is more than diversion. It serves as an anchor of sorts, a device and a practice dragging the unseemly and unexpected – including single parenthood and fragile mothers – back into more familiar realms of daily life. Perhaps the abnormal is to be acknowledged as nothing more than a portion of the new normal, a normal defined by 'the schedule', by the set that can always draw eyes away from disturbing, even frightening, events. Suburban life in this period, skewered by sociologists and cultural critics at the time and ever since has become the 'culture' in which frustration grows and leads to multiple versions of 'break down'.

It's Catharsis. That's Hard to Come By

At the heart of such matters, of course, is advertising. As Don Draper's speech to the Lucky Strike clients in the first episode, 'Smoke Gets in Your Eyes' (1:1), makes clear, the social successes developed after the Second World War were due, at least in part, to the construction, the articulation and the promised fulfilment of emotional needs.

> Advertising is based on one thing – happiness. And you know what happiness is? Happiness is the smell of a new car. It's freedom from fear. It's a billboard on the side of the road that screams with reassurance that whatever you're doing is okay. You are okay.

The irony, of course, made clear throughout the series, is that very little is okay and that almost everyone is desperately afraid of something. For the many who purchased them in the early 1960s, the smell of the new car may have provided the temporary happiness, but scents fade. So, too, does the nicotine hit, which made the two-pack-a-day habit necessary and kept tobacco companies in business. The elusive feelings attached to products also kept agencies busy turning out ads that could, in Don's reassurance to his clients, 'say anything'. Still, as *Mad Men* takes pains to show, the agencies, like television viewers, had to learn how to use, how to sell and how to think with the medium. When dealing with every product from presidential candidates to potato chips, however, thinking with TV wasn't always easy. This is made particularly clear in 'The Benefactor', (2:16).

In this episode Harry Crane, the 'media' guy at Sterling Cooper, opens a co-worker's pay envelope and discovers he makes much less. He tears the envelope on opening it and fears this will be discovered and that he will lose his job. He makes a desperate call to his friend Edgar at CBS. Their conversation is worth quoting at length.

Harry: Buddy. Harry Crane, how are you?
Edgar: I'm still at work, same as you.
Harry: How do you like it over there?

Edgar: Aww, did Sterling Coo lose some of its drunken luster?

Harry: I don't know . . . I was thinking I'd have to move out to move up.

Edgar: Well forget about here. They're picking us off. I'm one gone paleface.

Harry: Well, thought I'd ask. Keep an ear to the ground for me, will you. Doesn't have to be there.

Edgar: How 'bout some concern. I just lost Lever Bros. and Kimberly-Clarke from one of my biggest shows.

Harry: We're lousy with sponsors over here. What do you need?

Edgar: Don't get excited. Sponsors drop out for a reason.

Harry: Not always.

Edgar: OK, try this on. *The Defenders.* Top 20 show. E.G. Marshall and Bob Reed. Lawyers, you know. But they really care. So the writers turn in a script about a cannibal.

Harry: (laughing) A cannibal lawyer?

Edgar: The director eats up all this time refusing to do it. Like his resume isn't filled with crap. And surprise, the writers have only one other script ready. Something we threw away last year because they use the word abortion thirty times in fifty-one minutes.

Harry: Why?

Edgar: Because they show one. In the opening scene.

Harry: (Laughs uncomfortably)

Edgar: Exactly. The whole thing was a ploy to get us to shoot it. They think they're so clever. I tell you, I miss the Black List.

Harry: Send it over. I want to see it.

Edgar; Are you sure? It's going on the air, sponsor or no. I'll watch it with you at the bar where I'll be working.

Harry: Send it over. Let me see what I can do.

The Defenders (CBS, 1961–65) episode, of course, is a famous one, and it did air without sponsors. This conversation, however, exhibits a broader range of concerns linking television to advertising and to culture and society at large. For Harry, the question is what product can be sold with a television show dealing so specifically, so explicitly with such a topic. Edgar may lose his job because sponsors have pulled out and CBS will have to present the show without underwriting. Harry knows that CBS will accept any sponsor that will buy time on the episode. The significance of this storyline lies in questions regarding what television can and cannot do, what advertising will or will not do, what 'sponsorship' means. What could or could not be shown? Is cannibalism more taboo than abortion? That kind of significance continues after Harry reviews the episode alone, then convinces the Sterling Cooper creative and account group to present it to Bel Jolie lipstick, a client already looking for television opportunities. They screen the episode for Elliot Lawrence, the Bel Jolie representative. All of the agency's divisions are represented in the room. After a particularly harsh scene, Elliott stops the screening before it is completed.

Elliot: I do want to see the rest of this, but I get the idea.
Harry: Top 20 show. Prime time for pennies on the dollar. And it's a perfect match for Bel Jolie lipstick.
Elliot: Really? How does that work.
Don: Controversy means viewers. Women will find a way to watch this. Maybe, just because they don't want to get left out.
Elliot: (to Peggy Olson) Is that true?
Peggy: There's no doubt in my mind.
Ken: We can talk to them about putting on a warning. Research shows rules are made to be broken.
Harry: Thanks, Ken. (to Elliot) He has the research.
Elliot: This discussion . . . it's uncomfortable. This show is troubling.
Don: It's catharsis. That's hard to come by. What's better than tears to make a girl ready to hear she can be beautiful.
Elliot: I'd love to see a spike. But what do I do when Hugh Brody asks what the hell this is. Bel Jolie is a family company. This is not wholesome.
Don: There are limits to what you can get out of daytime.
Elliot: I don't want Bel Jolie to be part of this debate.
Harry: So you're thinking girls who buy lipstick aren't going to be interested in this? I don't care where they stand. So it's political. Politics are in. Women will be watching. Young women.
Elliot: I'm sorry.
Don: (recognizing it's no deal) Well, we thought you should know about it.
Elliot: I have to say, I'm very impressed you brought this to us. I wish we were a different kind of company.
Don: We all work for someone.

As in the exchange between Harry and Edgar, this scene is filled with cues regarding the rising significance of television, for society and culture, for the advertising industry and for the industry's attempts to 'interpret' the social and cultural roles of both TV and itself. Don's attempt to sell Bel Jolie on an attachment to controversy comes from multiple angles. Controversy is attractive. Women will find a way. Women don't want to be left out. When the generalizations fail Don, noted for his creative genius, he must become a salesman and pitch the product. But this is not cigarettes in print ads, where his admonition that anything can be said will work. His next attempt is more specific – brutal drama dealing with one of society's most charged topics leads to catharsis, which (as the Greeks well knew) is 'hard to come by'. Don's views on catharsis fall back on another generalization, the claim that cathartic tears make women – girls – want to think they can be beautiful. The attempt says more about Don Draper than about female desires for beauty, or for lipstick. Alongside such 'complicated' cultural analysis, Harry's desperate, 'Politics are in' seems a feeble last gasp and Don realizes they don't have a prayer of making this sale.

On his way out the door, Elliot, who has previously flirted with Sal, greets him again, quite warmly. Sal remains at his most professional remove from any suggestion of personal interest. But the juxtaposition of a reference to homosexuality, in the context of the significance of representing abortion on television, is telling. The management of desire and its potential consequences, whether pregnancy and termination or sexual attraction and disclosure, is in full display. Sal manages his behaviour. Elliott manages the interests of a 'family' company, even if he is more open about his own.

After all these events, Harry Crane is called into Roger Sterling's office. He enters like a schoolboy caught smoking in the bathroom. Roger's greeting is ambiguous and Harry is convinced he has been found out for opening a colleague's paycheck. But Roger is concerned about the risky move of pitching *The Defenders* to Bel Jolie. Despite his reservations, Bert Cooper approves. Roger asks what Harry wants. His first request is to have the agency create a 'television department' with him as the head. Roger blesses the idea. Harry then asks for a raise that will place him at a higher salary than Ken Cosgrove's $300 a week. Roger offers $225 and Harry eagerly accepts.

Harry will continue to watch shows, especially soap operas, on behalf of sponsors, making sure there is no dialogue that could be taken as an ambiguous but negative reference to a product. Joan Holloway, always the most astute employee at Sterling Cooper, becomes Harry's perfect assistant at this task. More than anyone, she understands how television culture intersects with advertising and the larger commercial world it serves. When Harry secures the services of a man as his script analyst, Joan is relegated to her clerical status. Still, a new age has begun for Harry and for Sterling Cooper. The agency takes a chance with the pitch to Bel Jolie because television has taken a chance with *The Defenders*. *The Defenders* took a chance on controversy. American culture had taken a chance with television.

Since When Do You Have a Television?

Such complex issues emerge clearly in these and other scenes involving specific advertising campaigns, character choices, products and programmes, but they were also deeply embedded in the kinds of interpersonal and domestic arenas examined earlier. In these explorations, the 'big' questions of what television would mean are linked to how people would learn to live with something that touched and influenced every feature of sociocultural experience. They are pointedly placed in one of Don Draper's early scenes. It is the sort of scene we come to take for granted with his character, and takes place in 'Ladies Room' (1:2).

Don is engaged in an affair with Midge, depicted as his 'bohemian' lover, a woman with 'beatnik' friends. The dalliance seems exciting for Don, a strong alternative to his life as an organization man, suburban husband and father. After making love with Midge in this episode, Don looks up from bed and the following conversation takes place.

Don: What's that?
Midge: What?
Don: That.
Midge: That's a television.
Don: Since when do you have a television?
Midge: I don't know. I think it's been at least ten days. It's amazing. I may have lost track.

Don: I seem to remember a woman wasting a good piece of a beautiful afternoon reciting a diatribe against television that should have ended with her banging her shoe on a table.

Midge: Well, Don, darling, if you want to ask a question. Ask it.

Don: Where'd you get the TV?

Midge: I got it.

Don: Same place you got that wig?

Midge: Someone gave it to me.

Don: And you took it.

Midge: Have you seen this thing called 'People Are Funny?'

He ignores her question, sulks.

Midge: Jesus, Don.

She picks up the small 'portable' television set and heaves it out the window of her apartment.

Midge: All better?

Don: (smiling) Yes.

She runs to the window, looks down and both laugh.

In this brief exchange we should realize that already by this time in its social history television must bear the burden of multiple cultural references and forms of significance. Midge, who goes to 'poetry readings' where women expose their breasts, who smokes marijuana and enjoys her affair with the married executive, initially considers TV the 'bad object'. In this nascent 'counterculture' the conventional unconventionality had already determined that the medium is the 'bad object' and would be nothing more than a padlock on the prison house of conformity. Having accepted it as a gift, however, perhaps from another lover as Don suspects, she has found it pleasurable, so pleasurable in fact that she has lost track of how long she has used it. As yet another form of seduction, the corruption of the non-innocent, such enjoyment would confirm television's narcotizing function, a drug at the opposite end of the social spectrum from pot. But wait, there's more. To Don, the acceptance of the gift object is a betrayal. It is evidence of her bad faith, not only with her prior judgement of television, but bad faith in his unfaithfulness. In a scene almost too obvious, he enters his home that evening to find Sally and Bobby sprawled before the family set watching *People Are Funny* (NBC, 1954–61).

In short, a television set is far more than a technological device, more even than a meaningful cultural object. It is a precious object of personal significance. It is already defining the meanings of how people live together yet also disrupting and intruding on those relationships in ways that would alarm psychologists, sociologists and political scientists. It certainly intruded on the efforts of advertising agencies and their clients. And it intruded on, disrupted and ultimately became central to American culture writ large.

The Whole Country's Drinking

This mesh of public and private, personal and professional, dangerous and acceptable, familiar and new, producer and viewer provides the strongest sense of the 'problem' of television. In the *Mad Men* narrative the 'problem' was answered with a form of temporary solution in the penultimate instalment of the third season, 'The Grown-Ups' (3:38). In this episode television is far more prominent than in others. The medium is 'quoted' at much greater length than previously. More images are used, more recognizable faces appear, more characters are shown sitting before the set actively watching television.

This is, of course, the episode in which the assassination of President John F. Kennedy is the central event. For some viewers of *Mad Men* the images, the quotes, are perhaps new and informative, are 'history'. For some they are references, somewhat familiar, seen previously in documentaries or textbooks. For some, however, they are experiential. They are accounts of the experience of learning about the event, of watching for long stretches of time, of moments lived with television. For such viewers this episode has hovered over the narrative from the beginning. Cues and clues have pointed to its coming. From the first episodes in which Bert Cooper pegs Kennedy as appropriately young and vigorous, a good TV candidate, through off-hand remarks about Nixon's lack of make-up in the debates, and on to clips and audio bites that bring issues of Civil Rights and the Vietnam War into the stories, this narrative has been developed within the Kennedy years.

Finally, the assassination and its aftermath ripple through the intertwined stories of the key characters. As the day begins Pete Campbell and Harry Crane sit in Harry's office discussing their careers. A graphic announcing a news bulletin is visible on the screen but they do not notice. In a hotel room Duck Phillips sees the bulletin and hears that the president may have been wounded, but he unplugs the set because Peggy is about to arrive for an afternoon of lovemaking. Office workers burst into Harry's office and everyone begins to watch Chet Huntley of NBC News describe events in Dallas. Don enters the empty outer office and asks 'What's going on?' Betty watches reports at home as Carla bursts in with the children and asks, 'Is he OK?' Betty tells her she just heard that the president is dead. Sally puts her arms around her weeping mother. At the hotel Duck plugs in the TV and both are astonished to hear of the president's death. Margaret Sterling weeps in another hotel room where she is trying on her wedding dress.

Don arrives at home where Betty and the children watch more reports. 'Why are the kids watching this?' he asks. 'What am I supposed to do, Don? Am I supposed to keep it from them?' His response offers key insight into his character, his marriage, his life. 'Take a pill and lie down. I can handle the kids.' He first tells the children to turn off the set, but when they don't, he joins them in viewing.

At Margaret's wedding Roger manages to console his daughter and entertain the guests. Later that night he puts his new wife to bed, drunk, then calls Joan Holloway to find his own consolation. As another morning begins, Betty watches as Jack Ruby murders Oswald. She screams. When Don rushes in, she yells, 'What is going on?' Later she drives alone to meet the man she may have fallen in love with. He consoles her, proposes marriage, makes her smile. Betty returns to tell Don she no longer loves him, that he has ruined 'all this'.

In the final scenes, set on the Monday after the assassination, funeral plans are being described on television. Don leaves the house and goes to the office. Only Peggy Olson is there. She's working on the story boards for a television commercial. 'Aquanette. We don't shoot 'til after Thanksgiving. We'll be OK.' Business, in short, will continue. The commercial will be produced and aired and the images of women in convertibles, their hair protected by the chemical spray, will translate into products sold.

Throughout the episode versions of this sentiment are expressed in bits of dialogue. Don consoles his children after sending Betty upstairs to take her pills. 'You two look at me. Everything's going to be OK. We have a new president and we're all going to be sad for a little bit and then one day there's going to be a funeral.' Trudy Campbell insists she and Pete should go to the wedding (though in the end they do not) by giving Pete a good reason. 'Because it's your bosses daughter's wedding. It's business, Pete and there's a system. You always say that. Have you been drinking?' To which Pete replies in a metaphor for the episode, 'The whole country's drinking'.

In many ways television came of age, or at least offered a new and significant definition for itself, in the coverage of events surrounding the Kennedy assassination. Perhaps, in some ways, those events indicated a new stage of American culture as well. *Mad Men* captures the trauma of those days as everything 'normal' seems to have stopped. But in other ways, everything goes on. As Don Draper says, 'We'll all be sad for a little bit', and as Trudy points out, 'there's a system'. But it is Joan's response to Roger Sterling that captures not only the sense of the day, of the times, but also of a central significance of television to those times, and perhaps to ours. 'People are still getting sick', she tells him. 'Car accidents are happening. Babies are being born.'

Add to her words that sets will be turned on. Programmes will be aired. Commercials will support the programmes. A war will continue. The Civil Rights movement will take on greater significance and energy. Marriages will break up. Companies will be sold. New companies will be formed. One employee will be surprised to be included. When Harry Crane arrives at the new firm's hotel room office, Bert Cooper recognizes him as 'the media man' and sends him to the bedroom. That's where the television set is located. To stretch the point, with television coverage of the Kennedy assassination and funeral, America realized it had learned to live with television – because it had to.

Works Cited

Spigel, Lynn. *Make Room for TV*. Chicago: University of Chicago Press, 1992.

8.
Space Ships and Time Machines:
Mad Men and the Serial Condition
Sean O'Sullivan

You know how it is: there was nothing, and then there was It, and now it's nothing again.

— Paul Kinsey, 'The Color Blue' (3:36)

Toward the end of the last episode of the first season of *Mad Men*, Don Draper embarks on what would become the most famous pitch in the show's history. Before an audience of two Kodak representatives and a handful of colleagues, Draper makes a case for an object that has been called the Wheel, but which he has chosen to redub the Carousel. His case depends essentially on a serial slide show, one taken from fragments of his family life – a family life which itself seems to lie in fragments at this point. Prefacing the slide show with a tale about 'an old pro copywriter', a Greek guy named Teddy who told him, many years ago, that the two most powerful words in advertising are 'new' and 'nostalgia', Draper proceeds to dazzle his audience by illustrating the Carousel's ability to move backward and forward across memory and experience. 'This device isn't a space ship', he announces; 'it's a time machine'. When the show finishes, and after Harry Crane – overcome by the reminder of his own troubled marriage – flees the scene, the Kodak representatives are stunned. Duck Phillips grasps the mood of the room, smiles, and sends the prospective clients out with a self-confident flourish: 'Good luck at your next meeting.' Duck's valediction reminds us not only that the Kodak guys are already in the midst of serial experience – a string of pitches from various agencies – but also that the art of advertising, and art in general, shuttles constantly between accident ('luck') and design ('meeting'). The magic show that Don has authored consists of 13 slides, or more precisely 13 clicks of the slide-changing instrument in his right hand. Thirteen is also the number of episodes in the first season of *Mad Men*.

At the end of the first episode of the second season of *Mad Men*, Don Draper embarks on a trip to a mailbox near his house, armed with a dog on a leash and a package addressed to a person whose name is withheld from the audience. Before a CGI rendering of early 1960s suburbia – a backdrop whose blurring of plausible photography and technological sleight of hand brings us back to the fusion of science and art that defined his pitch for the Carousel – Draper walks purposefully and silently to the corner of a block in Ossining, while we hear his voice on the soundtrack. He is reciting the last three stanzas of a poem, a poem that concludes the volume that he has slipped into that package – thereby connecting the end of the beginning of a new season with the end of a book that will begin a new storyline. This scene of performance is preceded by another scene of performance, when Draper asks his daughter Sally to 'show me what you learned in ballet'; her obliging enactment of a serial presentation of dance steps stages a moment of visual and soundless art, in contrast to the verbal and auditory art produced by Draper's reading of the coda of Frank O'Hara's 'Mayakovsky'. The slide show also featured Draper's narration; but that in the earlier case it was tethered to a visual medium, his words operating in concert with a sequence of images. In effect, Draper's marriage of sound and image, in his pitch for the Carousel, undergoes a divorce in the concluding minutes of the subsequent episode. The three stanzas that Don performs consist of 13 lines of verse. Thirteen is also the number of episodes in the second season of *Mad Men*.

What to make of this numerical pattern, this fractal replication? These iterations of 13 may also straddle the line between design and accident – although a later appearance seems unavoidably purposeful. In the thirteenth episode of the third season, when Lane Pryce, Bert Cooper, Roger Sterling and Don Draper decide to plot their escape from the company's upcoming sale to McCann Erickson, by allowing Pryce to fire the other three, Sterling cheerfully announces, 'Well, it's official: Friday, December 13th, 1963. Four guys shot their own legs off' ('Shut the Door. Have a Seat', 3:39). Friday the 13th: that traditionally unlucky confluence of day of week and time of month reflects in miniature cultural questions of fate and happenstance, of external agency and free will, that lie at the heart of both the subject and process of serial narrative; in one guise, it is the tension between a fully schemed plan that anticipates all the developments of a series and an improvisational spirit that allows potentially unanticipated changes of story and character. Putting aside that broader issue for the moment, the recurrence of the number thirteen – its evidence of an enumeration of pieces – is a reminder of the piecemeal nature of this particular serial narrative, and serial narrative in general. The putative unity of what we call '*Mad Men*', or even a specific season of *Mad Men*, is in fact a collection of pixels – pixels that we call episodes, or, at a smaller level, pixels that we call storylines within episodes; or smaller still, scenes (or 'beats', in TV parlance) within storylines; or, smaller still, shots within scenes; or, smallest of all, individual film frames within those shots. This is the pointillism of serial television – its apparent congruities, in fact, the result of a magic show put on by the Don Drapers of its universe.

We might turn, as a way of thinking about this, to another instance of thirteen – the celebrated aviary of Wallace Stevens' 1917 poem 'Thirteen Ways of Looking at a Blackbird'. Each of its 13 short stanzas – varying from two to seven lines, irregular in length – presents a distinct prosodic snapshot, of not just the titular blackbird but of perspective and experience itself, of space and time. The twelfth stanza offers one summary of the poem's modus operandi, a synthesis of juxtaposition, implied causality, and a critique of causal logic: 'The river is moving./The blackbird must be flying' (Stevens 94). As 'The Waste Land' and *Ulysses* would do five years later, 'Thirteen Ways' enunciates a modernist aesthetic committed to the conflict between fragmentation and unity, between art as pieces and art as a whole. Serial television, by its very process, is a potential inheritor of that central conflict; but it is fair to say that most shows have not chosen to highlight the fragment over the unity, the disjunction over the clarification.

One significant exception to that practice is *The Sopranos* (HBO, 1999–2007), the series on which *Mad Men*'s Matthew Weiner served as a staff writer and later executive producer for four years. David Chase, the creator and showrunner of *The Sopranos*, has always spoken of his disdain for television's conventions and limitations, and of his desire for a career as an art-house filmmaker; he notes that 'College', the fifth episode of the first season, came closest to his 'personal goal of making episodes that could be stand-alone feature films. It is self-contained' (Chase viii). Weiner has similarly spoken of a resistance to the connective tissue, and structure of familiarity, on which serial narrative – from Dickens onwards – has relied: 'I don't want there to be a formula, I don't want people to know what to expect ever when they turn the show on' (Sepinwall). We get an announcement about industrial art's preference for formula near the very beginning of the *Mad Men* pilot, when Draper's casual mistress Midge Daniels explains her job as an illustrator for greeting cards that celebrate the newly invented Grandmother's Day. In her words, Midge's iterative creations amount to 'Nine different ways to say, "I love you, Grandma"' ('Smoke Gets in Your Eyes', 1:1).

This echo of Wallace Stevens sets the tone for a show constantly resistant, but not overtly hostile, to the same-but-different production model of serial television. Episodes such as 'Three Sundays' (2:17), which dispenses with the typical two-or-three-day consecutive span of the serial hour in favour of Passion, Palm and Easter Sundays of April 1962, or 'Seven Twenty Three' (3:33), which begins with three brief, disorienting flashforwards to events that will transpire later in the episode, illustrate *Mad Men*'s compositional restlessness. Some critics complained, in reference to 'Seven Twenty Three', that this use of the flashforward was not exactly original (Keefe). But originality is an overrated criterion, as Eliot and Joyce emphasized in their writing: it is the variation, the shift, the unsettling of a work's own tendencies, that most fully marks modernist art, and modernist serial television. Don Draper's temporally and spatially disjointed slide show, and Frank O'Hara's elliptical poem, offer two prominent analogues of Stevens' staged battle between the many and the one.[1]

'For Those Who Think Young', the first instalment of the second season, is the episode subsequent to 'The Wheel', the last instalment of the first season. But is it? This depends on how we think of the first subsection of a television series, the stratum just below the narrative as a whole: namely, the season. Looked at from one perspective, as underscored by the method of episode-notation used by this volume of essays, episodes are part of a continuum: hence 2:14, as opposed to 2:1, as a way of indicating 'For Those Who Think Young'. This model most closely follows serial narrative's nineteenth-century traditions, where individual weekly or monthly numbers of *Great Expectations* or *Middlemarch* would be spaced at regular intervals, and separations within the larger narrative (such as 'The first stage of Pip's expectations', or 'Book Two') would function as movements within a symphonic work: a pause to gather one's thoughts and one's breath, before a return to business. The televisual season, however, is an unprecedented instrument in serial history – especially as practised in this last decade, by shows whose brief appearances (usually 12 to 13 episodes) often serve to punctuate long disappearances (up to 21 months, in the case of *The Sopranos*).

So the question of part and whole, discontinuity and continuity, has become a prominent element of serial television; and there may be no more glaring instance of that dialectic than 'The Wheel' and 'For Those Who Think Young'. In what is now a convention of sorts for 13-episode shows, the episodes were aired nine months apart: October 2007 to July 2008. But the gap in story time amounted to 15 months: November 1960 to February 1962. There seems to have been no precedent for such a significant diegetic leap in recent American television, although two months later the fifth season of *Desperate Housewives* would stage a five-year jump. I would distinguish *Mad Men*'s first break between seasons from *Desperate Housewives*' midcareer attempt at reinvention, or *Lost*'s fourth-season time-play prestidigitation earlier in 2008. This was not simply a reboot of an established system; rather, in was a first gesture toward making a system. Would this large elision turn into a pattern, or formula – into one of nine eventually familiar ways of saying, 'I love you, Grandma'? No and yes.

Season three began only six months later in story time than the conclusion of season two, thereby breaking the initial 'rule'. On the other hand, each of *Mad Men*'s first three seasons unfolded over approximately nine months of story time, roughly equivalent to the real-time gap between seasons, and thereby redolent of formula.[2] This alternating structural inconsistency and consistency works as a seesaw, a version of the contrast that Isaiah Berlin called the hedgehog and the fox. Berlin used those terms to classify writers into two categories: hedgehogs, such as Dante, who 'relate everything to a single central vision, one system' and foxes, such as Shakespeare, who 'pursue many ends, often unrelated and even contradictory, connected, if at all, in only some *de facto* way' (Berlin 3). As with the

13 stanzas of Stevens' poem, *Mad Men* persistently stages a conflict between a hedgehog, or a single central vision – a coherent narrative of characters and events unfolding through time via recognizable cause and effect – and a fox – many distinct narrative ends, straining the bonds of connectivity – evidenced through alterations or abandonment of formula, or through a persistent fraying of regular markers of time and space.

Time and space, of course, are the terms on which Don Draper pivots during his presentation of the Carousel. It is not a case of either/or, however: the Carousel, like serial television, is both a space ship and a time machine. Most particularly, serial television consists of joins between space and time, and breaks between space and time. While the joins may be what makes the narrative cohesive – what makes a show a hedgehog, in Berlin's terms – the breaks are the most important elements, at least in considering how a serial creates itself; we could say that the illusion of the hedgehog, of the synthetic unity of a show, depends fully on the particular manoeuvres of the fox, the specific ways in which the variances and interruptions force us to navigate seriality's inevitable lacunae of space and time – the negotiation among different physical environments, and the temporal omissions within and between episodes, and within and between seasons. One way to think about differences, omissions, gaps and fragments is to turn again to poetry, which offers a far more helpful pedigree than the novel in unpacking the methods and effects of serial television. Both serial television and poetry are broken arts – arts that are broken on purpose. Brian McHale has suggested that we think of segmentivity as the defining feature of poetry – its process of interrupting and reconnecting such syntactic units as feet, verses and stanzas – and the negotiation of gaps – between lines and stanzas – as poetry's system of creating 'meaningful sequence'. Serial television in particular depends on analogous strategies of segmentation and gapping – through such techniques as breaking each episode into separate storylines, and creating recurrent gaps or spaces between narrative segments, segments that we call episodes and seasons (McHale 14; O'Sullivan).

Paul Kinsey offers a description of the artistic process as a sequence of segments and gaps, of pieces and absences, in 'The Color Blue' (3:36), a third-season episode rich in crosstalk with 'The Wheel'. The most relevant storyline in this instance involves

Kinsey's battle with Peggy Olson over a campaign for Western Union – a campaign that is framed as the telegram versus the phone call, or the image versus the sound, another potential sundering of the two building blocks of television and film. One night at Sterling Cooper, while taking a break, Kinsey runs into his own inspirational old Greek guy, a janitor named Achilles. Kinsey informs Achilles that his is 'a mighty big name', and as they start to engage in small talk, Kinsey is suddenly struck with 'something very, very good', which he later calls perhaps 'the best idea I ever had' – maybe as good as Don's idea for the Carousel. I say 'maybe' because Kinsey returns to his office, pours himself a drink, and falls asleep – without writing down his career-changing insight. This is a fable about potential and actuality – another foundation of serial narrative, which operates by necessity on the prospect of possibility, of what might be in the next instalment – since neither we nor Kinsey nor anyone else ever discovers what the idea is.

When he and Peggy prepare to discuss their pitches with Don, he tells her his tragic narrative and cites a Chinese proverb: 'The faintest ink is better than the best memory'. Kinsey's model of Shelleyan, Romantic epiphany is undone by Peggy's postmodern *bricolage*, as she takes his throwaway cultural quotation and offers it to Don as an idea for Western Union, one that advertises the advantages of the permanence of image (the telegram) over the impermanence of sound (the phone call). Kinsey is as thunderstruck by Peggy's legerdemain as the Kodak guys are by Don's cool planning, in another staged *Mad Men* tussle between the planned and the improvised. Kinsey's description, to Peggy, of the fragility of his idea, and of artistic inspiration, is cited in the epigraph to this essay: 'You know how it is: there was nothing, and then there was It, and now it's nothing again.' The obverse way of considering this is as something, nothing, and then something – or, in serial terms, an episode, followed by a gap, followed by an episode. The gap, the nothing, in this case is primarily one of time – the principal property that Don Draper assigns to the Carousel; the gaps in time, not just between the airing of episodes but between the diegetic temporal excisions that separate *Mad Men*'s episodes, enact this serial narrative's Carousel-like movements.

Kinsey's lament about nothing, and nothing again, picks up a motif prevalent throughout the first season. Indeed, Don's celebration of the Carousel, or the Wheel, or the Doughnut (an alternative cited by Duck Phillips) – that is, the figure of a circle, which is also used to denote 'zero' – brings us back to the start of the pilot, where Don, sitting in a bar, is serenaded by the song 'Band of Gold', the circular jewellery that symbolizes marriage, which also may denote nothing. (In 'The Wheel', Betty Draper asks Don, regarding a neighbour's infidelities, 'Doesn't all this mean anything?' unconsciously echoing Hildy's assurance to Harry Crane that their one-night dalliance 'didn't mean anything' ('Nixon vs. Kennedy', 1:12). In the scene following 'Band of Gold', when Don visits Midge, he bemoans his lack of ideas for Lucky Strike cigarettes, twice saying, 'I've got nothing'. His later uses of the word include his plea, addressed to Rachel Menken, that they flee their New York lives – 'There's nothing here' (1:12) – and his self-identification with Richard Nixon, who, like Don himself, 'is from nothing' ('Long Weekend', 1:10). Sometimes the word appears in back-to-back scenes, deployed by very different characters in very different contexts: Betty's report that doctors think that 'there's nothing physically wrong with me' is followed the next morning by Kinsey's declaration that the aerosol can 'is nothing less than space age' ('Ladies Room', 1:2), while Adam's plaintive question to Don – 'You have nothing to say to me?' – precedes Trudy Campbell's ex-boyfriend saying that he wants to talk to her 'about something that has nothing to do with' her husband's short story ('5G', 1:5). These juxtapositions exploit seriality television's ability to cross-hatch – that is, to make parallel, interlaced connections that make something (a link between distinctly different stories and characters) out of nothing.[3]

Hence the fitting place of the Carousel at the end of the season. It functions by arranging a series of discrete images into sequence, and suggesting that they are narratively connected, purely by the existence of that sequence. In that respect, the Carousel is like a season of modernist serial television – its discrete images (episodes) intertwined as much by our desire to see patterns, to make stories out of separate events, as by any fixed narrative governing them. Don's show, which meanders gradually from scenes of 'nothing' – everyday glimpses of his children at play – toward scenes that denote 'something' – special events such as Betty's pregnant belly, Don carrying Betty over the bridal threshold and their kiss at a 1955 New Year's Eve party – weaves and unweaves a story, telling something and telling nothing all at once.[4] And how does the Carousel operate?

Through a chain of absences and presences, of nothings and some-things, namely the empty spaces into which each slide is dropped and the plastic dividers that keep each slide segregated. When set up and activated, the nothings magically become somethings – the photographic images projected through the filled spaces; while the somethings become nothings – the illuminations interrupted when the dividers rotate briefly before the lens. Harry Crane flees, over-come, not during the final recognizable shot – the New Year's Eve kiss – but after the final click, when the Carousel projects a space without a slide in it; the screen simply shows a white square of light, or nothing. The scene literalizes the act of projection, since it is only once Don's literal family disappears from the screen that Harry can project his own fractured marriage on to the narrative. It is the noth-ing, contextualized by the somethings that brings the story home to Harry.

And home, of course, is the subject of the story that Don tells through pictures. The conversation between home and work, or home and the world, is the subject of many television serials; nowhere is this more prominent than in *Mad Men*'s ancestor text, *The Sopranos*, whose entire pitch rested on the strife between Tony Soprano's two 'families', and the uncomfortable way in which home and the world get mixed up in the series. But the pilot of *Mad Men* tellingly keeps home off screen until the very end of the hour, when it is revealed that the apparently unattached Manhattanite hero in fact has a patient Penelope in the suburbs. The parallel to 'The Odyssey' lurks throughout the season, but it is brought into sharpest focus during the pitch for the Wheel, when Don cites a probably fictitious 'old pro copywriter, a Greek named Teddy'.[5] This old pro Greek guy – whom we should call by his real name, Homer – told him about the etymology of 'nostalgia', which supposedly means 'the pain from an old wound'. The fact that this definition is only half accurate is doubly appropriate. 'Nostalgia' more precisely means 'homesickness', and 'The Odyssey' is the most famous example of the narrative genre of 'nostos', or home journey. In Don's redefini-tion of 'nostalgia', the 'nostos' (home) drops out, and the sickness (or pain) now refers to an old wound. This slippage makes the link to Homer all the more explicit, since when Odysseus returns to Ithaca disguised as a beggar – a conceit that anticipates Don Draper's hobo code – his presence is almost given away by his old nurse Eurycleia, who while washing the visitor's thigh sees a familiar old wound, that is an old scar.

This recognition allows the narrator to stop the action and open up the history of the boar that stabbed Odysseus in his youth – a celebrated literary detail that serves as the starting point for *Mimesis*, Erich Auerbach's survey of 'the representation of reality in Western literature'. Auerbach claims that this backstory serves not to psychologize Odysseus, to create 'a sort of perspective in time and place'; rather, the Homeric style 'knows only a foreground, only a uniformly illuminated, uniformly objective present' (Auerbach 7). The parallels to Don's life are striking – his insistence on moving forward and not looking back at the past are advertised in his instruction to Betty, as she grieves for her mother, that 'mourning is just extended self-pity' ('Babylon', 1:6). The parallels to Don's slide show are even more useful, since his presentation is a lullaby about moving backward and forward, a story about how time and place collapse, where everything is foregrounded and made present. Odysseus' most memorable escapade, on his nostos, is the blinding of the Cyclops Polyphemus; Polyphemus demands to know the identity of his assailant, and Odysseus mockingly exclaims, 'No one', which Polyphemus takes to be not a denial of information but a proper name. When Don finds Peggy in his office in 'Nixon vs. Kennedy' – immediately after telling Rachel Menken that 'there's nothing here' – he barks at his secretary: 'Does this door mean nothing to you?' Given that the only distinguishing marks on that door are the perhaps meaningless words 'Donald Draper' – another hubristic alias – it is clear that both 'Donald Draper' and 'Odysseus' are, like 'Achilles', 'mighty big names'; but they are also bywords for 'no one' and 'nothing'.[6]

Another term for Don's slide show might be 'bullshit': the Greek guy named Teddy, the portrait of domestic bliss, the erasure of time and space. But that term, Harry G. Frankfurt suggests, might not be accurate. In his essay on the topic, Frankfurt distinguishes between the bullshitter and the liar. 'Telling a lie', he claims, 'is an act with a sharp focus . . . designed to insert a particular falsehood at a specific point in a set or system of beliefs', an act that 'requires a degree of craftsmanship'; the act of bullshit, by contrast, 'is more expansive and independent, with more spacious opportunities for improvisation, color, and imaginative play', and 'less a matter of craft than of art'

(Frankfurt 51, 53). In other words, the liar plans and pursues a deliberate strategy of substituting the false for the true – we might say substituting nothing for something – while the bullshitter makes things up as he goes along, relying on the whims of inspiration – we might say confusing the difference between nothing and something. These two approaches describe not just two recurring types of pitch that we get in *Mad Men* – the design and the improvisation – and two types of pitchers – Paul Kinsey the liar, and Peggy Olson the bullshitter – but specifically the two pitches that bookend the first season.

In the pilot episode, we get the show's purest rendition of bullshit. Stymied by the 'nothing' about which he has complained to Midge, and faced with the prospect of the firm's biggest clients walking out the door, Don suddenly conjures a feat of bullshit: 'It's toasted'. Not only is the act of inspiration a perfect piece of bullshit, an idea improvised from nothing; the idea itself is bullshit, since it replaces the lie that has been sold about tobacco – the carefully researched truth-substitution about the health benefits of cigarettes – with a line of bullshit – an evasion of the issue at end, an emphasis on the 'toasted' aspect of Lucky Strikes, a statement that blithely ignores the fact that everyone else's tobacco is toasted, and that the toastedness is neither here nor there, neither nothing or something. At the end of the season, by contrast, we get not pure bullshit but the pure lie: the carefully, cannily concocted sequence of Odysseus' home-images, choreographed to within an inch of his life, and his craft. The parallel with the art of serials is clear.

On the one hand, Matthew Weiner famously carried the pilot script around with him for years, planning meticulously the lie – to use Plato's term for art – that he hoped to screen for a rapt public of Harry Cranes; on the other hand, the production schedule and financial constraints of television require many of the improvisatory, occasionally obfuscatory decisions about script, performance, and mise en scène that we would classify as bullshit. Weiner has acknowledged that he had run out of show after the first season of *Mad Men*: 'I didn't know there was going to be a second season. I used *everything*' (Handy). We might be tempted to say that everything since then has been an act of bullshit. But really it has been a synthesis of the lie and bullshit, of the designed and the improvised – just as, finally, the slide show is a synthesis of design and improvisation.

After all, part of the magic of the show has to do with the apparently undesigned sequence of those slides, their glide around experience, their ability to bend time and space – not so much to substitute a different story as to smudge the whole notion of story. The slide show is a beautiful lie celebrating the beauty of bullshit.[7]

But it is not just Odysseus himself, or his scar, that matters here. 'The Odyssey' itself matters – since that poem is, arguably, the first serial narrative. Not because of its method of production per se, but rather its multiple plots, its logic of anticipation and expectation (i.e., Odysseus' impending return). 'The Odyssey's' negotiation between the home and the world – all absent from 'The Iliad' – have offered templates, as subject matter and narrative structure, for serial narrative since the nineteenth century. Most importantly, 'The Odyssey' is both linear and circular, since it tells simultaneously a story with a beginning, middle and end – Telemachus' efforts to bring his father back to Ithaca – and a story that turns around on itself – not just Odysseus' circular return home to the island where he started, but the many instances where stories of the past intervene, freezing the narrative of the present. This simultaneity of the line and the circle equally defines the process of serial television, especially in the case of a mutant hedgehog/fox such as *Mad Men*, which wants at once to move along and at once to pause and circle – fitting, of course, for a serial about the past, since its audience always wants both to push ahead with story events and loop back to the historical moment. Sal Romano articulates this duality when summarizing Paul Kinsey's pitch for Playtex, whereby all women in 1962 are divided between Jackies and Marilyns. 'A line and a curve', Sal informs Peggy – 'nothing goes better together' ('Maidenform', 2:19). But of course the line and the curve apply not just to 'The Odyssey', or to *Mad Men*, but to verse itself. 'Verse' indeed means 'turning'; each line of a poem is an act of pressing forward and an act of turning back. This double movement is enunciated, at the start of the second season, in the recitation of Frank O'Hara – not just by the very presence of poetic metre and rhythm but by the closing line of 'Mayakovsky': 'perhaps I am myself again' (O'Hara 54). The self not as line but as curve, or as both line and curve, represents the central subject of *Mad Men* and of lyric poetry, a subject most fully explorable through serial narrative's headless rush toward dawdling.[8]

To conclude, let us follow Don's lead and move backwards. 'Babylon', the sixth episode of the first season, represents another instance of propulsion and circumnavigation. In terms of plot, we get a signal discovery – Roger Sterling and Jane Holloway are having an affair – and a major development – Peggy Olson comes up with an artful (or crafty) description, and suddenly begins a career as a copywriter. That description, aptly, involves turning nothing (a trash receptacle full of used tissues) into something ('a basket of kisses'); her ability to transform one into the other marks her fitness as an ad man. Peggy's budding, not-quite version of Don crystallizes at the end of the season in 'The Wheel', as she attempts to coach a voiceover artist through a radio spot for the Relaxicisor. Peggy, increasingly frustrated by the talent's inability to provide what Peggy sees in her, finally instructs her to go 'back to being you'; the woman, tearing up, laments, 'I am being me'. Voiceover work, like acting for television, requires being something again and again, until it is what someone else imagines that something should be; being oneself again, or again and again, may be a trickier proposition.

By contrast with 'The Wheel', 'Babylon' is much more concerned with art that is fixed in time and place, resistant to the looping media of recorded sound and image – such as the performance art that Don and Midge witness at a bar in the Village, or the middlebrow Broadway shows that Midge's other boyfriend, Roy, assumes that Don prefers to the uncharted waters of experimentation. 'Babylon', far more prominently than any episode to this point of *Mad Men*, is full of explicit discussions of art, from novels (Rona Jaffe's *The Best of Everything* and Leon Uris' *Exodus*) to movies (Joan Crawford's eyebrows and Paul Newman's charisma) to paintings (Michelangelo's Sistine Chapel); Don, trying to leave the bar, declares, 'Too much art for me'. But none of the art that dominates 'Babylon' is like the art of serial television, or the art of poetry for that matter: novels, movies, paintings, and plays do not perform the line and the curve at the same time, do not embody the momentum and restlessness of TV and verse. For most of its hour, 'Babylon' offers a kind of catalogue of what *Mad Men*, and television, are not.[9]

Until the end. The closing sequence begins in the bar, as a trio sings the 'Babylon' of the title. The song, a traditional ballad, unfolds as a round – that is, as something explicitly both linear and circular, with some singers pressing onwards and some turning back, a sound that moves forwards and backwards. As the music continues on the soundtrack, we see a montage sequence: Rachel Menken arranging ties at her store, Betty putting lipstick on her daughter Sally; Don listening; and Joan and Roger putting their clothes back on after an assignation. This is the first montage sequence in the history of *Mad Men*, and it is a technique that the show does not use much – with a prominent exception, in a similar scene of clothing and appearance-making, at the very beginning of 'For Those Who Think Young'. Montage, as a way of organizing material, and playing with time and space, is of course borrowed from the cinema; but, as we have noted, originality is overrated. What's relevant, at the moment when the round underscores how serials operate prosodically, is that montage underlines how serials operate narratively – namely, by juxtaposing the disparate and asking us to see connections between the images, the enacted slides of people doing things.

The episode ends with Joan and Roger standing outside their hotel, waiting for cabs. On the soundtrack, once the song concludes, we get 'nothing' – that is, we hear only the diegetic sounds of the street, an unprecedented and unduplicated substitution of life, or the real, for art at the end of a *Mad Men* episode. But this auditory illusion of verisimilitude contrasts starkly with the visual, the posed presentation of Joan and Roger, in front of the Pierre. The two columns that frame the hotel entrance neatly separate Joan into a space on the left of the frame and Roger into a space on the right; in the middle, we get empty space, or nothing. Something, nothing, something. It's as pretty a picture of serial art as we're ever likely to get – all the lies and the bullshit, and all the craft and art of it.

Works Cited

Auerbach, Erich. *Mimesis: The Representation of Reality in Western Literature.* Trans. Willard R. Trask, Princeton: Princeton University Press, 1968.

Berlin, Isaiah. *The Hedgehog and the Fox: An Essay on Tolstoy's View of History,* New York: Simon and Schuster, 1986.

Chase, David. The Sopranos: *Selected Scripts from Three Seasons,* New York: Warner Books, 2002.

Frankfurt, Harry G. *On Bullshit,* Princeton: Princeton University Press, 2005.

Handy, Bruce. 'Don and Betty's Paradise Lost', *Vanity Fair*. September 2009. http://www.vanityfair.com/culture/features/2009/09/mad-men200909. Accessed on 20 November 2009.

Homer. 'The Odyssey'. Trans. Robert Fagles, New York: Viking, 1996.

Keefe, Patrick Radden. 'Cheap Tricks', *Slate*, 29 September 2009. http://www.slate.com/id/2225274/entry/2230814/. Accessed on 20 November 2009.

McHale, Brian. 'Beginning to think about narrative in poetry', *Narrative* 17.1 (2009): 11–30.

O'Hara, Frank. *Meditations in an Emergency*, New York: Grove Press, 1957.

O'Sullivan, Sean. 'Broken on purpose: Poetry, serial television and the season', *Storyworlds* 2 (2010): 59–77.

Sepinwall, Alan. '*Mad Men*: Talking "Out of Town" with Matthew Weiner', *What's Alan Watching?* 16 August 2009. http://sepinwall.blogspot.com/2009/08/mad-men-talking-out-of-town-with.html. Accessed on 27 November 2009.

Stevens, Wallace. *Collected Poems*, New York: Knopf, 1974.

Notes

1 We get a diegetic glimpse of another connected/disjointed modernist text in 'Nixon vs. Kennedy' (1:12), during Don's first flashback to the Korean War. Next to the cot of the real Don Draper, tucked in the background of the shot, there is a copy of Sherwood Anderson's *Winesburg, Ohio*. Anderson's 1919 experiment probed the fault lines between short story and novel, as modernist serial television probes the fault lines between episode and season, between the fragment and the whole.

2 This recurrence of this formula, which originated as a way to mirror the course of Peggy Olson's pregnancy, suggests that *Mad Men* (through its third season, at any rate) found a comfortable parallel between the diegetic length of a television season and the time required for human gestation.

3 The parallel word-motif in the first season of *Deadwood* is 'anyways', which (like *Mad Men*'s 'nothing') is used by many different characters in many different contexts. But 'anyways' suggests an instant ability to shift gears, to move on to something else and to tie everything together – fitting for a show, like *Deadwood*, whose episodes typically unfold in consecutive days, in other words with a minimum of gap and break. *Mad Men*'s 'nothing', by contrast, captures that series' aesthetic of interruption and abyss.

4   'The Color Blue' provides another fruitful connection, since it begins with a recitation of the end-of-year holidays (Halloween, Thanksgiving and Christmas) in the Draper kitchen – a conversation that eventually dovetails with Peggy and Kinsey's analysis of the telegram as an instrument for special occasions (wedding and births) and the telephone as an instrument of the everyday and transitory. Once again: the extraordinary and the diurnal, the something and the nothing.

5   The Homeric narrator first contextualizes his hero's prospective journey back to Ithaca thusly: 'when the wheeling seasons brought the year around,/that year spun out by the gods when he should reach his home' (Homer 78). The season, the wheel, the home and the gods – i.e., Matthew Weiner – are as operative in *Mad Men* as in 'The Odyssey'.

6   The door-name of 'Donald Draper' as a figure for nothing is first made explicit at the very end of 'The Hobo Code' (1:18), which concludes with that door being shut in the viewer's face. 'Donald Draper' – a first name (something) followed by a blank (nothing) and a last name (something) – gives us another hieroglyph of serial sequence. And, if we count the nothing, the space between, we get 13 typographic elements: six, one, and six.

7   It is worth noting that the final episode of each of the first three seasons includes a scene where Don pitches himself. In the second-season closer, 'Meditations in an Emergency' (2:26), he sabotages Duck Phillips' attempted coup by announcing that he does not have a contract – thereby pitching himself to the British buyers as a product they must privilege. In the third-season closer, 'Shut the Door. Have a Seat' (3:39), he pitches himself to Peggy in her apartment, asking her to join him in a new agency, after having taken her allegiance for granted. In each case, the pitch is planned, and not improvised bullshit.

8   We get both 'myself again' and the serial alternation between nothing and something at the very end of 'The Wheel', when Don's return home is seen twice. First, Don (Odysseus) comes back to find a delighted Betty (Penelope) and the kids – the lie of Ithaca that he would like to believe. Then, we get the exact same entrance, seemingly the exact same filmic sequence; this time, no one is home. A blunt reminder of the nothing, the absence that will obtain until the start of the next season.

9   What things are, and what things are not, comes up explicitly in the episode when Don and Rachel talk about Israel, as a potential utopia. Rachel recollects that she learned at Barnard that 'utopia' can mean 'the good place' or 'the place that cannot be'. Something, or nothing, or both.

9.
'The Catastrophe of My Personality': Frank O'Hara, Don Draper and the Poetics of *Mad Men*

David Lavery

> I'm not saying that I don't have practically the most lofty ideas of anyone writing today, but what difference does that make? They're just ideas. The only good thing about it is that when I get lofty enough I've stopped thinking and that's when refreshment arrives.
>
> — Frank O'Hara, 'Personism: A Manifesto'
> (*The Collected Poems* 498)

> Advertising is based on one thing, happiness. And you know what happiness is? Happiness is the smell of a new car. It's freedom from fear. It's a billboard on the side of the road that screams reassurance that whatever you are doing is okay. You are okay.
>
> — Don Draper in 'Smoke Gets in Your Eyes' (1:1)

In *The Last Avant-Garde*, a discerning study of the New York School of Poets (hereafter NYSP), a coterie of Gotham-based writers, John Ashbery, Kenneth Koch, James Schuyler and Frank O'Hara, active in the 1950s and 1960s, David Lehman summarizes at the outset their revolutionary effect on their time. 'In an age of split-level conformism', Lehman writes, the NYSP

> put their trust in the idea of an artistic vanguard that would sanction their devotions from the norm. The liberating effect of their writing became increasingly evident in the passionate, experimental, taboo-breaking early 1960s, when the nation's youngest president was in office, men discarded their hats, women started using the Pill, the

acceleration in the speed of social change seemed to double overnight, and America finally left the nineteenth century behind (1).

A striking claim, no doubt, but more striking still is the assertion's relevance to the subject of this book. Written at the very end of the last century, these words could almost be taken as Matthew Weiner's charge in creating *Mad Men,* a series in which the pill, hats, JFK and poetry play a not insignificant role.

Poetry in *Mad Men*

> I don't think you'd like it.
> – O'Hara reader in a bar to Don Draper in
> 'For Those Who Think Young' (2:1)

In Bruce Handy's profile of *Mad Men* in *Vanity Fair,* we are offered several tantalizing glimpses behind the scenes of the AMC series, including the disclosure that 'Before shooting began on the second season, during which Betty would finally confront Don about his infidelities and throw him out of the house, Weiner suggested the actress read "Ariel"'. Sylvia Plath's 'abstract howl of female rage and despair' – Handy's words – 'confused . . . and freaked . . . out' January Jones, who, '[n]ot knowing the coming plotlines . . . assumed this was his way of telling her Betty would be sticking her head in an oven for the season finale' (282). At the end of season three, Betty has yet to turn on the gas. 'Shut the Door. Have a Seat' (3:39) ended with Betty and baby Gene on their way to Nevada to acquire a divorce from the man who is not really Don Draper so she might marry Henry Francis.

The poetry of Plath (1932–63), who would take her own life in a North London flat about two months before the events of season three (and Don and Salvatore Romano's London Fog trip to Baltimore) begin ('Out of Town', 3:1), remains behind the scenes, deep background, one of many literary influences on Weiner's period drama. (The unmentioned death of Plath – 2/11/63 – and the assassination of President Kennedy – 11/22/63 – bookend the epochal year in which *Mad Men's* third season primarily transpires.) Unless, of course, we count the scene in 'A Night to Remember' (2:8) in which Betty struggles to ride a horse at full gallop, just as Plath herself did, as she recorded in the eponymous poem (and horse) that would give its name to Matt Weiner's recommended reading.

Mad Men gives numerous works of fiction cameo appearances: Joan and the Sterling Cooper office staff are tantalized by D. H. Lawrence's controversial *Lady Chatterley's Lover* ('The Marriage of Figaro', 1:3). Bertram Cooper pushes Ayn Rand's *Atlas Shrugged* on Don as essential reading in 'The Hobo Code' (1:8). Don plunges into Leon Uris' *Exodus* as research for securing the Israeli tourism account ('Babylon', 1:6). Betty reads F. Scott Fitzgerald's *Babylon Revisited* (in 'Three Sundays', 2:4) and Mary McCarthy's *The Group* ('The Color Blue', 3:10). Jet-setter Joy travels with William Faulkner's *The Sound and the Fury* ('The Jet Set', 2:11). Even Sterling Cooper's own Ken Cosgrove and Pete Campbell write fiction (published, respectively, in the prestigious *Atlantic* and the plebeian *Boy's Life*). Poetry, however, seems substantially less prominent. True, a very stoned and, as always, pretentious, Paul Kinsey does declaim some Eliot ('The Hollow Men') in 'My Old Kentucky Home' (3:3).

> *This is the way the world ends*
> *This is the way the world ends*
> *This is the way the world ends*
> *Not with a bang but a whimper.*

Like most television series, quality or not, *Mad Men* is hardly a poetry fest.

But then again we are offered poetic utterances like the following:

> Technology is a glittering lure,
> but there's the rare occasion
> when the public can be engaged
> on a level beyond flash
> if they have a sentimental bond with the product.
> Nostalgia.
> It's delicate but potent.
> In Greek nostalgia means
> literally the pain from an old wound,
> it's a twinge from your heart
> far more powerful than memory alone.
> This device isn't a spaceship,

it's a time machine.
It goes backwards and forwards.
It takes us to a place where we ache to go again.
It's not called the wheel.
It's called the carousel.
It allows us to travel
the way a child travels,
round and round, and back home again
to the place where we know we are loved.

These moving, powerful lines are not really poetry, of course. They are Don Draper's contract-securing pitch to Kodak (from 'The Wheel', 1:13), ventriloquized by Weiner and Robin Veith, rearranged as if they were verse.

Don Draper, whose real name, Dick *Whitman*, evokes twentieth-century American poetry's greatest precursor, may not be a true poet – his nemesis Duck Phillips belittles his ability to author 'a prose poem to a potato chip' as a dime-a-dozen gift ('Meditations in an Emergency', 2:26) – but Sterling Cooper's creative director demonstrates significant interest in the genre in the very next episode after 'The Wheel'. In season two's initial outing, 'For Those Who Think Young' (2:14), we find him sitting at the bar in a mid-town tavern, taken aback by his doctor's earlier revelation that he has high-blood pressure, delaying his arrival at Sterling Cooper. A few feet away a young man reads Frank O'Hara's *Meditations in an Emergency,* a 1957 collection, like all of the poet's work 'wry, light, a little naughty' (Schmidt, 906), the third by a then-in-his-thirties curator at the Museum of Modern Art on West 53rd. Don inquires, 'How is it?' and is informed that he – O'Hara – wrote some of it 'right here', on 23rd St., in a place since torn down. When Don quips that reading poetry 'makes you feel better about sitting in a bar at lunch', the poetry-reader replies derisively 'That's what it's about – getting things done'. Don again asks, 'Is it good?' Having already pegged his bar mate as a prosaic businessman, the O'Hara reader ends their colloquy by snidely insisting 'I don't think you'd like it'. The look on Don's face suggests he takes the rebuke as a challenge.

When Don finally shows up, late as usual, at a confab regarding Mohawk Airlines, his normally inspired extemporaneous gifts fail him in mid-sentence and he ends his trial pitch with an anything-but-poetic 'blah blah blah'. At the end of the episode, however, we find Don in his home office reading *Meditations*. One blogger observantly notes that it seems unlikely that Don could have found the Grove Press book so readily,[1] but impossible or not, Don has evidently read its 52 pages cover to cover, for we hear part four of 'Mayakovsky', the book's final poem, in Don's own voice as we look upon his meditative face:

> Now I am quietly waiting for
> the catastrophe of my personality
> to seem beautiful again,
> and interesting, and modern.

The second and third stanzas of 'Mayakovsky', heard in voiceover, accompany Don's inscribing of *Meditations* to an as-yet unknown recipient ('This reminded me of you'), placing it in an envelope, and walking to the corner mailbox:

> The country is grey and
> brown and white in trees,
> snows and skies of laughter
> always diminishing, less funny
> not just darker, not just grey.
> It may be the coldest day of
> the year, what does he think of
> that? I mean, what do I? And if I do,
> perhaps I am myself again.

So ends the first episode of season two as we find ourselves contemplating the relevance of the lines – about the poet's wrestle with the problem of his own identity – for understanding the mysterious Don Draper.[2]

O'Hara's place in the series is not yet over. In 'The Mountain King, (2:25)' the season's penultimate episode, during Don's California sojourn, we learn the identity of the recipient of his gift of poetry: Anna, the real Don Draper's widow, who responds to Don's question 'Did you read it?' with 'I did. It reminded me of New York and made me worry about you'. The very next episode, 'Meditations in an Emergency', the season finale, will draw its title from O'Hara, with the grave threat of nuclear war between the U.S.S.R. and America now having taken the place of the 'catastrophe of... personality'.

'Always Looking Away': Frank O'Hara Meets Don Draper

> My eyes are vague blue, like the sky, and change all the time; they are indiscriminate but fleeting, entirely specific and disloyal, so that no one trusts me. I am always looking away.
>> – Frank O'Hara, 'Meditations in an Emergency'

In the eventful 'Guy Walks into an Advertising Agency' (3:32), Conrad Hilton summons expert Manhattan mixer Don Draper for a sit-down at the Waldorf Astoria, and his role in Don's life will be pivotal in a season that will end in an almost complete reboot of *Mad Men's* narrative givens. But what if it had been Frank O'Hara, another real toad in *Mad Men's* imaginary garden,[3] not the eccentric hotelier but a man Michael Schmidt describes as 'cleanshaven and unobtrusive, keeping his own rather than everyone else's counsel' (906), who had asked the ad man to journey only a few blocks further west from the legendary hotel to stop by MOMA in order to compare creative processes and the state of the culture? Connie's name was already legend to Don Draper (and all of Sterling Cooper), but he would have recognized as well the name of *Meditations in an Emergency's* author, even if he had no idea the poet was a fellow New Yorker ('the most New York of the New York poets' [Schmidt, 906]) and a Manhattan professional like himself.

Draper and O'Hara might have found much in common.[4] Almost the same age ('Don'/Dick Whitman was born in 1925; O'Hara one year later), both were veterans (a very young O'Hara in the Navy in World War II; 'Don'/Dick in the Army in the Korean War). Both were considered visionaries by their inner circle. Don's ability to pull a brilliant new campaign idea out of thin air (or, for that matter, a new ad agency out of the dregs of its predecessor) has made him legendary. O'Hara was a prolific author of poems who seldom kept track of his prodigious output. For the New York School of Poets, as it came to be known, O'Hara was its acknowledged leader. 'Substitute Frank O'Hara for [Guillaume] Apollinaire [1880–1918] and Abstract Expressionism for Cubism, and you get an eerie fit', Lehman observes. 'The poets of the New York School were as heterodox, and belligerent toward the literary establishment and as loyal to each other, as their predecessors had been. The 1950s and early 1960s in New York were their banquet years' (2). By general consensus, it was only when O'Hara came to work in New York in 1951 that the movement coalesced (Lehman 7).

For two ardent movie fans, the subject of motion pictures would probably have come up. Draper's taste in cinema, we know, was broad enough to include an existential foreign film like Michelangelo Antonioni's *La Notte* (1961) ('The New Girl,' 2:18), while O'Hara would famously offer, in one of his many prose poems (none devoted to a potato chip), both advice and love 'To the Film Industry in Crisis':

> Not you, lean quarterlies and swarthy periodicals
> with your studious incursions toward the pomposity of ants,
> nor you, experimental theatre in which Emotive Fruition
> is wedding Poetic Insight perpetually, nor you,
> promenading Grand Opera, obvious as an ear (though you
> are close to my heart), but you, Motion Picture Industry,
> it's you I love!

O'Hara's poem alludes to some of the latest technological advances of the medium – technicolor, Cinemascope, Vistavision, stereophonic sound – but salutes the intrinsically superficial art form he loves: 'Long may you illumine space with your marvellous [sic] appearances' (5). Somewhat surprisingly for a cutting edge American artist, it is largely home-grown and more lowbrow talent to which he alludes: Jeanette MacDonald, Ginger Rogers, Fred Astaire, Johnny Weissmuller, Mae West, Harpo Marx, Marilyn Monroe, Myrna Loy, William Powell and Elizabeth Taylor.

O'Hara and the NYSP were under the influence of the painters of the period: Robert Motherwell, Jackson Pollock and Willem De Kooning. James Schuyler, a NYSP practitioner who also worked at MOMA, would observe that

> New York poets, except I suppose the color-blind, are affected most
> by the floods of paint in whose crashing surf we all scramble ... In
> New York, the art world is a painters' world; writers and musicians
> are in the boat but they don't steer. (Lehman 2)

More than any of the other members of the school, O'Hara was, in Marjorie Perloff's phrase, 'a poet among painters'.

We have no reason to believe the man who was once Dick Whitman was even in the boat, but in 'The Gold Violin' (2:20) the contemporary art world infiltrates Sterling Cooper. Bertram Cooper has acquired a painting for his office by Mark Rothko (1903–70), the Russian émigré whose deeply spiritual work was often grouped – against his protestations – with the Abstract Expressionists who powerfully inspired the NYSP. The painting of 'smudgy squares' – 'New Girl' Jayne's characterization – prompts an illicit visit to Cooper's office by Harry, Ken and Sal, led by Roger Sterling's future trophy wife, and results in a revealing discussion among the four. Art director Sal immediately identifies the artist. Harry speculates it may be intended as an 'Emperor's New Clothes' trap and goes in search of a 'brochure or something that explains it' that might tell them what to think about the painting. When Ken suggests, 'It's like looking into something very deep. You could fall in', Sal thinks he must be quoting some commentator. (The Rothko pilgrimage does have one immediate effect: Joan attempts to fire Jayne for her transgression.)

Later, in a one-on-one meeting in Cooper's office, Harry engages in some awkward dialogue with the Rothko's owner. When Harry can't take his eyes off the painting, he is told 'not to concern himself with aesthetics. You'll get a headache' and, in the end, Cooper admits the Rothko is an investment. We never get to hear Don Draper's take on the painting, but assuming he has taken note of it on his shoeless visits to Sterling Cooper's inner sanctum, he might have been ready to discuss, albeit superficially, Abstract Expressionism with his MOMA host. O'Hara might want to know in advance, however, that, like Bertram Cooper, Don is a bit disdainful of mixing art and advertising, the life of the mind and business: Sterling Cooper, he tells Pete Campbell in 'New Amsterdam' (1:4), 'has more failed artists and intellectuals than the Third Reich'.

What the NYSPers, including O'Hara, learned from the painters was, according to Lehman, 'that it was okay for a poem to chronicle the history of its own making – that the mind of the poet, rather than the world, could be the true subject of the poem and that it was possible for a poem to be (or to perform) a statement without making a statement' (3). Or as Don Draper would put it, in advice to Peggy Olson, 'Just think about it deeply and then forget it . . . and an idea will jump up in your face' ('Indian Summer', 1:11).

Or O'Hara and Draper could have discussed poetry – the poetry, at least, with which Don was familiar from his immersion in *Meditations in an Emergency*. We know from his 'For Those Who Think Young' reading of the lines from 'Mayakovsky' – 'Now I am quietly waiting for/the catastrophe of my personality/to seem beautiful again,/and interesting, and modern.' – that O'Hara's confessional style must have spoken to the roguishly handsome, laconic, mysterious, Protean ad man. But these could not have been the only poetic thoughts of O'Hara that would have had resonance for Draper, poster-child for the self-made man. How could one who had fled his childhood and held a series of jobs (selling used cars and writing copy for a fur company) not have found resonance in O'Hara's confession (in 'To the Harbormaster') that 'I am always tying up/and then deciding to depart' (3) or his description (in 'Blocks', 7) of 'always losing something and never knowing what' ('Blocks', 7)? O'Hara's boast that he has 'mastered the speed and strength which is the armor of the world' ('Poem', 13) might well have been Don's secret faith, too – on his good days, though not, perhaps, after being drugged and robbed by grifter hitchhikers ('The Arrangements', 3:4). A resolutely heterosexual man who seemingly has everything, including a beautiful wife, and yet is still ready to bed every bohemian artist, Jewish department store heiress, insult comic's wife, jet-setting young California woman, hitchhiker, and elementary school teacher who crosses his path might have taken to heart O'Hara's description of 'the racing vertiginous waves/of your murmuring need' ('Jane Awake', 26). 'I am the least difficult of men', Don Draper, I mean Frank O'Hara, ironically confesses. 'All I want is boundless love' ('Meditations', 38).

O'Hara's perplexing admission in the title poem – 'It's not that I'm curious. On the contrary, I am bored but it's my duty to be attentive' – could have struck Don as a mission statement he, too, could follow (39). How could the man who is both an illusion and a perpetrator of them not have responded powerfully to O'Hara's insistence that '[i]t is easy to be beautiful; it is difficult to appear so' (39)? And would not the individual now reanimating a dead soldier's identity not have identified powerfully with O'Hara's acknowledgement in 'For James Dean':

Men cry from the grave while they still live
and now I am this dead man's voice,
stammering... (43)

Although it is unlikely the subject would ever come up, O'Hara's loosely disguised homosexuality – 'At no point', Schmidt observes, did the poet 'disguise his sexual imagination' (906) – would not have been all that shocking to Don Draper, a man who knows more than a little about keeping secrets and who realized before anyone else, thanks to a glimpse from a hotel fire escape, that Sal might be gay. In 'Wee Small Hours' (3:35), of course, Sal is fired after he refuses the advance of Lee Garner, Jr., the son and heir to the Lucky Strike Tobacco fortune, in order to placate Sterling Cooper's biggest cash cow, and while Don is away in California, the very European Curt openly admits his homosexuality in front of Dylan-date Peggy and the homophobic Paul, Ken, Harry and Pete.

David Lehman quotes an observation in the journal of the still-in-the-closet John Cheever (who like the Drapers made his home in Ossining – see 'Ovid in Ossining') that 1959, the year before *Mad Men's* narrative timeline begins, was 'the year everybody in the United States was worried about homosexuality' (13) – proof to the great chronicler of suburban malaise that Americans are 'an absurdly repressed people'.[5] With O'Hara in mind, Lehman goes on to establish a tentative but convincing connection between the new gayness and the new poetics:

[W]hile I would not want to overemphasize [the NYSP's] homosexuality as an element of their aesthetic practice, it does seem to me that one question some of these poets are asking some of the time is whether the American pursuit of happiness may be consistent with a poetics of gaiety in both the traditional and modern senses of the word. (13)

Beyond his one exposure to O'Hara's 'poetics of gaiety', a reading, let us remember, he undertook almost on a dare ('You wouldn't like it'), it is doubtful Don Draper knew a thing about the remaking of poetry in his time.[6] But Don was an expert on the pursuit of happiness (see the epigraph to this essay). He knew, too, all about allowing his libido to do his thinking for him.

Frank O'Hara and Don Draper would indeed have much to talk about, but in *Mad Men* time Draper has only two and a half years – until 25 July 1966, when a forty-year-old O'Hara will be killed, run down in the middle of the night by a dune buggy on Fire Island – to meet the poet. If Don hears the news, might he recall that time the British Don Draper lost a foot to a drunk driver on a John Deere tractor? ('Guy Walks into an Advertising Agency').

Poetry and Television

> [L]ast night I was stunned to find poetry in the episode, and not just a shot of a book cover or a poetry reading going on in the background of a scene. Poetry was actually incorporated into the plot of the episode. If ever there's a way to win me over to a show, that's it.
>
> – Joshua Robbins, poet and blogger

The New York of *Mad Men* was saturated with poetry, so it should not seem surprising that the most refined and esoteric of literary forms would find its way into the series. As influential as *Mad Men* has become at the end of the first decade of the twenty-first century, however, poetry and the small screen are likely to remain strange bedfellows. Revealingly, Lynn Spigel's ingenious, seemingly comprehensive new book, *TV By Design: Modern Art and the Rise of Network Television*, which examines television's external relations with painting (abstract expressionism receives extensive coverage), design, architecture, art cinema and Andy Warhol, but the word 'poetry' does not even appear in the index, and an entire chapter on television and MOMA yields nary a mention of Frank O'Hara.

The medium had been, for a variety of motives, quick to recognize the benefits of the literary. As Mary Ann Watson observes,

> As the war wound down in 1945 and broadcasters geared up for the expansion of television, another sales strategy, one as fundamental as targeting families with children, was implemented. The plan was to convince upper-income, well-educated men and women, those who could most easily afford TV, that their purchase of a television would

141

be an enlightened investment. The appeal of live drama to urban
sophisticates lent impetus to the sponsorship of several anthology
series by manufacturers of TV sets, automobiles, and upscale consumer products. (Watson 21–22)

Consequently, early television 'became a nursery for the talents
of young unheard-of performers, directors, and, most of all, writers'.
'[T]he period nostalgically referred to as the Golden Age of Television', Watson remarks, was in reality a period 'when writers were
actually thought of as stars' (Watson 22).[7] Those stars tended to be
dramatists, however, or fiction writers, not poets.

Golden Age TV was not solely literary in its inventiveness, Gary
Edgerton reminds. It was also a proving ground for the perfection
of television aesthetics (194–95). As a groundbreaking basic cable
quality show, *Mad Men* will likely prove to be a touchstone for
new televisual literariness. The subject for another essay, it might
even be argued that this slow-paced, meditative, urbane, taciturn
(see Maurice Yacowar's essay in this volume on *Mad Men*'s silences)
and visually stunning series is in its text and texture a fascinating
experiment in a new, poetic storytelling.

When we find Joshua Robbins, an admirer of *Mad Men*, enrap-
tured by *Meditations in an Emergency*'s emergence (see the epigraph
to this section), we catch a glimpse of the cause and effect of poetry
on *Mad Men*. And it should hardly surprise us to learn that series
creator Matt Weiner's primary allegiance is not to traditional narrative modes. When asked by Chris Brancato if his dream is to 'write
the great American novel', Weiner replies: 'I would like to read the
great American novel. No, I was a poet in college, and I don't feel like
I opted out of that. In *Mad Men* I tried to treat the creative process
in an honest way' (41).

Works Cited

'An Outside View: Frank O'Hara Scholar David Lehman on *Meditations
  in an Emergency*' at http://blogs.amctv.com/mad-men/2009/03/
  frank-ohara.php.
Brancato, Chris. 'It's a Mad, Mad, Mad *Mad Men* World.' *Written By*:
  The Magazine of the Writers Guild of America, West February-March
  2007: 36–43.

Brown, Norman O. *Life Against Death: The Psychoanalytical Meaning of History.* NY: Vintage, 1959.

Cheever, John. *The Journals of John Cheever.* Ed. Robert Gottlieb. New York: Knopf, 1991.

Edgerton, Gary R. *The Columbia History of American Television.* New York: Columbia U P, 2007.

Leddy, Michael. 'Frank O'Hara and Mad Men.' Orange Crate Art, 27 July 2008 at http://mleddy.blogspot.com/2008/07/frank-ohara-and-mad-men.html.

Lehman, David. *The Last Avant-Garde: The Making of the New York School of Poets.* New York: Anchor Books, 1999.

McLean, Jesse. *Kings of Madison Avenue: The Unofficial Guide to* Mad Men. Toronto: ECW Press, 2009.

O'Hara, Frank. *The Collected Poems of Frank O'Hara.* Ed. Donald Allen. 1971; rept. Berkeley: U P California, 1971.

———. *Meditations in an Emergency.* New York: Grove Press, 1957.

'Ovid in Ossining.' *Time Magazine* 27 March 1964 at http://www.time.com/time/magazine/article/0,9171,938562,00.html.

Perloff, Marjorie. *Frank O'Hara: Poet Among Painters.* 2nd Edition. Chicago: U Chicago Press, 1998.

Robbins, Joshua, '*Mad Men*/O'Hara.' Little Epic Against Oblivion. July 15, 2009 at http://againstoblivion.blogspot.com/2009/07/mad-men-ohara.html.

Schmidt, Michael. *Lives of the Poets.* New York: Vintage, 1998.

Spigel, Lynn. *TV by Design: Modern Art and the Rise of Network Television.* Chicago: U Chicago P, 2008.

Watson, Mary Ann. *Defining Visions: Television and the American Experience in the 20th Century.* Malden, MA: Blackwell, 2008.

Notes

1 '*Meditations*,' Michael Leddy reminds, 'was published in a very limited run: 90 hardcover and 900 paperback copies. Brad Gooch's O'Hara biography *A City Poet* notes that by 1960 the book was out of print. This episode of *Mad Men* focuses on Valentine's Day, 1962 (the night of *Tour of the White House* with Mrs. John F. Kennedy). How does Don Draper get hold of this book so readily? Well, it's television.'

2 For New York School of Poets scholar David Lehman's own take on O'Hara's presence in *Mad Men* see 'An Outside View' from AMC's own series blog.

3 It was in her famous *ars poetica* 'Poetry' that Marianne Moore insisted on the need for 'literalists of/the imagination' to bring us 'imaginary gardens with real toads in them.'

4 Jesse McLean's 'unofficial' *Mad Men* guide, *Kings of Madison Avenue*, offers a very good discussion of O'Hara's work in relation to the series.

5 Norman O. Brown's neo-Freudian *Life Against Death*, which would argue that homosexuality was indeed an act of cultural heroism against such repression, was likewise published in 1959.

6 'It came to me that all this time,' NYSP pivotal voice Kenneth Koch would proclaim in the poem 'Days and Nights,' 'There had been no real poetry and that it needed to be invented' (quoted in Lehman 5).

7 Early TV's literariness was governed as well by a cost-benefit economy: 'while staples of the movies like car chases and shootouts were difficult and expensive to do on TV.' Consequently, '[l]ive television drama became the perfect canvas for exploring internal landscapes' (Watson 22).

Part Four.
Sexual Politics and Gender Roles

10.
Mad Women
Mimi White

Mad Men, season one, Episode One, New York City, 1960. It is Peggy Olson's first day at Sterling Cooper. Office Manager Joan Holloway guides her through the office. Joan's advice includes recommending a doctor who prescribes the pill to single women. While Peggy tries to settle into the job, her very presence as the new girl attracts attention, inviting suggestive comments, furtive looks and blatant leering from the male employees. She faces more invasive scrutiny on her lunch hour, when she visits the doctor Joan suggested to her. Later that night, an inebriated Pete Campbell makes an unexpected appearance on Peggy's doorstep, fresh from his own bachelor party. She lets him in. Months later, at a hospital emergency room with crippling abdominal pains, Peggy is shocked to learn that she is in labour.

Peggy's conduct seems odd, if not downright irrational. To start with, she simply doesn't look like someone in the hunt for an office romance. Joan and another secretary both point this out, when they encourage Peggy to shorten her skirts and show off her cute figure. Pete Campbell's initial response to her is arrant mockery, 'Are you Amish or something?' However extreme, his comment indicates just how distinctively wholesome Peggy looks to the Madison Avenue office veterans. Well into *Mad Men's* second season, Joan again admonishes Peggy to stop dressing like a little girl. In addition to looking straight-laced, Peggy doesn't act like someone looking for sexual action. She seems openly uncomfortable with the sexual attention she attracts at work, and equally ill at ease at the doctor's office. Having gone to the trouble of securing a prescription, she then proceeds as if she doesn't know (or doesn't care) how the pill actually works, by ending her first day on the job in bed with the most offensive guy from the office. She remains oblivious to her own pregnancy even as she gains so much weight that her male colleagues take notice. Clearly, she is at a loss when it comes to knowing, and controlling, her own body.

Over time, Peggy also exhibits a flair for advertising, sufficient talent to merit a promotion to advertising copywriter. She is the only woman on the company's creative staff and the only secretary to advance in this way. She should shine as the most successful woman at Sterling Cooper. Yet she stumbles into her new position almost by accident. Her fledgling career success in fact results from her singular combination of personal ingenuousness and professional aptitude. In comparison, most of the other women on the show are more sophisticated and more calculating than Peggy, and they are more apt to use feminine wiles to get what they want. Peggy's contradictions are rather mystifying. But they are also typical, insofar as they help define a prototypical 'Mad Woman' on *Mad Men*.

Peggy has plenty to be mad about. She is mad about pervasive male lechery. At the office, men expound on the values of the family and the American way of life when developing ad campaigns while flirting with anything in a skirt and guzzling booze. After work these same men continue their drunken binges at strip clubs with girls on the side. Peggy is mad that friendly conversation with any male gets construed as an invitation to intimate advances. She is mad about the way she is treated as her career progresses, especially when she has to share an office with the company's first Xerox machine. When she finally speaks up for herself to ask for her own office, she can't maintain her professional cool; instead she acts stunned when her request is granted. From the start it seems puzzling – perhaps just plain mad – that she follows Joan's counsel when it comes to contraception, but is far less compliant with the rest of Joan's personal advice. And there is no apparent reason for her to end up in bed with Peter, especially when he is totally drunk, on the eve of his nuptials. All of this madness becomes literal after she gives birth, as she lies catatonic in a hospital bed.[1]

Peggy is hardly the only woman at Sterling Cooper, even if the historical 'Mad Men' label never extended to the myriad of women who worked in ad agencies on Madison Avenue. As a female character, Peggy is distinctive; but as a 'Mad Woman', she belongs to a much larger group. These other 'Mad Women' may exhibit more conventional feminine allure; in many cases their status is closely tied to the income and position of the men with whom they consort, which doesn't necessarily make their lives any easier. Women's connection to men as a yardstick for success is also something Joan discusses on Peggy's first day at work. By this measure, Peggy's achievements at Sterling Cooper pale in comparison to Jane, one of the secretaries who succeeds her. Jane gets fired by Joan for sneaking into the company head's office. But Jane goes behind Joan's back to cry on senior partner Roger Sterling's shoulder. She uses the oldest female trick in the book, a show of tears, to secure her position and then transcends her secretarial post when she becomes Roger's new girlfriend and subsequently, his second wife. (This demonstrates remarkable ruthlessness since Joan herself was previously involved with Roger; Jane outmanoeuvres her on multiple counts.)

Other crying women populate the world of *Mad Men*, women whose tears lack female cunning, but reverberate as a signpost of common female setbacks. In what is almost a running joke, sobbing women regularly appear in the ladies' room at Sterling Cooper. These women never speak, they only bawl; and they are assiduously ignored by the co-workers who encounter them. The programme doesn't need to explain their dilemmas because their weepy presence is a sufficient sign of female fury, rage and defeat. We all know (or can guess) well enough what their stories are. These women comprise an anonymous, fleeting backdrop of female plight, the pale echo of the more prominent 'Mad Women' on *Mad Men*.

Consider Betty Draper, the picture-perfect wife of Peggy's boss. She is afflicted with the quintessential nineteenth-century female disorder, hysteria; for no apparent reason, she suffers temporary paralysis in her hands. When she needs a friend's help applying lipstick in a restaurant powder room, she seems to seek reassurance that her condition is nothing out of the ordinary. 'Do you ever have that? When your hands go numb?' she asks. Of course, her friend doesn't. Yet Betty's query insinuates that other women are apt to harbour their own afflictions, even if they don't share her specific symptoms. Despite her polished appearance, her behaviour sometimes crosses the boundaries of decorum for a woman of her circumstance: a college-educated, upper-middle-class suburban wife and mother. She retaliates for one neighbour's verbal outburst by shooting at

Betty Draper is afflicted with the quintessential nineteenth-century female disorder, hysteria; she is seemingly mad for no apparent reason. Courtesy of AMC.

his homing pigeons. She responds, imprudently, to the affections of another neighbour's child, granting his request for a lock of her golden hair as a keepsake. She talks with him as if he were the only person who truly understands her until she decides he is, after all, just a kid, wounding him with her sudden grown-up disregard. And though her paralytic episodes abate, she gets really mad as she learns about her husband's philandering, his monitoring of her psychiatric sessions, and, eventually, his hidden past. At one point she buys an old-fashioned fainting couch and positions it prominently in her home, as if confirming the association of domestic identity and madness as her female condition.

Even the most prepossessed of the regular female characters, executive secretary Joan Holloway, is mad, though she rarely lets it show. She wears hyper-femininity boldly as she glides through the office supervising the girls who work at Sterling Cooper. She gives the impression that she fully controls her female masquerade, but she also endures the deprecation that comes with her carefully crafted image. While her self-styling provides a hard coat of feminine armour, it also literally inscribes her with its bindings; undressing in the privacy of her bedroom, she massages the marks her garments etch on her body. Her boss, Roger Sterling, ends their affair after he suffers a heart attack, returning to the security of his wife and family. Adding insult to injury, he then leaves his wife for the younger, newer Jane. Joan hits the marriage jackpot herself, with her engagement to a doctor, but also endures a date rape at the Sterling Cooper office one evening, as he acts out his resentment of the sexual favours he suspects she has shared with the men at work. She fares no better professionally. At one point, Joan seems to have an opportunity, like Peggy, to advance in the company, when she temporarily serves as a script reader for the company's burgeoning television department. She enjoys her new duties, and demonstrates a gift for the work involved. But as soon as the company turns it into a permanent position, she is replaced by an inexperienced man. Joan may be a crack secretary and office manager, but she is never going to be taken seriously beyond the clerical level. To the men at Sterling Cooper, she will never fit the part, no matter her ability.

The madness of the women on *Mad Men* is a response to the world they inhabit, a world of status quo white, heterosexual, upper- and aspiring middle-class privilege. The varied pleasures and opportunities afforded to women in this milieu can abruptly turn destructive. In this context, women's agency, such as it is, always comes at a price and with built-in limits. Peggy, Betty and Joan offer three salient examples; but they are hardly the only ones. Understanding the women in this way, and calling them 'Mad Women', by no means

puts them on an equal footing with their male *Mad Men* coun-
terparts. It is, rather, a means of highlighting gender issues on the
show. The 'Mad Men' appellation, both historically and as the programme title, identifies the men with a specific place and profession and simultaneously lays claim to a specific disposition. The
'Mad Men' designation directly affiliates the advantages of gender,
profession and class status with the right to be angry, crazy, zany,
creative, manipulative and excessive. 'Mad Men' get to behave however they want. By contrast, the 'Mad Woman' label points out how
women are denied claims to this same territory, even as they are fully
implicated – if not trapped – within it.[2]

Certainly *Mad Men* devotes considerable attention to exploring male discontents and the ways in which the exercise of male
prerogative and power disguises (or at least uncomfortably coex-
ists with) deep-seated uncertainty, fragility, absurdity and weakness.
Yet ultimately, the exposure of troubled masculinities alleviates the
blandness of the stereotypical one-dimensional men in gray flannel
suits without disrupting their privilege. Roger Sterling may suffer
an emasculating heart attack at the office, and struggle with his own
mortality. But from the start, he gets to have affairs at will. Even after
the heart attack, a new secretary becomes his second wife, arousing
no small degree of ressentiment among his peers.

By contrast, whether women are stereotypically complacent or
wilfully transgressive doesn't make much difference. They are still
apt to have the rug pulled out from under them. Joan may supervise
the secretarial staff; and she may be confident, attractive and talented.
But she can't compete for the permanent script reader position, no
matter how well she does the job. And she has to pay a price for her
active sexuality, just as Peggy, it seems, pays a price for her passive sexuality. Don indulges in a succession of extramarital affairs, but Betty's
'revenge sex' – once she learns about one of his trysts – takes the form
of a tawdry, one-time hook-up with a stranger in a bar. Frankly, it
hardly seems equal to the task of squaring extramarital sex accounts.

In some ways all of this is par for the course within the terms of
the programme's fictive world and the historical setting that is its
point of departure. In the context of *Mad Men*, the gender divide
is at once normal, normative and playful. The programme sustains
a delicate balance between relishing the era in which it is set and
gleefully exposing the chinks in its lush veneer of stereotypicality.

The laconic narrative pace and eschewal of explicit motivation puts all the emphasis on how things look and how they happen; the programme devotes relatively little narrative attention to exploring character motives or developing a sense of their 'interiority'. Indeed, *Mad Men* is far better known for its highly wrought surfaces, evident in its meticulous mise en scène. The preoccupation with surface readily extends to the characters, who come across as distinctive types, while the narrative reveals fractures and fault lines in the veneer of its slick visual appeal.

Mad Men's temporal setting – the early 1960s – is the context and licence for its play with surfaces and types, including gender. The programme opens at the start of the decade, as a whole series of familiar events in American history are about to erupt. These events, looming in the fiction's future, exert decisive pressure on the narrative. When Sterling Cooper takes on Richard Nixon's 1960 presidential campaign, the programme already knows (as viewers are in a position to know) it is a lost cause.[3] Similarly, it is pretty likely that at some point the programme will reach November 1963 (as it did at the end of the third season) when President Kennedy is assassinated. The programme exploits the historical perspective as part of its knowing narrational strategy, counting on historical markers to generate anticipation via retrospection, and interpretation, of narrative events. *Mad Men* amplifies this process by deploying overdetermined images and (stereo)types that highlight the disparities between the way things were back then, in the programme's historical fiction past, and the way they are now, in the present of the programme's production/reception. This starts with the programme's mise en scène, but extends to more specific images and incidents. It encompasses, and then goes well beyond the constant drinking and smoking of the adult characters. It permeates scenes that seem devised solely to index the difference between then and now.

For example, in 'The Gold Violin' (1:7), Sally Draper runs around the house with a friend. Betty reprimands her for running in the house, but says nothing about the large, clear plastic bag covering Sally from head to knees. As Sally stands centre frame, panting, the point is obvious: those 1960 mothers were oblivious to the dangers of children playing with plastic bags. A similar impression is made in the same episode when the Draper family car drives away from a roadside picnic spot where their trash lies prominent in the foreground, carelessly strewn on the grass. The very framing of the image seems designed to slap viewers in the face with the characters' offhand disregard for littering the environment. These deceptively incidental images and events, often of doubtful accuracy, serve as conspicuous signs of the era's alluring, disarming, irresponsible, and potentially lethal habits.[4]

Raising the stakes even higher, the programme flaunts types and stereotypes by referencing a wide range of media intertexts, infusing its depiction of the era with expansive reflexive artifice. The range of intertextual reference anchors the programme in the era, but also extends well beyond this to address the show's contemporary, media savvy audience. For example, many have noted how the opening titles emulate the look of a Saul Bass title sequence, such as that for Alfred Hitchcock's *North by Northwest* (1959), which is also about an advertising executive. Don's bohemian girlfriend, Midge, readily conjures another Midge, from Hitchcock's *Vertigo* (1958). Beyond their shared name, both Midges are single, working women who ply their design trade at drafting tables in their urban studio apartments. In this context, Betty Draper's resemblance to Grace Kelly is hardly accidental. Even post-World War II taste in high art is included. Senior partner Bert Cooper's predilection for Orientalist modernism is not only evident in his private office décor, but also necessitates that his colleagues respect the Zen atmosphere of his office by removing their street shoes. His artistic sophistication is clinched when he purchases a Mark Rothko painting for his office. And he is portrayed by Robert Morse, who starred as an earlier popular culture version of a Madison Avenue adman in the 1961 Broadway musical, *How to Succeed in Business Without Really Trying*.

More obscure references suffuse the programme, their improbability offset by the programme's pervasive, confident knowingness. In one subplot in 'Smoke Gets in Your Eyes' (1:1), Don is asked to consult an in-house psychologist to help inspire a new campaign for cigarettes. The researcher is a middle-aged woman with a German accent, evoking two other German females readily associated with mass media: celebrity sexologist Ruth Westheimer and public opinion researcher Elizabeth Noelle-Neumann. In 'Ladies Room' (1:2), the advertising subplot sounds like an inside joke inspired by Sigmund Freud. Don asks his staff to develop a campaign for the new aerosol canister of Right Guard deodorant by contemplating the question of what women want. (The answer that Don eventually supplies is 'any excuse to get closer.' A woman would more likely conclude 'for men not to stink.')

Other references are more contemporary. For example, Bert's sister, who also owns a stake in the company, is named Alice Cooper, an unremarkable woman's name which is also that of an American rock band from the 1970s. Pete Campbell's blueblood parents bear an uncanny resemblance to Jay Sherman's adoptive parents on the animated series *The Critic* (ABC/Fox 1994–95); indeed, they seem to be the 'live action' incarnation of these cartoon figures. Even *I Didn't Know I Was Pregnant*, an American reality show that premiered on TLC in 2008, seems like an intertext in respect to the credibility of Peggy's unrecognized pregnancy. After all, if a reality series can be developed around women in the 2000s who remain unaware they are pregnant until they are in labour, what would you expect from someone in 1960?

The programme thus produces an astute, dense visual and narrative palimpsest offering multiple historical and intertextual trajectories into and out of the show. This contributes to the double-edged sensibility whereby the programme both delights in the era in all of its retro lushness and simultaneously disdains it for being so retrograde. Since all of this is a product of the programme's knowing artifice, it might seem as if the whole issue of gender and women is almost beside the point. After all, this is by no measure 'the way we were' but a highly intermediated and reflexive version thereof. At times *Mad Men* hovers on the verge of being a wholesale parody of conventional white, upper and middle class images of the dominant media from the era in which it is loosely set. But there is gender trouble.

Despite its knowingness, despite its artifice, despite the historical context for the fiction, *Mad Men* seems worried by the very constraints of its own fictions, specifically when it comes to the question of women. This becomes most clear beyond the fiction itself in the extra features packaged with the season two DVD set of *Mad Men*, which includes a documentary, *Birth of an Independent Woman*, focusing on American women's social history after World War II.[5] The documentary poses something of a rhetorical conundrum in relation to the programme and its fictive female characters. Indeed, the very inclusion of the documentary in the DVD set could be considered an apology for the ways in which women otherwise appear on the programme. For all *Mad Men's* evident knowingness, the documentary suggests that perhaps the ways in which it tries to balance relishing/disdaining the era in which it is set malfunctions when it comes to gender. The very existence of the documentary could be seen as a tacit admission that the programme needs to both address and redress questions of women in history in different terms than it is able to offer within the bounds of its historical fiction.

The documentary itself is quite traditional in its format and relates, in broad strokes, a familiar history. There are experts who speak on camera about the major issues related to women's roles in the post-World War II era and discuss the emergence of the women's movement in the 1960s.[6] The on-screen experts are intercut with a variety of documents including newsreel footage, photographs and printed materials from the past. These add visual interest and serve as visible evidence of the issues and events discussed. But by far the predominant illustrative material in the documentary comes from *Mad Men* itself. As the experts describe the prevailing gender norms of the 1950s and 1960s, dramatic scenes from the show are inserted into the documentary. These are, patently, neither historical nor documentary images; on the contrary, as previously described, they are laden with reflexive artifice. They are seamlessly inserted into the flow of the documentary, as if they had the same status as the other documents, and thus come to serve as examples of the historical issues that are explored by the documentary experts.[7] At best, these scenes might be considered to be something along the lines of 'dramatic reenactments' of this history.

It is of course clear that the documentary was made after – and to serve the interests of – the programme after it had already been airing on television for two seasons. Thus, there are a number of rhetorical sleights of hand at work here, leading to a kind of moebius strip logic. First, the documentary authenticates, and even justifies, *Mad Men's* treatment of gender in general, and women in particular. It stands as a kind of proof – proffered explicitly by the programme – that this is the way things once were for women at one time in history, while also indicating that beyond the bounds of the programme's fiction (later in the 1960s), women's lot will change for the better. But this rationale/apology, already problematic in itself, is carried out in a documentary film that uses scenes from *Mad Men* as the faux-archival examples of what the experts discuss. The result is a particular and decisively non-reflexive concatenation of history, fiction and documentary that combines all of these in the context of the blatant commercial interests of the programme itself. In the process, it makes *Mad Men's* gender narratives self-legitimating, as they illustrate and stand in for the 'actual' history of women.

At the same time, this use of the programme as documentary illustration ends up skewing the programme's representation, especially when it comes to women. It implicates the women characters in a realist history and in a discourse of truth to history associated with the visual aesthetic of documentary film-making. This is the case even though the programme clips have a very different look than the newsreel footage from the 1960s, and at the very same time that the authority of the documentary portrayal of history props itself on the programme's historical fiction. Moreover, as discussed above, while historical events are routinely invoked by the programme, the programme's overall narrative and visual strategies engage a reflexive knowingness that avows the simultaneous artfulness and the artifice of this historical narrative at one and the same time. However, the documentary decisively pulls the women in one particular direction, associating them more explicitly with the historical setting at the expense of the more playful elaboration and turns of absurd artifice that comprise the programme's historical fiction.

This has the curious effect of exacerbating the gender imbalance, by affiliating the women with historical/realist representation, despite their often stereotypical referents. The rhetorical conundrum introduced by the documentary is thus redoubled. First, it seems to point to the programme's own problems with women, problems which are at once historical (hence the history of second wave feminism) and representational (for the programme in the present). Second, as an effort to resolve the problem, by making clear that the programme's images are self-aware as historical images, it ends up reconfirming the gender disparity, since the women are so closely bound by the documentary's idea of 'true' history, despite the female characters' heavy implication in stereotypes. Third, because the programme itself serves as the prevailing illustrative material for the documentary, the very artificial (sometimes parodic) representations of women are turned into the stuff of history. All of this combines to corroborate the issues discussed from the outset, in particular the ways in which exposing the cracks in the façade of masculinity somehow makes the men more interesting, enriching the historical masculine stereotype at the same time. By contrast, for the women characters, history and fiction become one and the same thing, each the alibi and snare of the other.

It is enough to make a woman mad.

Notes

1 A margin of doubt remains. The male doctors definitively diagnose her as having a complete mental breakdown. Peggy herself never speaks about these events. One is tempted to take her silence as a proto-feminist refusal to speak.

2 It is also intended to resonate with the title of Sandra Gilbert and Susan Gubar's 1979 landmark work in feminist literary criticism, *The Madwoman in the Attic: The Woman Writer and the Nineteenth-Century Literary Imagination* (New Haven: Yale University Press, 1979).

3 Viewers are also likely to know that Nixon ran for president again, and in 1968 won the election. He proved to be a criminal and resigned in ignominy in 1974.

4 As someone familiar with the era from personal experience, I can testify that parents were well aware of the dangers of playing with plastic bags and concerned about public litter. Many of these sorts of images/events in the programme clearly serve a function that has little to do with their referential accuracy, and much more to do with constructing and signalling concise signs of historical 'difference'.

5 The salutary aspects of the documentary are incisively assessed by Mary Celeste Kearney. My analysis is quite at odds with Kearney's perspective. Despite this difference, she raises some interesting points. She discusses the documentary's value both in presenting aspects of post-World War II women's history that may not be widely known, and for its innovative use of DVD sets of popular television programmes as an outlet for documentary film-making. Kearney, 'Honey, look what I found in the special features!' *FlowTV* 10.08, 19 September 2009 at http://flowtv.org/?p=4283.

6 Kearney identifies the participants as Diana York Blaine (USC lecturer), Emily Bazelon (Slate.com editor), Ellen Dubois (UCLA professor), Marcelle Karp (*Bust* co-founder), Michael Kimmel (SUNY professor), and Michelle Wallace (CUNY professor).

7 To its credit, the documentary's version of women's history addresses relations between race and gender, and women's participation in a variety of 1960s activist movements.

11.
Women on the Verge of the Second Wave

Mary Beth Haralovich

Set in the early 1960s on the verge of the women's liberation movement,[1] *Mad Men* presents a sexist work environment for women and men. Sexual innuendo and harassment is as common as smoking. In the Sterling Cooper offices, a landscape of sound underscores the gendered disparity in power. Robust male laughter careens through the softer sonic ambience of the secretarial pool where feminine voices mix with the keystrokes of IBM Selectric typewriters.

The period showcase is a reminder of women's advances, to be sure. Yet, *Mad Men* also offers an opportunity for businesswomen to talk about the need for continued progress. In a *Forbes.com* Leadership post encouraging 'gen y women' to watch the series, Jennifer Allyn ('a managing director of PriceWaterhouseCoopers LLP, where she is responsible for designing programmes to retain, develop and advance women in the firm') finds in *Mad Men* that 'breaking down barriers . . . is depicted as exhilarating. Peggy's struggle to find her voice and be treated as a professional is inspirational.' Allyn sees in *Mad Men* the reminder that 'profound cultural change is possible' (Allyn). Through *Mad Men*, women's past connects with women's present.

To explore this resonance with lived history and businesswomen today, this chapter explores how secretary-turned-creative Peggy Olson and her female mentors, Joan Holloway Harris and Bobbie Bartlett, evoke the Second Wave and Third Wave women's movements to find empowerment in this man's world of business. Although set in the early 1960s, Peggy, Joan and Bobbie are not trapped in the amber of the past. These women are (or become) comfortable

Secretary-turned-creative Peggy Olson evokes the Second and Third Wave women's movements to find empowerment in Mad Men's *world of business. Courtesy of AMC.*

with their own bodies. The series creators have thought deeply about the rendering of woman's condition in the 1960s. The combination of feminine empowerment and sexism engages a subtle critique of patriarchy.

In this regard, *Mad Men* has parallels to the femininity that Kathleen Rowe Karlyn finds in the young women of the *Scream* horror film series: 'an opportunity to examine cultural and individual fantasies as they relate to gender and power.' Like *Scream*, *Mad Men* 'invites female viewers imaginatively to "try on" a new model of femininity more suited to young women of the Third Wave' than to the impending Second Wave.[2] *Mad Men*'s synergy of period verisimilitude, confident femininity, and awareness of the need for cultural change is meaningful for women's situation today.

Although Peggy, Joan and Bobbie do not speak of sexism, the women are well aware that the gendered work environment contains, suppresses and enables their ambitions. Their negotiation of the workplace and their acceptance of its conditions illuminate the gendered power structure and contribute to the period verisimilitude.

As these women seek ways to manage their work and to progress in their professional lives, they exhibit moments of solidarity as women, although not with the feminist consciousness characteristic of the Second Wave.

Mad Men's ambitious women are aware that it is a challenge to be a woman in business and they harness their femininity to succeed. Peggy, Joan and Bobbie infuse themselves with feminine empowerment (the grrrl power of the time) through their strategic understanding of the need to participate, within limits, in the gaze of heterosexuality as they demonstrate their evident skills as professionals.[3]

In '*Mad Men* – Why Gen Y Women Need to Tune In' in *Forbes.com*, Allyn finds that *Mad Men*'s

> portrayal of the 'old boys' club has a lot to teach young women today. Senior businesswomen often complain that younger women don't appreciate how much trailblazing was accomplished by the pioneers before them.

She goes on to encourage Gen X and Gen Y to 'break new ground . . . to ascend from middle management to the executive suite' and to continue to close the gender gaps in the business world

> because the workplace needs pioneers today who will advocate for more expansive definitions of flexibility, dismantle any remaining stereotypes and embrace the next level of business leadership. (Allyn)

Mad Men, in its exploration of the past, resonates with the present.

To illustrate these gender politics and women's trailblazing in the workplace, *Mad Men* writers and actors draw on influential exemplars of the period – Betty Friedan's *The Feminine Mystique* (1963) and Helen Gurley Brown's *Sex and the Single Girl* (1962) – for cues to creating the verisimilitude of women's condition in the early 1960s.[4] Creator and Executive Producer Matthew Weiner finds these 1960s manifestos to be relevant to women today:

> I had this incredible experience of reading *The Feminine Mystique* and *Sex and the Single Girl* in the same week. And I said, 'oh, this is my show' . . . It is literally the choice of what kind of woman to be at that time and today . . . *The Feminine Mystique* spoke to so many

> people . . . Helen Gurley Brown [is] giving you this advice on how to
> be a woman and how to use womanliness to get success. (Rose)

It speaks to the continued relevance of Friedan and Gurley Brown
that their ideas contributed to the creation of women characters who
are grounded in the past yet still speak to the present.

As Mary Celeste Kearney points out, *Mad Men* has an assertive
feminist presence in its DVD set special features. The season two
DVD has a two-part documentary, *Birth of an Independent Woman*
('The Problem' and 'Independence') where feminist scholars and
critics present the history of the women's movement. The documentary intercuts scenes of Peggy, Betty or Joan, linking the series
to the movement. Kearney finds more remarkable the very existence
of a feminist documentary in a DVD set 'which will likely reach a few
million globally' and suggests 'the state of feminism among industry
professionals'. Kearney offers hope that the *Mad Men* DVD set 'may
very well signal a new moment in feminist filmmaking, particularly
distribution', which has long eluded feminist film-makers (Kearney).

While the DVD set has the documentary and *Mad Men*'s press discusses the significance of 1960s books about women, the series itself
does not have many period references to the women's movement.
There are close-up inserts of period objects (such as a car radio and
a cigarette holder) and fleeting yet meaningful images on television
screens about Civil Rights and politics. There are references to contraception, abortion, periods and pantyhose, but not to the politics
of the women's movement. One exception is Peggy's reference to the
1963 Equal Pay Act when she asks for a raise ('The Fog', 3:31).

Peggy, Joan and Bobbie live in the early 1960s yet they are designed for the twenty-first century. Their characters are infused with
period verisimilitude, as well as hindsight about women's liberation,
but skip over the Second Wave's 'censoriousness regarding sexuality, especially heterosexuality' (Karlyn, 'Feminism in the Classroom',
60). *Mad Men*'s women are strategic participants in heterosexuality
while seeking equal pay, equal work and equal authority. This confluence of Second Wave and Third Wave attributes contributes to
the complexity and appeal of these characters and their relevance
today.

The Third Wave is typically defined in terms of its difference from
the earlier, Second Wave, generation of feminists. In her *AlterNet*

interview with Jennifer Baumgartner and Amy Richards about their book, *Manifesta: Young Women, Feminism, and the Future* (2000), Tamara Strauss describes the key issues:

> On the one side are Second Wavers who lashed out against their sexually limiting roles as wives and mothers in exchange for equal pay and egalitarian partnerships. And on the other are Third Wavers who...want to continue the fight for equal rights, but not to the detriment of their sexuality. They want to be both subject and object, when it comes to their sexual roles, their political power and their place in American culture.

The manifesta argues that woman's objectification is not 'part of the backlash against feminism'. Rather, it is an 'embrace [of] femininity.' Blogger Naomi Rockler-Gladen concurs, 'Third Wave feminism celebrates women's multiple and sometimes contradictory identities in today's world' (Strauss, Rockler-Gladen).

While *Mad Men*'s period setting eschews the Third Wave penchant for post-modern and 'girlie' femininity, Peggy, Joan and Bobbie are certainly engaging for a Third Wave perspective. The retro outfits, foundation garments, make-up, and hairstyles deconstruct the women's femininity even as they help locate Peggy, Joan and Bobbie in a 1960s pre-liberation environment. Series Costume Designer Jane Bryant comments: 'It's all about the bra and girdle...there's a different way of feeling, there's a different way of carrying yourself, there's a different way of walking.' Christina Hendricks (Joan) affirms, 'Half your work is done for you. It puts you into character immediately.' Media critic Jeffrey Sconce quipped that *Mad Men* costumes should be nominated for Best Acting.[5]

In 'Feminism in the Classroom: Teaching Towards the Third Wave', Karlyn observes,

> And so, while retaining the critique of beauty culture and sexual abuse from the Second Wave, young women have complicated the older feminist critique of the male gaze as a weapon to put women in their place, and instead exploit the spotlight as a source of power and energy. Thus girls do not see a contradiction between female power and assertive sexuality. (Karlyn, 'Feminism in the Classroom', 64)

Peggy, Joan and Bobbie embrace the professional expectations of 1960s beauty culture as a means to their own authority and power. As Bobbie counsels Peggy on presenting herself as a woman in business, 'it's very powerful' ('The New Girl', 2:18).

While *Mad Men* presents an assertive feminine confidence in the professional work environment, the series also connects with the lived work environment of executive women. '[I]t's less a product of the decade than viewers might think. The truth is that a lot of these moments that seem period and horrible for women come directly from experiences that I and the other women writers have had in our lifetimes,' says *Mad Men* executive story editor Robin Veith in a *CNN.com* feed of an Oprah.com story, '"Mad Men" and the real women behind them' (Bertsche).

On *WSJ.com*, the *Wall Street Journal* posts a recap of every episode of *Mad Men*. Cheryl Berman, former chief creative officer of the Leo Burnett ad agency and founder of her own start-up agency, provides a detailed recounting, with editorial commentary that evaluates the realism of Sterling Cooper's agency processes. Berman sees in Peggy her own experience. Regarding Don's unyielding rejection of Peggy's request to work on the Hilton account, Berman observes:

> Peggy has just come from a demoralizing encounter with Don, who reminds her that she was his secretary and now she has an office and a job a full grown man would kill for. I remember encounters like this with my male bosses. Why do they always have to remind you how young and inexperienced you were when you started and how lucky you are that they discovered you and made you what you are today? (Berman)

Mad Men's work environment is relevant not only to women executives who came up the ranks in the past.

The 'ForbesWoman Feed' on *Forbes.com* posted a response to a LinkedIn thread on 'salary and self-esteem' where posters stated that 'women generally don't assert their value in the workplace' and 'sexism still exists (shocked! I'm shocked!).' In response, Anne Daley, Ph.D., executive coach and professional development specialist for women, put together 'the top 10 unwritten rules for working women.' 'You better know what you're up against', she advised, 'don't let them sabotage your ambitions' ('ForbesWoman Feed').

Most of Daley's 2009 rules apply to Peggy's situation at Sterling Cooper in the early 1960s:

1. Men get the benefit of the doubt – women get hired on demonstrated experience.
2. Looks matter. Bare those arms and legs at your own risk. Flesh conjures up images of the beach and the boudoir, not the boardroom.
3. You won't get sufficient feedback . . . unless you ask for it.
4. A working mother's commitment is assumed to be ambivalent.
5. Actually, it is personal . . . cultivate mentors, allies, champions.
6. Men are bred for self-confidence . . . design your own path to self-confidence.
7. Women are rendered invisible until they demonstrate otherwise.
8. Women don't take charge, they take care . . . dance that fine-line between assertive and pushy, authoritative and bossy, smart and arrogant.
9. Women are different . . . code for 'other'. . . to keep women positioned as outsiders.
10. Women make great worker bees, but visionary leaders – not so much.
    ('ForbesWoman Feed')

Consider how Peggy negotiates these rules at Sterling Cooper with the advice of her mentors. Joan and Bobbie counsel Peggy on how to be a woman in a man's business environment. Joan adjusts her advice as Peggy's career pathway evolves from admonishing Peggy to accept objectification of the Sterling Cooper male gaze to encouraging Peggy to dress like a player. Bobbie takes the opportunity for an extended mentoring session with Peggy and, in the process, provides a key piece of advice for Peggy's future. Don, not being in the business sisterhood, provides a contrasting 'masculine' mentoring style. With stern candour, he mentors Peggy on performance expectations, on her role as a creative, and on crossing the fine line between assertive and pushy. In the process, he comes to recognize in Peggy a particular quality that he sees in himself.

Rules 1 and 7: As a secretary in what Jimmy Barrett crudely calls the 'tomato farm', Peggy's intelligence is invisible until she demonstrates her difference from the other 'girls' ('The New Girl',

2:18). During the Belle Jolie lipstick focus group with the secretarial pool, Peggy and Joan are different from the other women in the room. Joan uses the mirrored one-way window to tantalize her lover Roger (and the other men) by leaning over to put out a cigarette. Peggy does not try on the lipstick. She sits, watching the others. 'Here's your basket of kisses', she says, handing Freddy Rumsen a wastebasket of lipstick-blotted tissues. Freddy tells Don that Peggy 'really stood out brainstorming-wise.' This is Peggy's entrée into the creative world of Sterling Cooper, when Freddy invites her to work on copy for the Belle Jolie campaign ('Babylon', 1:6).

Rule 2: Looks do matter in the business environment. Joan enforces dress decorum at the office, demonstrating the range of femininity appropriate for the Sterling Cooper office. As a secretary, Peggy, quite upset, complains to Joan about the passes men are making at her. 'It's constant from every corner.' Joan declines the opportunity for solidarity and advises Peggy that she is 'the new girl and you're not much. So you might as well enjoy it while it lasts.' Peggy, terse: 'Of course.' Joan: I'm just offering some perspective, that's all.' Their exchange is followed by a montage of men looking at Peggy as they walk past her desk ('Ladies Room', 1:2).

Yet, there's a fine line between participating in the male gaze and offering up the flesh of the boudoir. Joan advises Jane, Don's new secretary after Peggy is promoted, about office protocol. Joan interrupts the men ogling Jane's display of leg and décolletage, bra showing. Joan, wearing cinched waist straight skirt and a soft red blouse with a flowing tie at the neck, cautions Jane: 'I see what you're doing and I have to say I'm disappointed. Your décolletage is distracting. This is an office that hinges on professional decorum. Be reasonable. There's still plenty to see and you know that.' Joan walks away and Freddy emerges from his office to play Mozart on his fly ('The New Girl', 2:18).

Unlike Freddy's performance, the exchange between Joan and Jane is not ironic commentary about different standards. It is a statement about the appropriateness of sexuality for the office. Although Joan's dresses fit her foundation-moulded curves, her outfits might be termed 'business casual' today. 'She's a goddess in tailored office-wear!' exults blogger Wendy Atterberry in 'How Joan Holloway of *Mad Men* gave me confidence'. When considering her own shape and what to wear, Atterberry 'just thought of Joan Holloway and how well she owns her size . . . and did something I hadn't done in ages – I donned a very form-fitting dress' (Atterberry). While Joan is comfortable and confident in her form-fitting office wear, Peggy cannot move forward without changing her look and her demeanour toward the male executives.

Rules 3, 5 and 6: To accomplish this transformation, Peggy needs no champion from among the Sterling Cooper men. Peggy acts intelligently on the advice of her female mentors and executes her own makeover. As she matures in responsibilities, her clothing matures as well. Peggy arrives at Sterling Cooper for her first day on the job, fresh from Miss Deavers Secretarial School, dressed in a long skirt. Joan, without the crude tone of the men, counsels Peggy to show her legs: 'A girl like you, with those darling little ankles, I'd find a way to make them sing.' Peggy does not explicitly act on this advice, which would serve to make her more suitable for the 'tomato farm'. There are numerous instances of Peggy ignoring sexist and harassing situations, starting with her first elevator ride to the office.

However, Joan mentors Peggy on the need to be a team player for the organization, to protect the agency's executive assets. Peggy, in a panic, goes to Joan for help on how to cover for Don, who is absent when Betty and the children arrive for a family photo portrait shoot. Joan:

> You entertain her and her brats. You don't know where he is and you forgot to remind him. It is the truth. And when he comes back, let him have an excuse and he'll have one. You just start apologizing for, well, just how stupid you are.

At the end of the day, Joan recaps the secretary's role for Peggy: 'You have to do your job. Keep his record clean here and at home, honestly.' Peggy, incredulous: 'That's my job?' ('5G', 1:5).

As Peggy contributes sensitive and smart ideas to the creative process, she receives mentoring from Joan and from Bobbie that will help her to fit better into the world she wants to enter. In a scene key to Peggy's trajectory, one that Elisabeth Moss (Peggy) identifies as pivotal ('That's when everything begins to change . . . everything that happens to her, even into next season, stems from that bit of advice'),[6] Bobbie spends the night at Peggy's apartment, nursing a black eye after she and Don crashed the car and were picked up for drunk driving.

Bobbie probes Peggy's self-esteem. Peggy: 'He [Don] made me a copywriter.' Bobbie, 'I'll bet you made yourself a copywriter.' Bobbie: 'I was curious if you are aware of the value of your service.' Peggy, with confidence: 'I know what I'm doing.' Admiring Peggy's gumption but aware that Peggy is naïve about how to manoeuvre in the business world, the older more experienced woman provides the key advice:

> You have to start living the life of the person you want to be . . . you're never going to get that corner office until you start treating Don as an equal. And, no one will tell you this: you can't be a man, so don't even try. Be a woman. It's powerful business when done correctly. Do you understand what I'm saying, dear?

Peggy responds with quiet, yet timid, assurance, 'I think so' ('The New Girl', 2:18).

Later, Peggy – dressed smartly in a nice blue blouse, shiny hair in a ponytail, earrings, and make-up – apologizes to 'Mr. Draper' for not being prepared for a meeting and then asks him to return the money she loaned him to pay his drunk driving fine: '$110 is a lot of money for me.' Don pays her back with an apology that invokes their common bond of denial – his buried past as Dick Whitman and Peggy's 'psychoneurotic disorder' and discarded baby: 'When you try to forget something, you have to forget everything.' Peggy ends the conversation saying, 'Thank you, Don' with an air of confidence and the professional familiarity of equals. He notices and is a bit taken aback, at a loss for words. She leaves his office ('The New Girl', 2:18).[7]

However, Peggy's path to professional dress is not a smooth one. In 'Maidenform' (2:19), the episode that follows Bobbie's advice to 'be a woman', Peggy crashes the men's strip club party. Peggy complains to Freddy that the men are not keeping her in the loop on the Playtex account. Freddy brushes it off. Peggy goes to Joan, who knows how the office runs. Peggy: 'There's business going on and I'm not invited.' Joan: 'You want to be taken seriously? Stop dressing like a little girl.' Peggy is wearing a blue and black checked dress with white Peter Pan collar, her hair in a ponytail.

Peggy overhears the men and the Playtex clients arranging to meet at the Tom Tom strip club. Her interpretation of Joan's counsel is to exhibit sexuality rather than 'professional decorum'. Peggy arrives at the Tom Tom wearing an electric blue dress, décolletage, dangly earrings, and hair down, face made-up. She sits on the client's lap and watches the stripper. Pete Campbell looks at her, disapproving. She catches his eye. Peggy exhibits only the smallest embarrassment, moving her hand across her brow and her breasts before she smiles and goes back to watching the stripper. Trying to become an insider and unable to access information in the office, Peggy presents herself as a playgirl. This sexual display is not what Bobbie or Joan had in mind ('Maidenform', 2:19).

Toward the end of the second season, Peggy's transformation to a professional woman is completed with makeover advice from Kurt, the 'European Smith'. Kurt invites Peggy to go to a Bob Dylan concert. She assumes it is a date and then learns Kurt is gay. When he picks her up at her apartment for the concert, she wonders aloud, 'I don't know why I pick the wrong boys. What's wrong with me?' Kurt touches her hair: 'This is not modern office for working woman. I fix you.' To the excruciating sound of scissors slicing through mounds of hair, he cuts off her ponytail and hands it to her. Peggy next appears with a new look – a modernized young professional – in trendy business casual outfits and her hair in a 1960s flip ('The Jet Set', 2:24).

Rule 8: As she finds her way, Peggy walks 'the fine line between assertive and pushy, authoritative and bossy, smart and arrogant.' Rather than presenting this as a simple binary, *Mad Men* explores in subtle ways how Peggy negotiates the workplace and her progress in self-discovery as well as career advancement. After Peggy's success with her first pitch, for the Relaxicisor vibrator ('It's my little secret'), she asks Don for her own office and a raise. Don: 'Do not be timid. You presented like a man, now act like one.' In the end, Don gives Peggy a 15 per cent raise ($5.00 a week) and a place where she can work on her copy ('Indian Summer', 1:11).

However, when Peggy casts and directs the Relaxicisor radio ad, she creates a disaster. She follows her own preference of actress for the product ('confidence, a better you') instead of Ken Cosgrove's ('that voice, randy and knowing'). Her lack of experience as a director, inability to communicate and insensitivity cause the actress to break into tears. Interestingly, Peggy does not invest in her own feelings or personalize her failure. Rather, she stays focused on the project, sending Ken to console the weeping actress and to bring in the actress he wanted ('The Wheel', 1:13).

In the second season, Peggy receives a promotion after she covers for Freddy who passes out in a drunken stupor. In the aftermath, Don is the arbiter of professional decorum as Sterling Cooper forces Freddy to take a leave of absence and Don offers Peggy all of Freddy's copywriting work. Don chastises the men for their juvenile behaviour. He counsels Peggy that she is not responsible for Freddy's pain and has no grounds for feeling guilty that her rise depended on her colleague's fall. Don reproaches the men for making fun of Freddy ('Can't you find something else to do besides dining on the drama of other people's lives, like a bunch of teenage girls? It's just a man's name, right?'). Peggy cannot reconcile her affection for Freddy, who gave Peggy her start, with taking his place (and ultimately his office): 'I love Freddy.' Don: 'Don't feel bad about being good at your job.' Peggy: 'I wish it hadn't happened this way.' Don: 'That's the way it happened. Congratulations.' Peggy leaves Don's office, walking with confidence and direction to upbraid Pete for telling on Freddy ('Six Month Leave', 2:22).

Lest it appear that Peggy's pathway is becoming cleared for career advancement, Don reminds Peggy of the gendered power structure and that she has misstepped on the fine line between assertive and pushy, as when she asks Don for a raise or to be involved with the Hilton account. In Don's career mentoring of Peggy, he tends to treat her as a genderless individual, although there are punishing moments that reveal his awareness that she is a female in a male world.

The second time Peggy asks Don for a raise, she evokes the 1963 Equal Pay Act that attempted to address pay discrimination by gender, but this does not move her boss. Peggy: 'I don't know if you read in the paper, but they passed a law where women who do the same work as men will get the same pay, equal pay.' Peggy makes $71.00 more a week than her secretary does and less than her male peers. Unsympathetic, Don cites Sterling Cooper's economic circumstances: 'It's not a good time. It's not going to happen, Peggy, not now. I'm fighting for paper clips around here.' Don gives Peggy a drink, as he does with the men. She persists in her quest. Peggy: 'I don't think I can have been any clearer.' Don is moved neither by assertiveness, nor federal law, nor Peggy's equal contribution to Sterling Cooper ('The Fog', 3:31).

Typically, Peggy quietly accepts Don's perspectives, even when they are sternly delivered, except for his rejection of her request to work on the Hilton account. Courted by Duck Phillips to join a rival advertising firm, Peggy attempts to leverage her 'woman's point of view' to get on the Hilton account. She sees Don on 'a pretence'. Don, angry at the pretence and the request, demolishes Peggy's self-esteem:

> You were my secretary and now you have an office and a job that a lot of full-grown men would kill for. Every time I turn around you've got your hand in my pocket... There's not one thing that you've done here that I can live without. You're good. Get better. Stop asking for things. Close the door.

Visibly shaken, Peggy apologizes for... stepping out of line? offending Don? realizing that she may have threatened her position? Yet, she retains the familiar form of address, 'I'm sorry, Don' ('Seven Twenty Three', 3:33).

Rule 9: The male executives exclude Peggy from information, meetings, decisions and the social life of the company. As a woman creative, Peggy is stoic. She does not become embarrassed, react or fumble when participating in the string of potentially awkward sexist strategy meetings, such as the Relaxicisor campaign (Don: 'From what I understand, it provides the pleasure of a man without the man.') or the Mohawk Airlines account (Ken: 'If you want to go somewhere, go up her skirt.') or the Playtex account (Ken: 'Peggy, do you wear Playtex and, if so, why?' Peggy: 'I do and I agree with the 95 women we surveyed about how well it fits.' Ken: 'I find they both open easily.') With calm confidence and perhaps willing denial, Peggy ignores the sexism and is vigilant about positioning herself inside the agency process ('Indian Summer', 1:11; 'For Those Who Think Young', 2:14; 'Maidenform', 2:19).

Yet, to function successfully in the office, Peggy must also remember her roots as a secretary. Joan, ever mindful of office politics, advises Peggy, as she walks her out of the secretarial pool and into her first office: 'Don't forget that just because you now have a door, once you didn't. Think of the other girls, or they won't think of you' ('The Wheel', 1:13).

Rule 10: At the end of the third season, Peggy rejects Don's offer to join the newly formed Sterling Cooper Draper Pryce agency, until he can see and acknowledge her as a colleague. In their tense encounter in Don's office, Peggy angrily resists his assumption that she is going to come on board. Don: 'I'm not going to beg you.' Peggy: 'Beg me? You didn't even ask me.' Peggy has 'other offers that came with a sales pitch about opportunity.' She reproaches Don: 'I don't want to make a career out of being there so you can kick me when you fail.'

Later, Don goes to Peggy's apartment to apologize and pitch her role in their new relationship. 'You were right. I've taken you for granted and I've been hard on you, but only because I think I see you as an extension of myself. And you're not.' However, Don sees that he and Peggy can both tap into their traumatic lives ('something happened, something terrible... and the way that they saw themselves is gone'). From that profound understanding, Peggy and Don can both design ad campaigns that relate to deep motives on the part of consumers ('nobody understands that, but you do and that's very valuable'). Don: 'With you or without you, I'm moving on. I don't know if I can do it alone. Will you help me?'

Peggy, voice quavering, is concerned they may become estranged: 'What if I say no. You'll never speak to me again.' Peggy is emotional in her desire for a better working relationship with Don, but she is not willing to commit until her professional contributions are appropriately recognized. Don: 'No, I will spend the rest of my life trying to hire you' ('Shut the Door. Sit Down', 3:39). Now part of the team, Peggy joins the start-up. From Cheryl Berman:

> But thank you Matthew Weiner for what I considered a happy ending. I wanted to burst into that room at the Pierre and get down to work. There is nothing more exhilarating than the freedom of starting your own company. I envied this little group of people, who never looked happier. The truth is, many of the famous agencies started just like that, with a handful of people, a few clients, and a dream. I expect some brilliant ideas will come out of that little hotel room. (Berman, '"Mad Men", season three, Episode 13')

Perhaps the role of 'visionary and leader' will be open to Peggy in the fourth season ('Shut the Door. Have a Seat', 3:39).

Peggy's desire for a career is bonded with her desire to move to an apartment in Manhattan. As she moves up at Sterling Cooper, her life outside the office is mostly off-screen. Peggy explains to her sister the reality of her daily life. She has a commute of 'almost two hours total, every day, five days a week. That's an extra week of work each month.' The increase in rent would be offset by not having to pay subway and cab fares and not having pantyhose torn by the ragged seats of public transportation. 'Are you going to be one of those girls?' her sister wonders in awe. 'I am one of those girls', Peggy declares, proudly (even though it was Joan who crafted the fun-loving single girl ad after Peggy's abysmal failure to generate effective copy to search for a roommate) ('The Arrangements', 3:30).

'Those girls' are the 'single girls' of the 1960s. Moya Luckett, in her analysis of the *Peyton Place* television series (ABC, 1964–69), points out that 'the Grace Metalious novel...was the biggest selling work of fiction, as late as 1969.' It examined 'the period's struggle over definitions of femininity' and, Luckett argues, this attention to femininity is 'perhaps its most "progressive" quality'. The novel's popularity 'suggested that conventional representations of female characters as serene, self-sacrificing homemakers, dutiful daughters, or one-dimensional sex symbols were out of touch with contemporary women's fantasies' (Luckett 76, 80).

A single woman living on her own in the city is an ingredient of these contemporary fantasies. *Mad Men* shows only glimpses of Peggy's life outside the office. However, as Sarah Hepola observes in her *Salon.com* review of the second season DVD set, there is a lot to be learned in a '15 second shot'. Hepola leads with a lengthy description of the opening of the second episode. Peggy 'lies on the bed of her cramped Brooklyn, N.Y. apartment the morning after a late-night bash...her room is an artful tangle of clothes tossed across furniture and abandoned in heaps on the floor.' For Hepola, this short shot 'contains a clue' about Peggy: 'the tightly coiled good girl and relentless worker turns out to be a bit of a slob' (Hepola).

In '15 second shots', *Mad Men* offers clues about Peggy's life as a single girl – enjoying herself in crowded bars and clubs, making out with guys in narrow hallways. Luckett observes, in 'the period's single-girl myth, the big city stands for freedom, choice, possibilities, and adventures unfettered by social and moral restrictions' (Luckett 85). As *New York Times* op-ed columnist Gail Collins wryly notes in a *Salon.com* interview with Joan Walsh about *When Everything Changed: The Amazing Journey of American Women from 1960 to the Present*, the sexual revolution was the most popular revolution of the 1960s (Walsh). *Mad Men* has updated the single girl myth and, in the process, the series opens a space for intergenerational conversation between Second Wave and Third Wave women.

Works Cited

Allyn, Jennifer. '*Mad Men* – why gen y women need to tune in', *Forbes.com*. 14 August 2009 at http://www.forbes.com/2009/08/14/mad-men-peggy-olson-forbes-woman-leadership-gen-y.html.

Atterberry, Wendy. 'How Joan Holloway of "Mad Men" gave me confidence', *CNN.com*. 2009 at http://www.cnn.com/2009/LIVING/homestyle/09/07/tf.joan.holloway.confidence/index.html.

Berman, Cheryl. '"Mad Men" Season 3, Episode 7: Recap.' *WSJ.com*. 28 September 2009 at http://blogs.wsj.com/speakeasy/2009/09/28/mad-men-season-3-episode-7-tv-recap/.

——. '"Mad Men", Season 3, Episode 13: TV recap (Season Finale)', *WSJ.com*. 9 November 2009 at http://blogs.wsj.com/speakeasy/2009/11/09/%E2%80%9Cmad-men%E2%80%9D-season-3-episode-13-tv-recap-season-finale/.

Bertsche, Rachel. '"Mad Men" and the real women behind them', CNN.com. 2009 at http://www.bozkurtihsan.co.uk/2009/LIVING/worklife/08/17/o.women.and.mad.men/index.html.

Collins, Gail. *When Everything Changed: The Amazing Journey of American Women from 1960 to the Present*, New York: Little, Brown and Company. 2009.

ForbesWoman Community. 'Top 10 unwritten rules for working women', *Forbes.com*. 20 October 2009 at http://www.forbes.com/2009/10/20/workplace-sexism-gender-stereotyping-forbes-woman-net-worth-leadership.html.

Hepola, Sarah. 'Critics' picks: Secrets of *Mad Men*', *Salon.com*. 22 July 2009 at http://www.salon.com/ent/critics_picks/2009/07/22/mad_men_dvd/index.html.

Karlyn, Kathleen Rowe. 'Feminism in the classroom: Teaching towards the third wave', *Feminism in Popular Culture*. Joanne Hollows and Rachel Moseley, ed. Berg: 2005, 57–75.Karlyn, Kathleen. '*Scream*, Popular Culture, and Feminism's Third Wave: "I'm Not My Mother".' *Genders* 38 (2003): 1-26.

Kearney, Mary Celeste. '"Honey, look what I found in the Special Features!" or When *Mad Men* Pitches Women's Lib.' *FlowTV.org*. 10:08. 19 September 2009 at http://flowtv.org/?p=4283.

Luckett, Moya. 'A moral crisis in prime time: Peyton Place and the rise of the single girl.' Mary Beth Haralovich and Lauren Rabinovitz, ed. *Television, History, and American Culture: Feminist Critical Essays*. Durham and London: Duke University Press. 1999. 75–97.

Rockler-Gladen, Naomi. 'Third Wave feminism: personal empowerment dominates this feminist philosophy.' *Suite101.com*. 3 May 2007 at http://feminism.suite101.com/article.cfm/third_wave_feminism.

Rose, Charlie, 'a discussion of the television series *Mad Men*' with Matthew Weiner, Jon Hamm and John Slattery. *charlierose.com*. 28 July 2008 at http://www.charlierose.com/guest/view/6417.

Strauss, Tamara. 'A manifesto for Third Wave feminism.' *AlterNet.org*. 24 October 2000 at http://www.alternet.org/story/9986.

Walsh, Joan. Interview with Gail Collins. 'Has everything changed for women?' *Salon.com*. 1 December 2009 at http://www.salon.com/life/feminism/index.html?story=/opinion/walsh/feminism/2009/12/01/gail_collins.

Notes

1   The First Wave suffrage movement gained US women's right to vote in 1920. The Second Wave is the Women's Liberation Movement of the 1960s and 1970s. Growing up in an alleged post-feminist world, the Third Wave is a generation of young women who see a need for continued progress for women. For a discussion and history of the relationship between Second Wave and Third Wave, see Kathleen Rowe Karlyn. 'Feminism in the Classroom: Teaching Towards the Third Wave,' *Feminism in Popular Culture*. Joanne Hollows and Rachel Moseley, Ed. Berg: 2005. 57–75.

2   See Karlyn, '*Scream*, Popular Culture, and Feminism's Third Wave: "I'm Not My Mother".' Her essay explores the intergenerational tensions between Second Wave women and young women today.

3   The advertising agency appears to be a good setting for this. Gail Collins finds, in her women's history constructed from interviews and archives, that 'advertising, for all its discrimination, was more open to women than were most business fields' (Collins 26).

4   See the special features on the DVDs of season one and season two for informative discussions of creative roles on the show.

5 See 'Costume Design: Independent Women' and 'Establishing *Mad Men*.' Special Features. *Mad Men* season one DVD; and Jeffrey Sconce, *Facebook*. 24 August 2009.

6 See Sarah Hepola, 'Critics' Picks: Secrets of *Mad Men*.'

7 During Peggy's flashback to her hospitalization for a 'psycho-neurotic disorder' after having the baby, she awakes in a medicated haze to find Don sitting beside the bed. Don leans in to Peggy, his face half in darkness: 'Peggy, listen to me. Get out of here and move forward. This never happened. It will shock you how much it never happened.'

12.
The Best of Everything: The Limits of Being a Working Girl in *Mad Men*
Kim Akass and Janet McCabe

At eight-forty-five Wednesday morning, January second, 1952, a twenty-year-old girl named Caroline Bender came out of Grand Central Station and headed west and uptown toward Radio City. She was a more than pretty girl with dark hair and light eyes and a face with a good deal of softness and intelligence in it. She was wearing a gray tweed suit... Caroline hurried along with the rest of the crowd, hardly noticing anybody, nervous and frightened and slightly elated. It was her first day at the first job she had ever had in her life, and she did not consider herself basically a career girl. Last year, looking ahead to this damp day in January, she had thought she would be married. Since she'd had a fiancé it seemed logical. Now she had no fiancé and no one she was interested in, and the new job was more than an economic convenience, it was an emotional necessity. She wasn't sure that being a secretary in a typing pool could possibly be engrossing, but she was going to have to make it so. Otherwise she would have time to think, and would remember too much.

– Rona Jaffe, *The Best of Everything* (1958) 1–2

A bright, crisp morning in New York City: It is the first day at work for Peggy Olson, the bridge-and-tunnel girl from Bay Ridge, freshly out of secretarial college. A vertiginous sweep of a Manhattan streetscape nostalgically evokes the *North by Northwest* credit sequence. It tells of illusions. Of the deception of images. People scurry ant-like. Taxis cruise by. A revolving door disgorges human traffic. A woman's shapely legs; be-suited men sporting hats and briefcases flood into a building. Paul Kinsey, Harry Crane and Ken Cosgrove enter the elevator. They cannot help but notice Peggy: fresh-faced and virginal; full of hopeful innocence; neatly packaged, if slightly old-fashioned. Catching their eye she quickly turns and looks away, careful not to transgress what propriety dictates. 'Take the long way up', says Ken. He leans into Peggy leering, 'I'm really enjoying the view here.' Peggy uncomfortably bears the weight of their lascivious gaze.

New Dawns: Uncomfortable Beginnings; Poised for Change

Fifty years separate these two narratives – one, a best selling US novel and film from the late 1950s and the other, an award-winning US TV drama series from the late 2000s. Both protagonists start in the typing pool but soon rise through the secretarial ranks. Caroline takes home manuscripts to read, preparing book reports in her own time to further her editorial hopes at the publishing house. Peggy too burns the midnight oil. She quickly demonstrates a flair for writing copy, impressing her bosses with ideas for the Belle Jolie and the Rejuvenator accounts. Half a century apart, but these women have much in common. Taking initiative, aspiring to be more than just secretaries. Desiring independence, wanting the best of everything, although conflicted by what that might mean. But glass ceilings, entrenched misogyny and casual sexism condition aspirations.

Eliminating 40 years of women's rights – of the right to participate equally in the workforce – and retreating into a post-war US dreamscape with its chauvinistic sexual politics leads us to ask, and to borrow from Thomas Elsaesser: Why the *Mad Men* story, why tell it now – and why does this series belonging to an age of supposed emancipation glance backwards to these dislocated shadows of the past, pulling us back to a time when working girls had few opportunities, little chance of escaping the typing pool, and echoing the themes of a novel that electrified a generation on the cusp of revolution?

Neither male nor female critic failed to pick up on the 'chauvinism and often outright misogyny of the year 1960' (Cochrane 24). We could relax, safe in the knowledge that those ghastly days were far behind us. We could be comforted by the fact that 'the women's rights movement of the [1960s and 1970s], which . . . rode "a crest of activism"' (Rowe-Finkbeiner 197), swept away degrading sexist attitudes and gender inequalities. Given that women have supposedly achieved parity in the US workplace, legislated through the 1963 Equal Pay and the 1964 Civil Rights Acts, as well as the 1972 Equal Rights Amendment, prevailing wisdom at the end of the 1980s claimed that substantial gains had been made. Exceeding educational levels of past generations, women were now entering the workforce in unprecedented numbers; and, 'As of 2000, over 80% of women aged twenty-five to thirty-four were working' (115). Recently, it was announced that women have overtaken men and now make up the majority of the American workforce. These are generations who

> reaped the benefits of our mother's struggles and our race and class positions, having grown up with a sense of entitlement so strong that . . . we virulently denied that any form of sexism existed . . . that we [had] the same opportunities, [could] compete with men equally, man to man. (Heywood and Drake, 42)

And yet . . .

Long has the issue of working women been caught up in America's culture wars but since 9/11, argues Susan Faludi, the retreat of working women into domesticity has become a staple of mainstream media and political discourse: 'Talk of married, professional moms dropping out of the workforce to rear kids is all over magazines, talk shows and bookstore shelves' (Aikenhead 8). Faludi contends that the 9/11 attacks on American cities led to a widespread retrosexism, a regressive impulse, which reactivated a uniquely US historical imagining populated with strong manly men and vulnerable damsels. Or, to put it as Faludi does, while 'endeavoring to wish into the present our chosen "likeness of the past" . . . What [are] we struggling to overcome with our 1950s fantasies?' (8).

Such a discourse rigorously tugs at US cultural longing for prescriptive feminine roles, and to borrow from Michel Foucault, 'holds up well, owing no doubt to how easy it is to uphold. A solemn historical and political guarantee protects it' (5). Foucauldian insights have proved particularly fruitful for feminist enquiry into 'the fundamental link between power, knowledge and sexuality' (5). The contribution of feminist theory reveals how female subjectivity is positioned by power into a binary matrix: Subject and object, work and home, productive and reproductive; how power 'constructs' and regulates the feminine self – her body, her choices, her aspirations – in the process of knowing it; and how power's control of it is sustained through 'acts of discourse' (83), subjecting it to 'infinitesimal surveillances' (145) and schematic discussion which allows it 'no obscurity, no respite' (20). Post-feminist ambivalence relates to bringing this knowledge into discourse – but the right to speak is conditioned by politics. It means, often paradoxically, that what gets uttered bears traces of a halting logic.

> As 'feminists' such as Camille Paglia begin to evoke the myth of the femme fatale and push sexual power as a means to achievement and to controlling men, and as Katie Roiphe shrugs off second wave feminist concerns such as sexual harassment and date rape, and as the media at large hails the 'sexy' feminist and the 'return' of femininity, young women have more and more chimeras to fight, and the hard lessons of feminist history are forgotten and lived again. (Heywood and Drake 50)

No wonder we find it difficult to speak about what our liberation should look like, to adopt a different tone in fact (Foucault 6). Just as third-wave feminism redefines 'women as individuals, taking back the objectification of the female body, and forming a more diverse community' (Rowe-Finkbeiner 186), merely speaking unabashedly on the subject of our bodies, our aspirations and lifestyle choices, our pleasures and desires, is no easy matter, often condemning authors to critical opprobrium, theoretical misinterpretation and charges of historical amnesia. As Foucault describes it, 'Something that smacks of revolt, of promised freedom, of the coming age of a different law, slips easily into this discourse on sexual oppression' (7).

Perhaps some progress has been made with the adoption of legislation and gains in employment law; but traces, values, assumptions and old rules remain entrenched. Difficult as the pernicious sexism of *Mad Men* is to watch; shocking as it is to witness how women are complicit in an oppressive system that does them few favours; more alarming still, and despite half a century of social progress and legislative change, is how strangely familiar the world of *Mad Men* looks today. From the David Letterman 2009 sex scandal to how the post-9/11 media speaks ad infinitum about 'opting out', the infertility epidemic and the marriage crisis (Faludi 2007), while exploiting those very stories as a way of knowing the modern working woman. Adjusted to coincide with the latest developments in late-US capitalism, new formulations and ideas appear. But the *Mad Men* text, safely insulated in the recent historical past, provides a discrete space to talk of such matters. 'The past is a foreign country, they do things differently there' (1), to quote L.P. Hartley. It offers sanction: It allows sexism the right to forms of reality – and authorizes *Mad Men* to speak loudly about what is supposedly legislated not to exist (i.e., inequality and discrimination in the workplace – and has no right to exist (i.e., sexual coercion, sexist attitudes and abuses of power).

What sustains our interest in writing about Peggy Olson and Joan Holloway, the working women of Sterling Cooper, is how these seemingly archaic representational types that have fallen out of generic fashion are being revised and given new life on television. And yet this is not a simple remembering; it is about making strange, about the allure of surfaces and their deconstruction. *In* and *through* the dislocation between representation and critique, between silence and language, these women make visible the halting logic of our age of troubled emancipation with its divisive culture wars, uneasy legacy of second-wave feminism and the lingering trauma of 9/11.

Gender Matters I: Acoustic Mirrors and Distorted Desires

Office Manager Joan Holloway is a force to be reckoned with – both within the diegesis of Sterling Cooper and in the scripted performance of femininity enacted by her. Saturated *in* and *through* her generic DNA, Joan reawakens the 1950s Hollywood pin-up fantasy of a voluptuous female sexuality – combining erotic sex with a kitsch glamour. From the moment we first see Joan she commands the space with her 'to-be-looked-at-ness' (Mulvey 14–26). It is her thing, her strategy for asserting *her* authority inside the male-dominated, chauvinistic world of Sterling Cooper. Sashaying through the space. Perfectly fashioned. Impeccably coiffed. She is seductive; she *is* seduction. Paul Kinsey cannot help but swoon in her wake. 'Hello Joan', he says dreamily as she sails by. He quite literally cannot take his eyes off her. Joan stirs up what Molly Haskell calls,

Office Manager Joan Holloway is a force to be reckoned with in her scripted performance of femininity. Courtesy of AMC.

'the fifties' fiction, the lie that . . . she is there to cater to, or enhance a man's needs' (255). If she did not already exist, the ad men of Sterling Cooper would surely have conjured her up as a fantasy to sell nylons and lipstick – an idea of glamour, an icon of desirability, a new female subjectivity defined by consuming, consumerism and being consumed.

Paul may be beguiled by her, but so is Peggy – as are we. Escorting the new girl to her desk, Joan uses the time wisely to instruct Peggy on the sexual politics of Sterling Cooper. Her brevity belies the complexity and nuanced gendered landscape of the office. No instruction about lunch breaks, how the phone works or where the restrooms are from our Joanie. Nothing so simple. Almost purring, she lists the tools of the secretarial trade before offering the advice to which her archetype has long given representation: 'They may act like they need a secretary, but most of the time they are looking for something between a mother and a waitress. And the rest of the time . . . well.'

'Offering us a mistress-class in Laura Mulvey's 'Woman as Image, Man as Bearer of the Look' thesis (14–26), Joan schools Peggy in how she should display herself, 'an appearance coded for strong visual and erotic impact' (19). She instructs her to: 'Go home, take a paper bag and cut some eyeholes out of it. Put it on your head, get undressed, look at yourself in the mirror and *really* evaluate where your strengths and weaknesses are – and be honest.' Once Roger Sterling and Don Draper arrive Joan performs her 'to-be-looked-at-ness' for them – and for us. Her tiny gesture (smoothing down her skirt), her knowing look at Peggy, her sashay, beguiling the men, speaks of a feminine performance that compels us to think of the 'supplicating symbol of sexuality . . . the masturbatory fantasy that gave satisfaction and demanded nothing in return; the wolfbait, the eye-stopper that men exchanged glances over' (Haskell 254).

It is no small coincidence that this female chimera conjured up from a post-war Hollywood cinema resurfaces on a US cable TV channel with a reputation for airing classic American movies: A nostalgic yearning entrenched in and through its programme schedule and film choices. Appropriating filmic representational types – like the 'sexpot' (Haskell xiii) – long peddled in 'classic' Hollywood films, is ingrained in the institutional practices of AMC, but also remembered and revised in this contemporary, post-9/11 US television drama series. Joan consciously exploits the sex-bomb image that men, with their libidinous looks, impose upon her, while understanding the power (however limited) contained within that exhibitionist role. So much so that it explains her visceral reaction to the death of Marilyn Monroe in 'Six Month Leave' (2:9). So devastated is she by the news of Monroe's tragic passing that Joan must go and lie down in a darkened room to mourn. Discovering her in his office, Sterling says, 'Not you too'. She responds simply: 'This world destroyed her'. Monroe had everything and threw it away. Joan warns him that one day he too will lose someone important to him – and it will be 'very painful'. It is an extraordinary moment of candour from a character so cognizant of her spectacle, so seemingly in control of the display of her image.

No better example of woman as erotic spectacle and visual contemplation can be found than when the secretaries are invited to test Belle Jolie lipstick. Sexual imbalance is ordered by a two-way mirror, which in turn determines circuits of pleasure in looking, 'split between active/male and passive/female' (Mulvey 19). On one side are the men of Sterling Cooper, sipping drinks, smoking cigarettes, leering at and heckling the 'chickens' trying on lipstick. On the other are the women. Female exhibitionism is established by the giddy re-action of the secretaries rushing to put on the cosmetic. Painting an image of perfection. The women are invited to consume and take pleasure in their own objectification, gazing into mirrors and scru-tinizing themselves unaware ribald men are observing them. Gen-dered circuits of desire and looking confirm the paradigmatic logic of the cinematic gaze, 'oscillating between voyeurism and fetishistic fascination' (Mulvey 23).

So far, so sexist. Only Joan is aware of the male voyeurs behind the mirror. If, as Laura Mulvey argues, 'The determining male gaze projects its fantasy onto the female figure, which is styled accord-ingly' (19), then it is Joan that compels us to think about these deeply ingrained patriarchal ways of seeing and erotic looking. Whereas the secretaries work at applying that image, Joan displays her body as sexual object, 'coded for strong visual and erotic impact'. She 'holds the look, and plays to and signifies male desire'. Temporarily halting narrative flow; confirming what Mulvey describes as, 'The presence of woman [as] an indispensable element of spectacle in normal narrative film . . . her visual presence tends to work against the de-velopment of a storyline, to freeze the flow of action in moments of erotic contemplation' (Mulvey 19). The camera and its movements (determining her as spectacle through close-up, fetishization of her hour-glass figure) reanimate production practices that have long made such representational forms possible in the first place.

As if to drag us from our visual reverie, our dreamy scopophilia, Ken Cosgrove invites the men to stand and salute Joan after she bends over in front of the mirror displaying her voluptuous derriere for extra erotic allure. Circuits of looking and desire may be diegetically motivated by the 1960s time period, when men believed they had licence to look at, and talk about, women in such an unabashed way, but what *Mad Men* does is to make visible the complex gendered terrain of the public sphere before such attitudes and habits were labeled 'misogynistic' and legislated against as 'sexual harassment'.

If Joan evokes the reflection theories of Haskell, and reminds us of the Mulvey thesis, then it is because the circuits of desire inspired by her representation draw us back to a moment when feminists felt compelled to theorize such cultural forms. These pioneering studies underpinned the radical political action of second-wave feminism and named the problem. Feminism spoke out against patriarchal power and knowledge, pronouncing different truths and determined to change discourse. These writings on the politics of representation presented new knowledge on female oppression, sexual inequality and gender exclusion – and gave language to the feminist movement. What Joanie does with her body – objectifying it, believing she has some agency in that objectification, taking pleasure in that process – thus makes visible the continuing confused and confusing feminist debate about female sexuality, empowerment and the female body as object. Is there empowerment in objectification? Or is it another form of false consciousness and oppression?

We need look no further than the 2009 media reporting of the workplace politics of CBS's *The Late Show with David Letterman*, which uncannily echoes the sexual shenanigans of the offices of Sterling Cooper, to see how this debate reverberates today. As Jill Filipovic says in *The Guardian*, 'Letterman acts like a sleaze, humiliates his wife and is outed as a textbook hypocrite. And he still comes out on top'. This story is not so much about how Letterman has set about his public rehabilitation, or how feminist groups have taken up the sexual harassment in the workplace debate as a ground for renewed political action, but the silence of the women involved with the talk show host. No woman has yet come forward with allegations of sexual harassment. Indiscretion has been shrouded in feminine silence. As author of *Girl on Top: Your Guide to Turning Dating Rules into Career Success* Nicole Williams says, it 'either means we're so much more evolved and no one cares or [women haven't had] the voice with which to complain' (Ravitz). And is this not what lies at the dark heart of *Mad Men*'s gender politics?

In 'Nixon vs. Kennedy' (1:12), Ken Cosgrove drunkenly chasing Allison, one of the secretaries, tackling her to the floor and hiking up her skirt to check the colour of her panties. In 'Long Weekend' (1:10), Roger Sterling asserting his seniority in classic casting couch fashion by mounting a young wannabe and riding her around the office. (His heart attack may be textual retribution but it is short-lived and he is soon up to his old tricks.) Puritanism around sex, sexuality and sexual relations exists in office hours and in bourgeois marriage; but the office party, the hotel room, the cocktail bar become places of tolerance. It is reasoned that the men must make mischief elsewhere. Their behaviour is 'quietly authorized' only in these places where an untrammeled misogyny has 'a right to (safely insularized) forms of reality' (Mulvey 4). Attitudes and male action are enacted in a context, in which the right and privilege to act in this way go unquestioned.

No wonder the women are often left to stand and look on in expressionless silence. Marge turns to Peggy after silently witnessing Ken wrestling the hapless Allison to the ground: 'I used to think I'd find a husband here.' Is this what Joan truly desires from her first season sexual dalliance with Sterling? Or, is it the only way for her to achieve a minute shift in power? Afternoons spent in hotel suites; gifts of birds and stolen intimacy behind closed doors. Never once does Joan confess her affair with Sterling or speak of her desire – even privately. Her discretion insures (limited) access to power, compliance guarantees authority.

It is not long before Joan gets the opportunity to leave her secretarial duties behind in 'A Night to Remember' (2:8), when recently promoted Head of TV, Harry Crane, requires help with vetting the suitability of TV scripts for clients (2:8). He may purport to know what women want, but Joan has done her homework. Reading scripts late into the night, learning how television serial narratives work and identifying the best spots for 30-second commercials makes Joan uniquely qualified to select the most lucrative timeslots for Sterling Cooper clients. The ad men may take charge of a feminine desire and absorb it into the serious business of consumer capitalism; but Joan *lives* that desire. She pitches the perfect strategy. Her skill makes visible the emergent demographics, new subjectivities being identified, spoken about and addressed for the first time. Joan is sent into the meeting with two Maytag executives. Of course the clients like what they see – and what she has to say. What man could resist those womanly wiles?

No sooner has the deal been brokered than Crane replaces the 'hour glass' with another 'suit'. It is a shocking moment. But it should be no surprise. Speaking in and through a representational type that codifies patriarchal fantasies of a feminine ideal is a precarious business; and Joan's participation in *reproducing* the sexist culture of *Mad Men* has deep implications. Crane calls her into his office. He needs Joan to explain to his new hire, Danny, what she has learnt about reading TV scripts and negotiating with the networks. As the exchange of looks makes visible, Joan never owns the gaze – she probably never did.

The scene heralds Joan's return to silent spectacle, only able to speak through those verbose looks, pregnant pauses and loquacious gestures. It is not long after this that fiancée Greg forces himself upon her behind closed doors during office hours in 'The Mountain King' (2:11). It is a confusing moment. Emerging Joan says nothing; and tacitly accepts Peggy's comment that Greg is 'a keeper'. But what *can* she say? What language, in fact, does she have to eloquently speak about what has happened to her on the floor of Don Draper's office? Silent discretion translates into quiet confusion. She is again lost for words when Sterling decides to leave wife Mona and marry the young college graduate briefly hired as Draper's secretary. And, after all, she is politically outmanoeuvred by Jane, who manages to get herself reinstated by Sterling after being fired by Joan, and snaring a gold wedding band into the bargain. Has Jane, not Joan, achieved the best of everything – a home in the suburbs, a rich and powerful husband and no need to return to work?

Gender Matters II: Glass Ceilings and Quiet Aspirations

Unlike Joan, Peggy tries to keep her distance from these circuits of looking and (erotic) desire, wanting to behave differently and change the script; while at the same time remaining deeply conflicted about what that might mean. For no one exists beyond laws governing sexuality and gender politics, but always remain subject to rules, prohibitions and controls. As Foucault observed, '[One] is always "inside" power, there is no "escaping" it, there is no absolute outside where it is concerned' (95). She may be the only woman not to fall under the spell of free samples of Belle Jolie lipstick, but it does not go unnoticed that 'little mouse ears' is not joining in the fun. Peggy is, after all, subject to the same surveillance practices as the other women. When questioned by Freddy Rumsen over why she did not choose a lipstick, Peggy simply answers that her shade had been taken. Setting herself apart from the other women: She is not just another colour in the box. Peggy's answer bespeaks of a different attitude towards female subjectivity: The 'Mad Men' may busy themselves constructing identities and telling women what they want, but it is how women like Peggy struggle for identity *in* and *through* those representations that is at stake here.

Aspiring to be more than just Don Draper's secretary, Peggy, like Caroline Bender in *The Best of Everything* before her, takes her opportunities when she can. After impressing Rumsen with her description of the discarded tissues as 'a basket full of kisses', he later suggests to his colleagues that Peggy write the copy for the Belle Jolie account. What harm can it do? She may come up with new approaches, formulate different ideas, but it is how male authority – their superior status, their perspectives and their right to speak – manages those ideas and put them into discourse that matters: It is about Peggy being given permission to speak; it is how her concepts are sanctioned. She may devise the 'mark your man' campaign, but it is the ad men's translation that renders her words acceptable and useful for the campaign.

The more Peggy establishes herself the more alone and isolated she becomes. Her move out of the secretarial ranks is initially accompanied by a considerable weight gain. (Explained in the first season finale when, much to her surprise, chronic stomach cramps turn into labour pains.) Her changing body shape means that nobody is taking Peggy too seriously. Men dismiss her as unattractive while the women remain uncertain of her motives. She later complains to Joan that she is not being included in memos to the creative team. (Joan tells her that she needs to 'learn to speak the language' of the creative staff, take herself seriously and 'stop dressing like a little girl' in 'Maidenform', 2:6). Unsure of how to market a new weight-loss invention aimed at women, who better to ask than Peggy? The project is abandoned to her in 'Indian Summer' (1:11). Taking the 'Relaxicisor' home Peggy soon discovers its hidden pleasures. The next morning sees her struggling to find words to explain its good vibrations. 'It vibrates, and that coincides with how you wear it', she tells Don. 'It's probably unrelated to weight loss.' Don instructs Peggy to find a way of bringing female pleasures into discourse. Addressing the team, swollen with pregnancy weight, Peggy pitches her campaign: 'Women lose weight so they'll feel good about themselves. Combined with a sensible diet, the Rejuvenator – you'll love the way it makes you feel'. The men love the pitch but remain confused until Don translates the coded message: 'It provides the pleasure of a man without the man'. Humour aside, Peggy's copy offers a new language of female (sexual) liberation. But to speak differently, to adopt a different pose, is an uneasy process and subject to censure.

Peggy knows this process only too well. On the pretext of Christian duties, her priest pays a visit to the office in 'A Night to Remember' (2:8). Father Gill is desperate to elicit a confession. Pregnant throughout season one with Pete Campbell's child, Peggy knows only too well what he wants to hear. But she is not going to put her experience into a discourse that will subject her to endless moral judgment and pastoral recrimination. Foucault tells us that 'to speak about sex is to play directly into power. Telling the truth about one's sex . . . is to relinquish sexuality to the authorities who use the knowledge gained about it for purposes of social control' (15). In a Foucauldian twist, Peggy refuses to speak. Only the relentless clickety-clack of the photocopier can be heard.

Sex for Peggy is a private matter. Her one-night stand with Campbell when he pays her a booty call in 'Smoke Gets in Your Eyes' (1:1); the early morning tryst in his office witnessed only by someone without any legitimacy to speak, the African American janitor, 'The Hobo Code' (1:8); and her liaison with a Brooklyn College engineering student in 'Love Among the Ruins' (3:2). Less about taboo, Peggy recognizes that talking about sex exposes a woman to censure and transforms her desires into a language beyond her control.

Season three finds Peggy maturing as a copywriter (despite Draper's dismissals and rebukes), competing with Princeton graduate, Paul Kinsey, with cleverer ideas and smarter words. In 'Love Among the Ruins' she, along with Ken, Harry and Salvatore Romano, watch Ann-Margret sing 'Bye Bye Birdie', the title song from the hit film of the same name. The client wants a similar look to front the campaign for Pepsi's new diet soda. While the men revel in Ann-Margret's ingénue performance, Peggy is planning the strategy. Asking why men like women in their twenties acting like teenagers, she questions whether this is the best way to attract the targeted female consumer. Immediately her male colleagues think she is talking about her own first season weight gain. Momentarily rattled, fleetingly frustrated by their assumptions about her, she holds strong to her opinion. Draper may later chide her for 'feeling uncomfortable' with how the men responded to Ann-Margret – 'Men want her. Women want to be her' – but Peggy has the last laugh. For her part, she is not averse to mimicking Ann-Margret's sensuality, but Peggy has got it right. Despite doing exactly what the client wants, the advert does not work. The client cannot put his finger on what is wrong with it. But Peggy knows. Her knowing look to Draper says it all. As the series progresses, Peggy pitches new ideas and offers different ways of looking; and in so doing makes visible a new language and way of seeing the world that (post)feminism will later loudly proclaim.

Conclusion

Gendered habits, attitudes and behaviours are carried out in the context in which women struggle in silence, with no language (as yet) to express their ambitions and do things differently. And this may explain why men bond while women remain isolated – forced to go it alone. Peggy must prove herself better than the men. Ensconced at last in a decent office, maybe not the corner one, but next to it nonetheless. Deciding not to go up onto the roof to contemplate the universe with the men, she instead returns to her office with a Dictaphone and bottle of water in 'My Old Kentucky Home' (3:3). Women like Peggy hold out the promise of change, however heavily circumscribed that may be. Her secretary Olive frets about the marijuana smoking, but Peggy reassures her: 'I'm not scared of any of this'. Reminiscent of the feminist conversation with our mothers she tells the older woman, 'I am going to get to do everything you want for me'. But what exactly does that mean?

In a sequence which reworks the Sirkian moment when Jane Wyman is left home alone to consider her reflection in the new TV set bought by her son in *All That Heaven Allows* (1955), Peggy surprises her mother with a new television in 'The Arrangements' (3:4). With Peggy, her mother and sister fleetingly reflected in the screen, Peggy breaks the news that she is getting an apartment in Manhattan, moving out of the old neighbourhood and turning down the offer to stay in the family home. Her mother's response is brutal: 'You'll get raped'. Nothing her daughter can say will appease her mother. Isn't Peggy just trying to buy her mother off with the new television? Peggy must leave nonetheless.

Like the working women from *The Best of Everything*, Peggy and Joan have romantic aspirations for the possibilities of professional lives that liberate them from old familial patterns that traditionally defined them only as wives and mothers. They are not alone. From

Rachel Menken, the Jewish department store owner with romantic yearnings and whose affair with Draper ends with her refusal to run away with him (she later marries Tilden Katz) to Midge the beatnik artist who lives an existentialist morality but ends up in a very conventional relationship. Joan too plays the piano accordion for her husband's colleagues (at least it is not the ukulele). But still.

Time and again women may try to change the scripts of their lives only to find themselves confronted with the same old traditional roles and impossible choices. The pernicious casual sexism of the 1960s may boggle us. It is shocking to see how women are complicit in their own denigration; and more alarming is how we still have not entirely liberated ourselves from those sexual politics, despite half a century of social progress and legislative change.

Works Cited

Aitkenhead, Decca. '9/11 ripped the bandage off US culture', *The Guardian: G2* 18 February 2009: 6–15.

Cochrane, Kira. 'A woman's world', *The Guardian: G2* 5 May 2009: 24.

Elsaesser, Thomas. 'Postmodernism as mourning work', *Screen* 42.2 (Summer 2001): 193–201.

Faludi, Susan. *The Terror Dream: What 9/11 Revealed About America*, Conshohocken, PA: Atlantic Books, 2008.

Filipovic, Jill. 'Letterman's sex isn't a scandal', *The Guardian: G2* 9 October 2009 at http://www.guardian.co.uk/commentisfree/cifamerica/2009/oct/08/david-letterman-affairs-sex-harassment. Accessed on 15 December 2009.

Foucault, Michel. *The History of Sexuality, Volume 1, An Introduction*, New York: Penguin, 1990.

Hartley, L. P. *The Go-Between*, New York: Penguin Classics, 2004.

Haskell, Molly. *From Reverence to Rape: The Treatment of Women in the Movies*. Chicago: University of Chicago Press, 1987.

Heywood, Leslie and Drake, Jennifer. 'We learn America like a script: Activism in third wave; or, enough phantoms of nothing', *Third Wave Agenda: Being Feminist, Doing Feminism*. Eds. Leslie Heywood and Jennifer Drake. Minneapolis, MN: University of Minnesota Press, 2003: 40–55.

Jaffe, Rona. *The Best of Everything*, New York: Penguin, 2005.

Mulvey, Laura. *Visual and Other Pleasures: Language, Discourse, Society.* London and New York: Palgrave Macmillan, 1989.

Ravitz, Jessica. 'Letterman affairs spotlight sex, romance in the workplace', *CNN.com/Living* 7 October 2009 at http://edition.cnn.com/2009/LIVING/10/06/sex.at.work.guidelines/index.html. Accessed on 15 December 2009.

Rowe-Finkbeiner, Kristin. *The F Word, Feminism in Jeopardy.* Berkeley, CA: Seal Press, 2004.

Part Five.
Cultural Memory and
the American Dream

13.
Men Behaving as Boys: The Culture of *Mad Men*
William Siska

'Love and work are the cornerstones of our humanness.'
  – Sigmund Freud (*Civilization and Its Discontents* 48)

The men in the fictional advertising firm of Sterling Cooper feel free
to comment, favourably or unfavourably, in earshot or out, on the
endowments of the women in the workforce. The women toil in
a version of English philosopher Jeremy Bentham's panoptikon, a
central enclosed space in which they can be viewed at all times. Men
work singly or in pairs in private offices that surround the women's
area. Those privileged with corner offices or other large, window-
lined domiciles access well-stocked liquor cabinets at any time of
day to suit any emotion. They light and puff cigarettes ritualistically
and compulsively. Somebody else empties the ashtrays.

If this reads like the description of a latter-day male heaven, think
again. The male employees of Sterling Cooper, save its eccentric co-
founder Bert Cooper, are unhappy, often desperately so. At any rung
of the career ladder, though more frequently towards the bottom,
the spectre of dispensability and fear of backstabbing competition
permeate the atmosphere. What has gone wrong with these self-
styled Mad Men? They were lucky enough to have gotten in on
the ground floor of America's longest-running binge of priming
the nation with consumer goods. Why are they experiencing such
misery? For all the apparent success, riches and gratified egos of the
men of advertising circa 1960, and the vicarious pleasure or amused
outrage we take in watching them flout rules of behaviour that bind

us in our own time, by analyzing the reality beneath the image, we find in *Mad Men* a stern, even subversive critique of American capitalism and consumer culture.

The post-structuralist Michel Foucault made his mark by provocatively overturning items of conventional wisdom accepted by most people in the late twentieth century. In the first volume of *The History of Sexuality*, he rejected the notion that Victorian abjuration of displays of sexuality bespoke a profound repression, and argued that our contemporary hyper-sexualized advertising and popular culture was itself evidence of neurosis and inhibition regarding sexuality. In this assertion, Foucault places himself in the tradition of Sigmund Freud, who theorized in *Beyond the Pleasure Principle* that in the neurotic individual's conscious motivations often mask unconscious drives much the opposite. Thus, the overtly hedonist Roger Sterling (who came to power the old-fashioned way: his father was co-founder of the firm) rationalizes his excessive smoking, drinking and womanizing as a pursuit of life's pleasures – just payment for having survived the terrors of World War II combat. In contrast, this behaviour can be read as an unconscious desire for his own demise.

These theories are impossible to prove, but provide a useful template for understanding the male culture of *Mad Men*. In Matt Weiner's series, what appears to be the celebratory cataloguing of the behavioural indulgences of adult alpha males during the period of economic expansion in 1960s America turn out to be symptoms of regression, the 'acting out' of a longing to return to a pre-industrial way of living. The formula of the 'workplace as family' ('tribe' might be a more accurate term sociologically) has been a network television staple for 40 years, and some of the medium's most successful and highly regarded shows fit this paradigm. Beginning in the 1970s with *M*A*S*H* (CBS, 1972–83) and *The Mary Tyler Moore Show* (CBS, 1970–77), TV showed us workplaces that performed important social functions in high stress environments that brought the participants into close friendship with each other. More recent manifestations of this formula are *Boston Legal* (ABC, 2004–08) and *Grey's Anatomy* (ABC, 2005-present). In the most honoured of these programmes, *The West Wing* (NBC, 1999–2006), the running of the United States government itself is seen as a process accomplished by a cohort of workers coalescing as a family, mutually supportive and uniting against outsiders, of whom even the President's wife is treated as a problem to be solved rather than as a member of the group.

The formulation of the early German Swiss sociologist, Ferdinand Tönnies, regarding the shift from a pre-industrial and highly rural society to an industrial, urbanized citizenry helps explain the popularity of these programmes and the psychological function they fulfil. Tönnies theorized that in pre-industrial Europe persons were united by common bonds – by shared beliefs, interests and blood – into a gemeinschaft, a community based on friendship. In the gemeinschaft, an individual is valued for who he or she is, existence alone confers value. With the move to cities, where persons are given tasks of building and operating complex commercial and social institutions, individuals experience a separation from their communities and from the security their social identity once gave them. Now they are in a gesellschaft, a formal social organization based on the contract, where people's sense of worth, indeed their very survival, is based not on who they are but on how they fulfil their end of a contract, on what they can deliver to another, often impersonal company or institution (De Fleur and Ball-Rokeach 143 ff).

'Workplace as family' programmes work out a social fantasy of turning the gesellschaft into a gemeinshaft, providing reassurance that though the individual must labour to fulfil his or her contract, the real reason for being in the workplace is because it provides a stronger sense of community than exists in the world outside it. Family life outside the workplace rarely intrudes into the worlds of *M*A*S*H* and *Mary Tyler Moore*. One can logically speculate that this formula has resonated so strongly with American audiences of the last 40 years because the typical working American spends half his or her waking hours surrounded not by family, but as part of an arbitrary group of persons thrown together to perform tasks, and it's comforting to think that in a social environment that provides for our livelihood based on what we can deliver, we can still be appreciated for who we are.

Network television has always seen itself constrained to present life in the workplace as comedy rather than drama or tragedy, and it is no surprise that all the popular series mentioned earlier are comedies. Police procedurals such as *Law & Order* (NBC, 1990-present) and *CSI: Crime Scene Investigation* (CBS, 2000-present) provide representation of the opposite experience of the world outside the home, playing on audience fears of life 'outside' in our impersonal and highly competitive commercial society. *Mad Men* more realistically turns this formula on its head, moving the paradigm from comedy to drama. The fantasy is still there, that the workplace (Gesellschaft) can embrace us as community (Gemeinschaft), but the energy for this comes not from an overlay of a bourgeois wish-fulfilment ideology onto workplace shows, but as an expression of the emotional needs of the characters in the drama itself.

At the centre of *Mad Men* and commanding its screen time is its lead, Don Draper (Jon Hamm), the Sterling Cooper advertising firm's 'golden boy'. Novelist Barbara Kingsolver says, in reference to her novel *Lacuna*, 'the most interesting thing about a character is what we don't know about him' (*Bob Edwards Weekend*). If this is true, the opacity of Don Draper on *Mad Men* solidifies his position as the show's lead, for disclosure of crucial parts of his backstory are intentionally withheld from the audience to be revealed at moments that heighten the drama of his situation at the time of revelation. Gradually, we learn about his hardscrabble upbringing, his birth to a prostitute and his biological father's early death. We learn in a jolting episode the mystery of how he came to change his name in an attempt to wipe out his wrong-side-of-the-tracks roots. But even after three years we don't know how he came to court and win Betty, his wife, nor how he has risen to the prestigious and powerful position of creative director at a mid-sized advertising firm.

Jon Hamm and the character he portrays has been promoted as a 'new-old' romantic leading man, in the mould of iconic strongmen of few words like Clark Gable, Gary Cooper and John Wayne. It is Cooper that Jon Hamm most resembles physically. The Cooper persona is shy, even deferential around women, and in moments of tense conflict never loses his composure. Cooper said little, and let women talk. This, according to biographer Jeffrey Meyers, allowed women to share their inner feelings with him, and that made them love him all the more.

Don Draper seems to be cast in this mould. Joy, the youthful hedonist who seduces him on his California trip tells him, 'You're beautiful and you don't talk too much' ('The Jet Set', 2:24). He can therefore become hers and other peoples' fantasy. Don's reticence can also come across as cold and disinterested. Don often doesn't have much to say to other people because he just doesn't care all that much about them. He doesn't have room in his psyche for anyone else. Indeed, Don veers so close to being an unsympathetic protagonist, with his resistance to his wife Betty's emotional needs and his serial betrayals of his marriage, his lack of affect and his general unavailability towards his children until the last few episodes of season three, that he seems sometimes not worth the effort of the characters close to him or similarly of viewers to stay with him. Don challenges everyone not to care.

Yet the intensely loyal audience of *Mad Men* stays with him week after week because Don Draper is a character on an inner quest for self-understanding and self-acceptance. He is a common character in the best American literature of the last half of the twentieth century – Bellow's Herzog, Updike's Rabbit, and Roth's Zuckerman. Don is opaque to us because he is opaque to himself. His 'man of mystery' exterior is an expression of his inner life; he's a figure who knows he wants to escape his past, is frustrated by his present, but by the end of season three is only beginning to formulate an idea of where he wants his future to lead.

The first clue to understanding Don's troubled psyche occurs in 'The Marriage of Figaro' (1:3) where the claustrophobia induced by the domestic demands of his daughter's birthday party leads to a panic attack. Don drives off to fetch the birthday cake and fails to return until after the guests have left, taking his car anywhere just to keep moving. The audience's knowledge that something is wrong with Don is challenged by the suave, cool certitude with which he handles his job and his co-workers. Initially, Don appears a near descendent of the 1950s 'Man in a Gray Flannel Suit' overcome by anxiety, but as events unfold we come to see him as an anxious and insecure adolescent who hasn't fully accepted the entitlement of his position.

Flashbacks during season one reveal two critical facts of Don's existence that fly in the face of his identity as a crack Madison Avenue executive with the glamorous wife, comfortable suburban home, and substantial bank account. During a flashback in 'The Hobo Code'(1:8), however, young Don is shown as dirt poor, raised by a diffident stepmother whose remarriage to a brutal man results in Don being treated as a pariah in his home. In this episode, an out-of-work Depression era wanderer shows up at his parents' farm begging for work. Don instinctively identifies with the man and wants to help him. This incident echoes Don's psychic state as a lost man despite his surface persona as a leading advertising executive, and prefigures the wandering 'hobo' he will become in season two when he flees his family and work in California.

So repelled is the young Don by the life he might return to after the Korean War that when his commanding officer dies in a freak battlefield accident, Don exchanges his identity with the dead man ('Nixon vs. Kennedy', 1:12). With this act, Don Draper becomes a quintessentially American figure, shedding his past to reinvent himself, unaware that the tenuousness of the re-created self will lead him to doubt his own authenticity. Don's flight from his past and desire to become a different person leads him into some despicable behaviour. When Don's admiring younger half-brother Adam shows up in Manhattan, having come in search of some recognition from his successful sibling, Don rejects him harshly ('5G', 1:5) and his brother eventually commits suicide ('Indian Summer', 1:11).

Don's several affairs are affronts to his wife Betty and threaten his family life, but he pursues them relentlessly, out of a need for both escape and self-definition. The women he chooses are remarkably similar to each other and contrast strongly with his wife. With the exception of the sybaritic Joy, all are women with professional identities that give them an independence that his stay-at-home wife Betty lacks. Midge, the commercial artist, and Rachel, the department store heiress, are conspicuously dark-haired compared to Betty's icy-blond coiffure. The affairs end when Don flirts with deeper commitment by suggesting rash flights from his present-day reality by asking Midge to move with him to Paris ('The Hobo Code', 1:8) or Rachel to run away with him to San Francisco ('Nixon vs. Kennedy', 1:12). The women are not lost souls, however, as they confidently move on with their lives instead. In their own ways, Midge and Rachel are mirror images of Don, and in his affairs with them, he is looking at, and looking for, himself.

In screenplay parlance, the hero's mirror is the character who can talk back to the hero and get him to level with himself, which is what occurs when Don flees the perfect image of a cardboard marriage for the arms of other women. The hip Midge brings Don into a circle of Greenwich Village bohemians in season one, but their aimlessness, arrogance and judgmentalism repels him. His season two sojourn in California leads him first into a brief liaison with Joy and her family of tanned hedonists, proving only to Don that he can't live a life of useless indolence ('The Jet Set', 2:11). In that same journey he reconnects with Anna, the wife of the real Don Draper, and relives his early post-Korean life as her surrogate husband. In this episode, Don learns that he cannot live a buried life as a blue-collar married man, working on hot rods in the alley with the guys ('The Mountain King', 2:12).

Still, Don is unsure of what in his life is worthwhile. Midge questions his choice of work in season one, as does the idealistic school teacher Suzanne in season three. Don admires Suzanne for her dedication to both her demanding vocation and her lost and ungrateful brother. 'Are you dumb or pure?' he asks her in admiration, though this only points up his own lack of purpose ('Wee Small Hours', 3:35). Don is feted by Sterling Cooper as the embodiment of the American Dream, moving from an obscure background to prominence in the advertising profession ('The Color Blue', 3:36). Ultimately, it is an empty and sad occasion for Don; he is a 'golden boy' who hates himself in spite of his own good luck.

Don is a foundling, a Moses or Huck Finn character; Bert Cooper reminds Don that he has come from nothing and could be returned there if he doesn't sign the contract the firm has placed in front of him ('Wee Small Hours', 3:35). Don has behaved with an air of exceptionality. He flouts his independence with frequent unexplained absences from the office; he is an individualist in the age of the organization man. Bert and 'Connie' Hilton, the legendary high-profile client he lands and loses, recognize the unique perspective Don's individualism gives him that the more conformist executives lack. At the same time, they paradoxically feel obliged to rein him in: Bert with the contract; Connie with his rigid and unrealistic demands.

If Don is a character who exhibits significant neurotic symptoms, his cohorts at the top, Bert Cooper and Roger Sterling, are no less 'Freudian' in their behaviour. Bert's eccentricities are modelled after Howard Hughes, who was compulsive about cleanliness and sequestered himself in luxurious quarters well-separated from his employees. Don and Roger do not even grin conspiratorially as they remove their shoes before entering the president's office, as Bert's power precludes them from finding him humourous.

The male patriarchy that rules in *Mad Men* insists that women want to present themselves for men's delectation in ways that men choose. They assert that what they want to see is either Marilyn Monroe or Jacqueline Kennedy. They also believe that all women want to be either one of the other ('Maidenform', 2:9). Office manager Joan Holloway is an almost cartoonishly top-heavy version of Marilyn, and gets her share of looks; Draper's new secretary, Jane Siegel, is a Jackie who becomes an increasingly troublesome trophy wife for firm partner Roger. Beyond that, though, the men think of Marilyn and Jackie less as cultural figures than as convenient icons to facilitate the sale of brassieres. When news of Marilyn Monroe's sad death of a drug overdose at age 36 in 1962 spreads through the office, the males take little notice; only one of the secretaries and later Joan express strong emotions over her death ('Six Month Leave', 2:22).

In fact, the advertising executives in *Mad Men* seem remarkably detached from the events of the day. They take a fleeting interest in aiding – gratis – the campaign of Richard Nixon, but when the politician's operatives don't follow up, the lukewarm Republicans at Sterling Cooper return to their moneymaking pursuits. The first thing that strikes us about *Mad Men* is that they are not mad in being capable of outrageous creativity, but instead, they are mad as being angry at the way the higher-ups dismiss their efforts and frustrate their ambitions. The title 'Mad Men' is a moniker the advertising aces apparently gave themselves, playing on the location of their firms' offices on or around Manhattan's Madison Avenue, and to give the illusory impression that their jobs were filled with madcap excitement and the freedom to imagine.

The relatively well-off young executives of Sterling Cooper are doing alienated labour but are not wholly aware of this situation. They blame their unhappiness on other things, usually the failings of their wives to excite them in the way they thought they deserved. Pete cannot maintain a healthy sexual relationship with his wife, and becomes a predator taking advantage of women of lower social status, as he does with Peggy during the first few episodes of season one as well as later on with Gudrun, a young European nanny in his apartment building ('Souvenir', 3:34). It's not until the end of season two, when the firm is sold to a British corporation that cares only about advancing its bottom line that the lower level executives at Sterling Cooper begin to realize their unease stems from their own work environment. These characters are descendants of W. H. Auden's four ennui-ridden urbanites in his 1948 long poem 'The Age of Anxiety', melancholic souls adrift in a dreary world of commerce.

One way Weiner and his creative team depict this theme is through the early 1960s set design and décor. The ad men at Sterling Cooper sweat to sell products for profit rather than for the improvement of society, and the dissonance between their energy and talents and the purpose to which they are put is best expressed by the office furniture. Stern sharp lines, hard surfaces and muted colours reflect the impossibility of soul craft in such a space. Only the crassest of human interactions take place in the offices of Sterling Cooper, such as Roger's after-hours exploitation of a young aspiring model on the office rug ('Long Weekend', 1:10), and the myriad muggings and betrayals of co-workers that pepper each episode, such as Pete's attempt to blackmail Don in order to secure a promotion for himself the easy way ('Nixon vs. Kennedy', 1:12).

When account executive Ken Cosgrove publishes a short story in *The Atlantic*, the combination of envy and admiration that this accomplishment arouses in his male peers suggests a traditional cultural hierarchy that values literary art over crass commercial enterprise ('5G', 1:5). Still, the junior executives at Sterling Cooper are not overly cynical about their profession. While Richard Yates' acclaimed novel of unhappiness in the 1950s corporate milieu *Revolutionary Road* is an influence on *Mad Men*, its embittered would-be writer Frank Wheeler stands in marked contrast to the young advertising men in *Mad Men*. Pete, Paul, Ken, Harry and Sal never talk down about the work they do. They instead follow the lead of legendary advertising guru David Ogilvy who exults in any kind of advertising that sells a product. In *Confessions of an Advertising Man* (1963), Ogilvy begins with the basic premise that a product should be something consumers want to buy, if only they had the facts. The integrity of the advertisement is therefore connected to the quality of the goods to be sold.

What sets Don Draper apart is a much more contemporaneous attitude towards selling than the one espoused by Ogilvy. Don presciently tells a client and assembled co-workers in *Mad Men's* inaugural episode that 'advertising is based on one thing, happiness. And you know what happiness is? It's a reassurance that whatever you are doing is okay. You are okay' ('Smoke Gets in Your Eyes', 1:1).

Despite a sense of privilege, advertising men Ken, Harry, Sal, Paul and Pete are generally unhappy, often desperately so. Courtesy of AMC.

For Don advertising is a metaphor for moving beyond the traditional concern with a product's quality to the personal preoccupation with how the consumer feels when he or she consumes it. If Don can create a sense of satisfaction in a consumer buying one of the products he's selling, whether it is an item in Menken's department store or a night in one of Conrad Hilton's hotel rooms, there is also a chance that Don might one day find that same kind of happiness for himself.

Mad Men is a show told in hindsight. It carefully plays up the audience's image of the 1960s as a decade of tumultuous social upheaval rambling headlong towards cultural modernization. Part of the show's critique of the culture at Sterling Cooper lies in the nonchalance with which the advertising executives ignore the tidal wave building up behind them. Pete Campbell's wife retreats to the Jersey shore for the duration of the October 1962 Cuban Missile Crisis, but with few other expressions of fear, the work of selling continues unabated. Only Peggy and the European 'youth' brought in reluctantly as a bellwether for the buying tastes of the new generation share the excitement of discovering Bob Dylan, and rock music in general seems not to exist. You wouldn't know that the last works of the giants of twentieth-century American literature, Faulkner and Hemingway, were finding their way posthumously into print, and that Updike's Rabbit, Bellow's Herzog, and Philip Roth's stories of suburban discontent were imminent.

Mad Men, like other historical allegories, is about the time in which it is set and about the time in which it is produced. Up through Halloween 1963, the range of experiences of the Mad Men has been narrow and cloistered. The penultimate episode of season three, 'The Grown-Ups' (3:38) encompasses 22 November 1963, and the dazed weekend that followed. *Mad Men* dramatizes the Kennedy assassination as a sea change that rocked the American psyche and lifts the veil of safety and innocence behind which Americans discover they have been fecklessly living. Roger Sterling lamely tries to rally the decimated crowd at his daughter's 23 November wedding to some degree of joy with little success. Several scenes later Don Draper says to Peggy Olson, 'We know things will never be the same', which holds special meaning for current viewers because they can relate to the similarly life-changing events of 11 September 2001.

This sombre episode is then followed by 'Shut the Door. Have a Seat' (3:39), which is one of the liveliest in the whole series. 'Shut the Door. Have a Seat' is fast-paced and crowded with incidents that dramatically reboots the drama and revivifies Don Draper with a reenergized personality. Don's bravado returns as he transforms from an enervated and beaten man faced with divorce and the dismantling of his picture-perfect suburban family to a charismatic leader exhorting Bert Cooper to abscond with him from the resold Sterling Cooper to strike out on their own with a brand new advertising firm.

He becomes a humble supplicant to both Roger Sterling and Peggy Olson, convincing them to sign on to the new venture, despite their resentment at Don's past behaviour to them. In 'Shut the Door. Have a Seat', we see Don transformed from a boss to a leader. The importance of Don's transformation to shore up his vulnerable identity is revealed in a powerful flashback as young Don watches his father, stretched past breaking by low Depression era grain prices, pull out of a farmer's cooperative to go it alone. Fortified by drink which encourages his hot temper, he unwisely bends down behind a horse in his barn, which kicks him in the head killing him instantly. Don will not repeat the ill-advised act of independence that brought down his father in such a stubborn and short-sighted way.

'Shut the Door. Have a Seat' also possesses the verve of a 'caper' film like Robert Redford's *The Hot Rock* (1972) or *Sneakers* (1992) as the partners of Sterling Cooper arrange for their own dismissal, then bring into their conspiracy the man who fired them (Lane Pryce), while also collecting the other men and women they need to pull off the 'heist' and set up their own shop. The 'caper' recalls Howard Hawks' last films with John Wayne, *Hatari!* (1962), *El Dorado* (1967) and *Rio Lobo* (1970), which share the same narrative pattern, in which Garry Wills writes in his insightful *John Wayne's America,* 'an improbable band uses its combined skills to overcome its obvious flaws.' Wills continues, 'The "caper" need not be a crime . . . it can be any feat that a disparate little band pulls off against long odds'(275). 'The high-spirited cooperation' of the people in the band gives this kind of narrative its tone and removes any possibility of tragic results (276).

When the remaining employees show up at the emptied offices of Sterling Cooper on Monday morning, pipe-smoking Paul Kinsey is visibly dismayed that he is not one of the chosen members of the group. There is much pleasure to be taken in the formation of the new members of Sterling Cooper Draper Pryce, as one person after another is added, akin to the gathering of the gunmen in *The Magnificent Seven* (1960). Don insists, 'We need an art director', leaving the door open for the wrongly fired Sal Romano to eventually be taken back by the re-energized band.

A signature characteristic of *Mad Men* during its first three seasons has been its toughness, its hard edge both in its treatment of characters whose less appealing qualities have been allowed to shine along with their sympathetic and amusing sides. Leaving the ravaged confines of Sterling Cooper for the last time, Don remarks that he never wanted to work in a place like this one anyway. The new workspace is an upscale albeit homey suite at the Pierre. For example, nerdy Harry Crane gets comfortable and right to work by eagerly claiming the bed as his desk. The 'workplace as family' theme is given a certain added nuance by the ambience and layout of the location.

Mad Men will tell its Busby Berkeley, 'Let's put on a show' story of the birth of a new advertising firm, and we will get a dramatization of the skills that Don Draper possesses, which have always made him a respected creative advertiser and a leader who inspires his subordinates. The sensibilities of Weiner and his team suggest that the workplace worlds of *M*A*S*H* and *Mary Tyler Moore* are ideals that might flourish for a time, but the new firm will inevitably develop its own fissures and intrigues that marked life at Sterling Cooper, because that is the eventual consequence of corporate capitalism.

The regressively 'boyish' behaviour of the men at Sterling Cooper has never been a desire to recapture authentic feelings of childhood. None of the men, so far as we know, had an idyllic upbringing, especially Don Draper and Pete Campbell who apparently grew up in familial atmospheres that were cold, harsh and unfulfilling. Instead, the mad men behaving as boys in this series demonstrate a desire to escape to a future free of the tensions and need for conformity required by corporate America. The founding of a new company by a group of enthusiasts results in a temporary gemeinschaft: the reason Roger and Don must coax Peggy and Pete to join them is to assure them that they are wanted for who they are, and not just for what they can do. But the cracks in the armour of good feeling in this gemeinschaft are fated to appear and grow because the demands of the gesellschaft require that persons be evaluated by how well they fulfil the contract. As Charlie Chaplin's character tells the court that judges him at the end of *Monsieur Verdoux* (1947): 'Business is a dirty business.' Tension caused by the desire for gemeinschaft relationships in a gesellschaft world will inevitably bedevil the 'boys' of *Mad Men* in the seasons to come.

Works Cited

Bob Edwards Weekend. 'Interview with Barbara Kingsolver', 14 November 2009.

De Fleur, Melvin L. and Ball-Rokeach, Sandra. *Theories of Mass Communication*, New York: David McKay, 1975.

Foucault, Michel. *History of Sexuality Vol. 1: The Will to Knowledge*, London: Penguin, 1976.

Freud, Sigmund. *Beyond the Pleasure Principle.* James Strachey, trans. with a biographical introduction by Peter Gay, NY: W. W. Norton and Company, 1990.

Freud, Sigmund. *Civilization and Its Discontents.* James Strachey, trans., NY: W. W. Norton and Company, 1969.

MAD MEN

Meyers, Jeffrey. *Gary Cooper: American Hero*, New York: William Morrow, 1998.

Ogilvy, David. *Confessions of an Advertising Man*, New York: Dell, 1963.

Wills, Garry. *John Wayne's America*, New York: Touchstone, 1997.

Yates, Richard. *Revolutionary Road*, New York: Vintage Books, 1961.

14.
The Strange Career of *Mad Men*: Race, Paratexts and Civil Rights Memory
Allison Perlman

Over the course of its first three seasons, *Mad Men* has continually coupled the gorgeousness of its mise en scène with the ugliness of its characters' actions. The glamour of their clothing and hairstyles, the decadence of their drinking and smoking and the sleek style of their workplace are juxtaposed with their sexist barbs, anti-Semitic views and, most importantly, blindness to the racial discrimination that is so much a part of their fictional lives. Set in the early 1960s, *Mad Men* certainly is not the first popular text to address racism during the Civil Rights era and to position shifting race relations as an integral part of how we remember the 1960s. Yet unlike other narratives, *Mad Men* finds racial discrimination in the modern offices of a New York advertising agency and the posh suburban homes of its executives, rather than in the brutal climate of the Jim Crow south. A shocking expression of racism takes the form not of physical violence rained down on innocent African Americans, but of the blackface serenade by the head of a prominent ad agency who sings lyrics of old 'darkies' for his guests' amusement ('My Old Kentucky Home', 3:29). *Mad Men* offers a revisionist look at race relations in this era. The power of its critique is enhanced by reading the series intertextually, in recognizing the ways in which *Mad Men* overturns how previous popular texts have coded and defined what was Civil Rights in the early 1960s.

Mad Men's paratexts – those extra-textual features that surround a text and contribute to how audiences approach and interpret its meanings, such as promotional posters, DVD special features, interactive websites, reviews, interviews with cast and crew – paradoxically work to authenticate the show as an accurate representation of the past, others operate to undermine the central historiophotic[1] critique of the series itself, especially on the topic of race relations. *Mad Men*'s official website and the special features on its DVD box sets serve many of the same functions media scholars have identified as the crucial work of paratexts; they privilege certain readings of the episodes, establish showrunner Matthew Weiner as the series' auteur and reiterate the myriad ways the series should be seen as 'quality' television.[2] *Mad Men*'s paratexts have the additional task of certifying the series as a history lesson and verifying the accuracy of its depiction of the early 1960s. In audio commentaries, web interviews, and a 'making-of' documentary, Weiner and his cast and crew underscore the authenticity of nearly every facet of the mise en scène, and discuss the meticulous research conducted for each *Mad Men* episode. In addition, the '1960s Handbook' (online) and the 'time capsules' (DVD) offer viewers features that flesh out, and verify the historical legitimacy of references embedded in the programme. Significantly, though, the paratexts on Civil Rights also undermine *Mad Men*'s central critique of popular memory of race relations.

This chapter examines the interaction between *Mad Men*'s depiction of race relations in the 1960s and the treatment of Civil Rights in the online and DVD special features that accompany the show. It explores how *Mad Men*'s narrative challenges what counts as the history of racism and race relations in the early 1960s and overturns many of the hallmarks of Civil Rights narratives presented in popular film and television. The essay then investigates how its paratexts undo this critique by reasserting conventional narratives about the Civil Rights movement, while also reinforcing hegemonic meanings implicit in its legacy.

TEXT: *Mad Men*'s Revisionist History of Race Relations

Popular media has continually played an important, if not controversial role, in Civil Rights history, historiography and popular memory. Scholars have noted how television broadcasts, during what historians have labeled the 'classic civil rights era', publicized the campaigns of activists, made visible the racism and injustice African Americans encountered in the southern United States, and elicited the sympathy of moderate whites for the cause of Civil Rights. These broadcasts also have provided an archive of the Civil Rights era, utilized in documentaries and museum exhibits on the history of Civil Rights; the existence of this footage has yielded powerful audio-visual evidence of this past, though one that often limits how to remember Civil Rights through the events and individuals captured by the television camera. *Eyes on the Prize* (1987) series, for example, draws on these texts and in mapping its seminal documentary history of Civil Rights replicates the emphasis on leaders and iconic encounters found in the Civil Rights telecasts (Bond 2001; Torres 2003; Brasell 2004).

Throughout the 1980s and 1990s, films and television series took the Civil Rights movement as their focus or backdrop, and provided consistent narrative tropes and messages to audiences on how to remember Civil Rights struggles. The overwhelming majority of these narratives contain racism and Civil Rights activism to the southern United States. They tend to centre on white characters who either unlearn their racism through their encounters with noble, virtuous black people (e.g., *The Crisis at Central High*, CBS, 1981; *Heart of Dixie*, 1989; *The Long Walk Home*, 1990; *I'll Fly Away*, NBC, 1991–93), operate as the heroes of the Civil Rights movement who fight more uneducated, working class whites on behalf of black victims (e.g., *Mississippi Burning*, 1988; *Ghosts of Mississippi*, 1996), or function as innocents whose colour-blindness contrasts to the racist society that engulfs them (e.g., *Forrest Gump*, 1994; *American Dreams*, NBC, 2002–05). The black characters who appear in these narratives, what *Time* media critic Richard Corliss (2003) labels 'fables of reassurance for white folks', often are not fully developed individuals but, in Corliss's words, 'props for their white neighbours' learning curve' in which an 'orphan child or stray puppy would serve the same function' (16). These films and television series ultimately offer a triumphalist narrative of racial progress in which racism, embodied by redneck southerners, is tamped out and American ideals of equality and justice are affirmed and strengthened. These texts simultaneously ask viewers to acknowledge the violence and discrimination of the past and comfort that, through excising bad people for the national body, Americans have overcome this blight on their history (Graham 2001; Montieth 2003; Fuller 2006; Morgan 2006; Hoerl 2008, 2009).

Mad Men has offered an alternative narrative of race relations in the 1960s in multiple ways. The Civil Rights movement is directly integrated into the show through the Civil Rights subplot in its second season, in which copywriter Paul Kinsey travels with his African American girlfriend to Mississippi, and via the radios and televisions within the show's diegesis that report and chronicle iconic events of the Civil Rights era. In addition, African American characters are consistently part of the mise en scène as elevator operators, doormen, food cart vendors, maids and janitors. Except for the Draper's maid Carla, African Americans are largely invisible to our main characters even though they do much of the labour that enables their worlds – both occupational and domestic – to function. The presence of African Americans on screen both lends credence to the atmospheric racism that is part of the show's narrative and provides opportunities for the main characters to exhibit the spectrum of prejudices held by whites towards people of colour. In each of these ways, *Mad Men* disrupts the familiar 'fables of reassurance' of other texts and challenges the tropes of Civil Rights narratives that had been circulating since the 1980s such as the aforementioned *Mississippi Burning* and *The Long Walk Home*.

Though racism has been part of the series since its first scene, when a black waiter is put back in his place by his white boss, the series avoids discussing the Civil Rights movement until its second season when Paul Kinsey has a romance with an African American woman and a brief foray into Civil Rights activism. Within the œuvre of Civil Rights representations, Paul is an atypical Civil Rights hero: he lacks the moral sensibility, personal integrity or commitment to civic equality that often defines these characters. Instead, like Norman Mailer's 'White Negro', Paul's investment in African Americans has more to do with his own search for meaning and style than a commitment to the rights and lives of actual black people.

Within the first season, Paul is set up as the character most likely to take an interest in Civil Rights. Paul remarks in episode '5G' (1:5) that he had written a story about hanging out one evening with 'a bunch of Negroes' where they 'all got along'. He then asks, 'Can you imagine how good that story is?' Paul's comment both attests to a segregated social world and the improbability of forging personal relationships across the colour line. It also exposes his own fetishization of African Americans and his sense that to be accepted by them would confer something special and authentic upon him. When, in 'Flight 1' (2:15), Paul introduces Joan to his African American girlfriend Sheila, the narrative leaves open the possibility that he is dating her to show, 'how interesting' he is, as Joan puts it. Their romance is revealed in the context of Paul's party, in which he denounces the cultural barrenness of New York, prances around with an ascot featured prominently around his neck and displays openly the typewriter he had stolen from the offices of Sterling Cooper. Paul, by this episode, had been established as the office blowhard, one whose countercultural aspirations are signified by the absinthe in his office and the dreadful play he's written in his desk drawer ('Nixon vs. Kennedy', 1:12). His romance with Sheila can be plausibly read as another pretension to cultivate his bohemian credentials.

Though he initially is reluctant to make a trip to Mississippi to register voters with Sheila, preferring to go to California on business, Paul ultimately joins the Civil Rights struggle ('The Inheritance', 2:23). Paul's motives are questioned twice in this episode. When Sheila gets angry that Paul had not prioritized this trip, he asks impatiently 'Can't it wait?' Later, he agrees to 'make a stand' with her only after Don decides to go to Los Angeles in his stead. As he tells Sheila that he'll go, he grumpily shoves his airline ticket and badge into an envelope. At best, these two scenes undercut Paul's commitment to Civil Rights; at worst, they reveal his decision to travel south is an act of petulance and resentment about his work environment that he sees as undervaluing him. When Paul returns two episodes later, he is hailed as 'our man from the evening news' and he states that he believes they 'made a difference' in their work and it was 'the adventure of a lifetime'. The hollowness of these claims is quickly underlined. The conversation shifts when the lads learn that fellow copywriter Peggy Olson had been given a new large office, and Paul exclaims, 'Why don't you just wear Draper's pants?!' ('The Mountain King', 2:25). In this scene, Paul's outrage is unleashed by the politics of office assignments, seemingly more so than the brutality and injustice he must have witnessed while in Mississippi. The courageous white northerner has been recast as a buffoon whose participation signifies an act of personal pique rather than a commitment to racial justice.

If the series denies admiration for Paul's actions, it also emphasizes how cavalierly all the characters in the series respond to the Civil Rights struggles going on at the time. While in the south, Paul's colleagues at the ad agency discuss and watch on television the riots that accompanied James Meredith's enrolment in the University of Mississippi ('The Jet Set', 2:24). References to James Meredith are woven into a conversation in which topics jump from work concerns (marketing deodorant to women) to the merits of popular culture (an episode of *The Loretta Young Show*). In a sentiment that will be echoed by Betty Draper in season three, Harry Crane scolds the integrationists for stirring up trouble in the south, while his colleagues briefly shake their heads over the riots in between discussing lunch plans. As the mid-level staff at Sterling Cooper watch President Kennedy address the mob violence at Ole Miss on television, they engage in office gossip and appear nonplussed by what they are seeing. The television reporting that exposes the violence inflicted upon Civil Rights workers elicits neither moral outrage nor a rethinking of racial politics from its white viewers; instead, it operates as another mundane topic of conversation, one that is secondary to the insular politics of office life.

This use of Civil Rights broadcasts recurs in season three when in the 'Wee Small Hours' (3:35) Don and schoolteacher Ms. Farrell listen to a bit of Martin Luther King, Jr.'s 'I Have a Dream Speech' on the radio and later when the Drapers' maid Carla listens to King's eulogy of the four girls murdered in the Birmingham church bombing. The two scenes parallel each other in a couple of ways: Don and Carla both go to turn the station rather than continue listening to the broadcast, only to be advised by Ms. Farrell and Betty, respectively, that they should leave it on. Ms. Farrell tells Don that she'll read King's speech to her students, and responds to Don's query of whether they'll understand it with 'they already know it', while Betty expresses tepid dismay over the bombings then says to Carla that perhaps the time is not right to push for Civil Rights. Ms. Farrell's comment registers as naïve, perhaps poetic in its sentiment but entirely unsubstantiated in its claim – she teaches an all-white student body in an affluent suburban school with youngsters whose only contact with African Americans is with the domestic help employed by their parents. Betty's comment misunderstands the urgency of Civil Rights activism, here exposed by the innocent young victims of an act of horrifying violence. While quite different in sentiment, both comments seem inappropriate: one for its hippie-dippy idealism; the other for being unfeeling and callous.

These moments – the Ole Miss riots and the King speeches – are significant both for how they are integrated into the narrative and for how characters within the series respond to them. *Mad Men* denies viewers the iconic *images* associated with southern Civil Rights: white mobs attacking peaceful activists and the visual footage of King delivering his speech in Washington. Instead, the focus remains on our characters' reactions, which are alternately blasé, simplistic or dismissive. The responses of *Mad Men*'s characters, furthermore, trouble the way we have imagined radio and television broadcasts of Civil Rights to have mobilized northern white support, igniting the moral outrage of their audiences. Here, our primary characters are seemingly unaffected by what is happening, and their behaviours and political commitments remain superficial or untouched by the broadcasts.

In addition to the explicit referencing of the Civil Rights movement, *Mad Men* has also continually challenged how we understand race relations in the 1960s. In its first season, racism functions as a backdrop, but never a primary storyline in which viewers witness casual acts of racial discrimination. In the first scene of the series, a white waiter behaves rudely towards a black waiter, whom Don defends and interrogates on his cigarette preferences ('Smoke Gets in Your Eyes', 1:1). Pete Campbell, put out for having to share an elevator with an African American janitor, chastises the African American elevator operator who had brought him into the car ('The Hobo Code', 1:8). Paul, as he tries to charm Peggy, teases an African American food cart vendor, who responds cordially to the light-hearted if insulting barb ('Ladies Room', 1:2). *Mad Men*'s atmospheric treatment of racism fills out the portrait of racial discrimination beyond horrific acts of violence to include not only more subtle expressions of prejudice – mundane condescensions, snide remarks, and belittling attitudes as well as forms of economic discrimination that constrain the opportunities of African American workers.

Importantly, the show presents racism not as a peculiar and hazardous facet of southern culture, but as a form of prejudice that infects the entire country, including its northern urban centres. Almost all of the white characters in the show exhibit racial prejudices.

In the world of *Mad Men*, racism is not equated with lack of education, income or manners; rather, it is as much a part of the world inhabited by our characters as their fedora hats, martini lunches and incessant cigarette smoking. One of the most controversial moments of the series occurs in its third season ('My Old Kentucky Home', 3:3) when Roger Sterling serenades his young bride and their guests at a Kentucky Derby party by singing 'My Old Kentucky Home' in blackface. The powerful and affluent on *Mad Men* are perhaps the worst practitioners of racial prejudice, and the programme destabilizes the comforting gestures of previous popular narratives where racism is the sole purview of the poor and the uneducated who cling to their hatred, but who ultimately can be excised from the rest of the community for their bad behaviour.

Mad Men topples the 'fables of reassurance for white folks' by reframing how we remember Civil Rights and race relations in the 1960s. Through both explicit references to the Civil Rights movement and the attitudes and behaviours of its characters, *Mad Men* challenges the nostalgic view of previous popular texts such as *Ghosts of Mississippi* and *The Crisis at Central High* that racism was the purview of bad individuals in the south, while the justness of the Civil Rights struggles was apparent to most thoughtful white citizens, who rooted out the horrors of racism when they became visible and thus restored the ideals of justice and equality. This intervention is undone by the series' paratexts, however, which reassert dominant and familiar narratives of the Civil Rights era.

PARATEXT: Reaffirming Civil Rights

Both *Mad Men*'s official website and its DVD box sets have included features, or paratexts, to not only promote and extend the pleasures of – and viewer investment in – the series, but also to legitimate the series as a history lesson and construct for viewers how to read *Mad Men* as a window onto the past. The DVD 'time capsules' and the web-based '1960s Handbook' entries affirm the appropriateness of the material objects, political events and cultural texts embedded in *Mad Men*'s individual episodes.[3] Importantly, the Civil Rights paratexts reinscribe the hegemonic construction of race relations that the series seeks to displace. They thus operate paradoxically to authenticate *Mad Men*'s faithfulness to historical chronology and to undermine the series' critique of our popular memory of the Civil Rights era.

The '1960s Handbook' on James Meredith, for example, narrates a progressive history of southern racial integration. The feature begins with lyrics to Bob Dylan's 'Oxford Town', a song that chronicles Meredith's struggles in integrating Ole Miss. It then discusses not only Meredith's legal battle to gain entry into the university, but also the mob violence that met him when he enrolled. The short piece quotes Constance Baker Motley, Meredith's attorney who suggests that though people 'have forgotten about it', this event marked the 'last battle of the Civil War.' The handbook entry ends with an overview of Meredith's 'varied' career – including his work advising Jesse Helms – and the legacy of his struggles vindicated when he was able to see 'his son graduated first in his class from the university with a doctorate in business administration' (Koo 2008, 'James Meredith'). This short piece on Meredith hits many of the notes typically associated with the Civil Rights era: the viciousness and brutality of southern racism, the import of the battles over legal discrimination, and the ultimate triumph of Civil Rights activism that paved the way for today's more equitable society. The opening quotations from Dylan's song, which sympathizes with Meredith's plight and excoriates white brutality, acknowledges and reiterates the position of the white outsider (Dylan) who champions the cause of Civil Rights activism.

Similarly, the '1960s Handbook' on King's Birmingham Church Bombing Eulogy provides a brief overview of the facts of the bombing and the Birmingham Campaign and quotations from King's eulogy. Though the post offers that the bombing marked 'one of the darkest hours of the Civil Rights movement', it suggests that it galvanized '[o]utraged citizens – both black and white' to join the movement, and inspired musicians to compose songs about the tragedy. In addition, the post ends by intimating that the bombing and King's eulogy helped usher in the 1964 Civil Rights Act, stating that 'without the tragedy in Birmingham, it might very well have been much longer' for this important piece of legislation to pass (Neuman 2009). Much like the 'James Meredith' piece, this paratext emphasizes the viciousness of southern whites and the compassion and solidarity of liberal-minded whites, and offers a victorious conclusion – here signified by the Civil Rights Act – to southern struggles.

The 1960s Handbook web feature and the time capsule that accompany 'The Inheritance' (2:23 – the episode where Paul and Sheila travel to Mississippi) reiterate these themes, yet are odd departures from the other evident paratexts. They provide brief histories of the Freedom Riders. This choice is curious, because the Freedom Rides are never mentioned in *Mad Men*. Paul and Sheila go south to register voters, not to test – as the Freedom Riders did – a Supreme Court ruling that banned segregation in public transportation facilities. The Freedom Rides took place in 1961, whereas *Mad Men*'s second season takes place in 1962. The Freedom Riders paratexts are outliers, the only supplemental features to provide the context and significance for a historical reference not explicitly mentioned in the series. However, such a choice is consistent with how *Mad Men*'s paratexts narrate the history of Civil Rights.

The web feature on the Freedom Riders emphasizes that the individuals who participated, both black and white, were heroes and victims, risking violence and arrest to test the Supreme Court decision that integrated interstate travel. The violence and brutality that met the Freedom Riders combined with their tenacity to continue their journey, according to the 1960s Handbook entry, forced President Kennedy to involve the federal government and to enforce desegregation. Labelling the Freedom Rides as 'an important milestone in the Civil Rights movement', they are credited with enabling people of all 'race, color, or creed' to ride any bus or train or use any facility (Koo 2008, 'Freedom Riders'). Congressman John Lewis is singled out as one of the Freedom Riders, who has been a member of Congress for over 20 years.

The Freedom Rides time capsule is narrated by Jeffrey Sammons, history professor at New York University, and Robert and Helen Singleton, both of whom had participated in the Freedom Rides. The short documentary crosscuts between talking head shots of Sammons and the Singletons and images from the Civil Rights era. They establish the historical conditions for the Freedom Rides of 1961: the cold war context, in which American claims of a free society rung hollow against evidence of domestic racism; the nonviolent orientation of the activists, who ironically were jailed for testing the limits of federal law while those who beat them were not; and the import of transportation as a stage for Civil Rights activism, and segregation laws that limited behaviours signified and reinforced a system of racial hierarchy. Sammons suggests that the Freedom Rides may not have immediately brought about change, but certainly contributed to the environmental shifts that ended segregation. The time capsule ends with Robert Singleton discussing the day that Obama was elected, and how he and fellow Freedom Riders reflected that they helped knock down some of the barriers that enabled this victory. He remarks, 'We didn't want the president to have to ride at the back of the bus.'

While the time capsule offers a more thorough account of the Freedom Rides, both paratexts offer a triumphalist narrative in which the activists ended a particular form of segregation and paved the way for the more equitable society we now inhabit, embodied by the long political career of John Lewis (mentioned in the Handbook) and the election of Barack Obama (discussed in the time capsule). In addition, the Freedom Rides were a form of true interracial cooperation in which white activists put their bodies on the line as much as black activists, a moment when the lines between good (the riders) and evil (the mob of white southerners) were clear. The paratexts affirm the nobility and courage of black and white Civil Rights activists who successfully root out the racism that impeded the full integration of African Americans. Like the other special features, they reiterate familiar tropes of Civil Rights narratives and suggest a progressive narrative of race relations in which the cruelties and inequalities of the past had been challenged and eradicated by the actions of brave individuals.

In addition, all of these paratexts provide what the series itself has denied viewers: iconic images of southern Civil Rights struggles. Each of the Handbook posts are accompanied by photos that show white and black activists (Freedom Riders, James Meredith) and the mourning of black victims of white violence (King's Bombing Eulogy). The time capsule showcases myriad images of brutality towards African Americans (the back of a man who had been whipped, for example, and an image of a lynching) and of Civil Rights leaders and activists, including photos of King. These images underscore the pathos of the narrations and legitimate the urgency of Civil Rights activism described in the texts.

Conclusion

Mad Men presents another side of race relations in the 1960s, over-turning what historian Emily Rosenberg (2003) has termed 'event-centered history' (188) by showcasing decidedly unheroic, often disinterested, and sometimes callous responses to the Civil Rights movement in the 1960s. To be sure, *Mad Men*'s treatment of Civil Rights, like much of the series, is open to multiple readings. As the sumptuousness of the show's mise en scène constantly foregrounds the past-ness of the series, we can view the racist comments, actions and attitudes of the characters as a relic of an earlier era, the ugliness beneath the beautiful surfaces on parade in the programme. On the other hand, by expansively exposing racism and by showcasing an indifference to discrimination and inequality, the series indicts nearly all white Americans in the propagation of injustices. *Mad Men* provokes white viewers to think through their own complicity in less dramatic forms of racism and to question whether the myriad ways that racial discrimination operated in our society then have been truly upended.

By constructing a narrative of progress that defines *de jure* dis-crimination as *the* fight of Civil Rights and that asserts that legal inequality was overcome, popular Civil Rights narratives have sug-gested that the sins of the past have been eliminated and that racism is no longer a major problem in the United States. Such narratives, as Jacqueline Dowd Hall (2005) has argued, have served the politi-cal agenda of the New Right as they imply that the victories of the Civil Rights era have yielded a 'color-blind' society, whereby any programme or policy that considers race is by definition racist – even those looking to remedy past discriminations – and in which any achievement gap between communities is understood to be the result of the personal failures of individuals, not systemic or struc-tural inequalities. The stakes in how we remember Civil Rights are still important, as they can structure how the past is mobilized to prop up political positions in the present (Montieth 2003; Hall 2005; Morgan 2006). *Mad Men*'s more subtle treatment of race relations rejects many of the hallmarks of how we have remembered the Civil Rights movement and thus throws into question the reassuring mes-sages of racial equality and progress offered by other popular texts. In its exposure of the pervasiveness of racial discrimination, the series requires us to consider the legitimacy of claims to 'post-racism' or of a 'color-blind society', especially those that point to the legal victories of the Civil Rights era as evidence. The triumphalism of *Mad Men*'s paratexts, not only is out of sync with the tenor of the programme, but also works against the important revisionism of the series.

Perhaps this is just what paratexts do. The tension between *Mad Men*'s text and paratext is not confined to the issue of race relations. For example, while the Port Huron Statement – a seminal document of the New Left – is sanitized of its political critique and quickly co-opted for a coffee advertising campaign in 'The Gold Violin' (2:20), its time capsule reaffirms how the document captured the idealism of the early 1960s and evokes the 2008 election, the Obama presidency, and the subsequent surge in participatory democracy as its inheritance. The Cuban Missile Crisis, which provides the backdrop for 'Meditations in an Emergency' (2:26), is presented as a time of fear and uncertainty, and focuses on the terror experienced by individuals outside the halls of power, while its time capsule rehearses the familiar chronology of the crisis and the clever diplomatic manoeuvrings that brought about its end.

In the weeks leading up to the premiere of season three, AMC similarly launched a number of promotional tie-ins which included a Banana Republic clothing line based on the fashions of the series and cocktails inspired by the show that were served in hotel bars in New York. Viewers could also create avatars bedecked in the style of *Mad Men* characters by using the site's 'Mad Men Yourself' application, while profile photos of Facebook friends and Twitterers appeared for a time as animated *Mad Men*-inspired characters, martini in hand, cigarette in mouth, and dashingly dressed in outfits resembling those that had appeared in the show. On *Mad Men*, the fashion and habits of the characters underscore the repressiveness and rigidity of gender expectations in the early 1960s. The costumes accentuate and underline the physical and social differences between men and women, as well as the copious drinking and smoking, which expresses the discontent that otherwise cannot be voiced in their milieu. In siphoning off and decontextualizing these and other elements of the mise en scène, the tie-ins relegate the historical reconstruction of the series to its style and fashion and erase the incisive criticism of the era's gender politics that they signify. *Mad Men*'s promotions ultimately inoculate the critique of the series, much as the '1960s Handbook' and DVD 'time capsules' have done.

History and memory are always processes of selection, of determining which facets of the past – which events, perspectives, ideas and sensibilities – are remembered and which discarded. One of the primary allures of *Mad Men* has been its recovery of a 1960s previously absent from our collective memory of the decade. *Mad Men* offers us the conditions that spurred the social movements of the decade – the repressive gender roles and pervasive prejudices – rather than a heroic narrative of those who fought them. *Mad Men* does not reassure, as some texts have, that the struggles of the 1960s delivered the nation into a more just and equitable society. Its critical depiction of race relations is consistent with the series' revisionism and importantly challenges the celebratory and triumphalist narratives that have dominated how we remember Civil Rights. Consequently, it has denied viewers the reassurance that accompanies most nostalgic looks at the past which typically suggest that we are the inheritors of a better world than the one that previously existed. Instead, the idealism in *Mad Men* is restricted to the advertising campaigns that Sterling Cooper's creative staff designs.

And to its paratexts. They reassert the nostalgic and familiar narratives of the past that *Mad Men* explicitly questions. While *Mad Men* undermines celebratory glances backwards, and refuses audiences the pleasures of seeing wrongs righted, of injustice challenged, of racism eradicated, its paratexts do just that. Thus in extending viewer engagement with the series, the paratexts simultaneously sanitize its historical critique and undo the pessimism that engulfs its reconstruction of the 1960s. If the series asks its viewers to look at the ugliness beneath the glamour and to reckon with whether we see ourselves in it, the series' paratexts return our glances back to more comforting narratives about the past, allowing us to take the gaze off ourselves and return it to where it more comfortably rests: on familiar iconic images that signify the triumph over prejudice which is characteristic of a 'color-blind' society that some would have us now believe we have achieved.

Works Cited

Bond, Julian. 'The media and the movement: Looking back from the Southern Front', *Media, Culture, and the Modern African American Freedom Struggle*. Ed. Brian Ward. Gainesville: University Press of Florida, 2001, 16–40.

Brasell, R. Bruce. 'From evidentiary presentation to artful re-presentation: Media images, civil rights documentaries, and the audiovisual writing of history', *Journal of Film and Video* 56.1 (2004): 3–16.

Brookey, Robert Alan and Westerfelhaus, Robert. 'Hiding homoeroticism in plain view: The *Fight Club* DVD as digital closet', *Critical Studies in Media Communication* 19.1 (2002): 21–43.

Corliss, Richard. 'Flashbacks in black and white', *Time* 13 January 2003: 16.

Fuller, Jennifer. 'Debating the present through the past: Representations of the Civil Rights Movement of the 1960s', *The Civil Rights Movement in American Memory*. Eds. Renee C. Romano and Leigh Raiford. Athens: The University of Georgia Press, 2006. 167–196.

Graham, Allison. *Framing the South: Hollywood, Television and Race during the Civil Rights Struggle*, Baltimore: The Johns Hopkins University Press, 2001.

Gray, Jonathan. *Show Sold Separately: Promos, Spoilers, and Other Media Paratexts*. New York: NYU Press, 2010.

Hall, Jacqueline Dowd. 'The long Civil Rights Movement and political uses of the past', *Journal of American History* 91.4 (2005): 1233–63.

Hills, Matt. 'From the box in the corner to the box on the shelf: TVIII and the cultural/textual valorisations of DVD', *New Review of Film and Television Studies* 5.1 (2007): 41–60.

Hoerl, Kristen. 'Burning Mississippi into memory? Cinematic amnesia as a resource for remembering civil rights', *Critical Studies in Media Communication* 26.1 (2009): 54–79.

———. 'Mississippi's social transformation in public memories of the trial against Byron de la Beckwith for the murder of Medgar Evers', *Western Journal of Communication* 72.1 (2008): 62–82.

Koo, Carolyn. '1960s Handbook: Freedom Riders', *Mad Men*. 8 October 2008. Web. http://blogs.amctv.com/mad-men/2008/10/freedom-riders.php. Accessed on 18 October 2009.

———. '1960s Handbook: James Meredith', *Mad Men*. 16 October 2008. Web. http://blogs.amctv.com/mad-men/2008/10/james-meredith.php. Accessed on 18 October 2009.

Monteith, Sharon. 'The movie-made movement: Civil rites of passage', *Memory and Popular Film*. Ed. Paul Grainge. Manchester: Manchester University Press, 2003. 120–43.

Morgan, Edward P. 'The good, the bad, and the forgotten: Media culture and public memory of the Civil Rights Movement', *The Civil Rights Movement in American Memory*. Eds. Renee C. Romano and Leigh Raiford. Athens: The University of Georgia Press, 2006. 137–66.

Neuman, Clayton. '1960s Handbook: Martin Luther King Jr.'s Birmingham Church Bombing Eulogy', *Mad Men*, 13 October 2009. Web. http://blogs.amctv.com/mad-men/2009/10/martin-luther-king-birmingham-eulogy.php. Accessed on 18 October 2009.

Parker, Deborah and Parker, Mark. 'Directors and DVD commentary: The specifics of intention', *Journal of Aesthetics and Art Criticism* 62.1 (2004): 13–22.

Rosenberg, Emily. *A Date Which Will Live: Pearl Harbor in American Memory*. Durham: Duke University Press, 2003.

Torres, Sasha. *Black, White, and In Color: Television and Black Civil Rights*. Princeton: Princeton University Press, 2003.

White, Hayden. 'Historiography and historiophoty', *The American Historical Review* 93.5 (1988): 1193–99.

Notes

1 I employ Hayden White's (1988) term historiophoty, the 'representation of history and our thoughts about it in visual images and filmic discourse' (1193) as opposed to historiography, the representation of history through written discourse.

2 Media scholars have identified a number of functions of paratexts: they privilege readings and confer value (aesthetic, moral, educational and political) on a text; they can establish generic expectations and can gesture to a preferred or targeted audience; they often reinvigorate an auteurist approach and can privilege authorial intention as a mode of textual analysis (Brookey and Westerfelhaus 2002; Parker and Parker 2004; Hills 2007; Gray 2010).

3 The 'time capsules' include topics drawn from popular culture (e.g., Marilyn Monroe, *The Man Who Shot Liberty Valance*, 1962; *The Defenders*, CBS, 1961–65), social history (e.g., 'hot rod' culture, the restaurants Lutece and Sardi's, Maidenform brassieres), art and design history (e.g., Mark Rothko, Jackie Kennedy's renovation of the White House), and political history (e.g., the Port Huron Statement, the Freedom

Rides, the Space Race, and the Cuban Missile Crisis). Many of the topics of these time capsules first were addressed as '1960s Handbook' posts. The variety of topics covered in the 'time capsules' and the handbooks reinforce *Mad Men*'s emphasis that what counts as history is not only the political events that come to define an era, but also its cultural milieu and the sensibilities and perspectives that such texts reveal.

15.
Mad Men: A Roots Tale of the Information Age

David Marc

Appreciation of forbidden acts from a safe distance has always been among the compelling attractions of drama. In the franchise series that have dominated network drama in recent decades (*CSI: Crime Scene Investigation*, CBS, 2000-present; *Law & Order*, NBC, 1990-present; *NCIS: Naval Criminal Investigative Service*, CBS, 2003-present), those acts are almost always murders, often committed in conjunction with other horrific crimes bearing antique pedigrees, such as sexual and/or family violence. With so much TV production energy given to homicide, relatively sparse attention is paid to another compelling attraction of drama: the self-examination of society through depictions of contemporary manners in what amounts to consideration of society's lesser crimes, de facto and de jure. What little there is of this in the popular police procedurals[1] is typically packed into facial expressions and one-liners delivered by hard-working police officers at the crime scene as they note, with a kind of wistful disgust, the evident debauchery of the not-so-hard-working spoiled rich kids, ruthless executives, religious fanatics, amoral trendoids, and pathetic loners who do most of the killing.

Other popular scripted hour-long dramas, such as docshows and ocshows, are focused on other types of death, and do little to take up the slack in depicting borderline social behaviour. Medical dramas as different in tone as the piously romantic *Grey's Anatomy* (ABC, 2005-present) and the existentially haunted *House* (Fox, 2004-present) tend to rely on the psychological dysfunctions of characters to create dramatic tension. While predisposed viewers are free to blame society, writ large, for driving everybody nuts, contemporary medical series are not big on exploring cultural particulars. They rarely, for example, build episodes around the wellness messages that are so much a part of middle-class culture: red-meat eating, artificial sweetening, sedentary living, and the like. An old-school reason for the reluctance persists: calling attention to public health issues can play havoc with sponsorship options from here to rerun eternity.

There is a more recent concern as well: death by lifestyle has become the bread and butter of television news, a genre whose writers and editors are highly skilled at sounding alarms without assigning blames. Occult dramas, from *Buffy the Vampire Slayer* (WB, 1997–2001; UPN 2001–03) and *Angel* (WB, 1999–2004) to *True Blood* (HBO, 2008-present) and *Vampire Diaries* (CW, 2009-present), position themselves to scoff at the bourgeois shallowness of human-American life, but rarely make good on the promise. Their voracious need for supernatural exposition – 'sorry, that spell only works if performed by a virgin on a Thursday because . . .' – leaves little time for developing the particulars necessary for a convincing critique of manners.[2] That job, once at the heart of situation comedy, now falls almost exclusively to a distinctive subgenre of animated sitcoms (e.g. *King of the Hill,* Fox, 1997–2009; *The Family Guy,* Fox, 1999–2002 & 2005-present), perhaps because the mask of 'kid stuff' affords a degree of jester's privilege to cartooning. Since cable competition liberated comic drama from the lively battles the genre fought during the 1970s with the old network Standards and Practices offices, sitcoms have generally exercised their passion for free speech by testing the limits of one-liner vulgarity in an endless permutation of non-traditional family set-ups.[3] Among sitcoms using onscreen actors, *Scrubs* (NBC, 2000–08; ABC 2009-present) is perhaps the only recent success that can claim the legacy of *The Mary Tyler Moore Show* (CBS, 1970–77), *All in the Family* (CBS, 1971–79), and *M*A*S*H* (CBS, 1972–83).

Mad Men does not fall gracefully into any of the major genres of television drama, past or present, which helps explain its freshness as well as why it was passed on by HBO and other networks higher than AMC in the first-run-series pecking order. At first glance, *Mad Men* can be mistaken for a self-consciously retro prime-time soap about rich big shots in a glamorous racket living lusty, sinful, hypocritical lives in the big city; *Dynasty* (ABC, 1981–89) on the Hudson. But loyal viewing reveals a complex hybrid drawing energy from multiple sources: an oddball crime show primarily concerned with misdemeanors, in which guilt is in the eye of the beholder more often than on the books; a gothic medical sci-fi series in which a team of specialists are paid by corporations to experiment on the psyche of a nation; and an occult tale where, behind the mounds of data generated by taste tests and focus groups, dark arts rule. There is even a suggestion of post-*Smallville* (WB, 2001–06; CW 2006-present) Metropolis in a series whose main character crash-lands in prime time, complete with secret identity, Euclidian jaw and powers beyond those of mortal men. It does not, however, take a Braniac to discover that *Mad Men's* definitive dramatic qualities grow from its setting in time and space.

A New York advertising agency in the 1960s hasn't been seen on a hit television series since *Bewitched* (ABC, 1964–72) used Darren's office at McMann & Tate as a secondary location.[4] Although Madison Avenue circa the New Frontier has a wealth of features to commend it as an ideal setting for TV drama (including glamour, sophistication, product placement opportunities and plausible appearances by male and/or female models at any given moment), it has been avoided like the plague for more than 40 years by generations of television producers, probably because they had no stomach for feasting on the hand that feeds. Supported by a full sponsorship package, Matt Weiner has staked a credible claim on one of the last great tracts of virgin mythic territory in post-television American cultural history. After all, it was on Madison Avenue during the Sixties that the ice was broken for any number of the public conversations that continue to resonate in American society. Whether the subject is birth control (including abortion), cancer-causing products (including cigarettes) or the evolution of species (including humans), advertising has been there to mark the cultural battlefields upon which the chattering classes wage war.[5] *Mad Men* is a glimpse at the big bang of the universe seen through the lenses of CNN, MSNBC, and FOX News.

Broadcast Advertising and the Birth of Neo-conservatism

Radio, which was invented in the 1890s to solve the age-old practical problem of two-way communication between ship and shore, did not become a significant mass entertainment or advertising medium until the late 1920s. It almost didn't become an advertising medium at all. Political conservatives opposed allowing commercials on the radio, fearing that the traditional cultural authority of family, church and school would be undermined by tradespeople. Some, including Secretary of Commerce Herbert Hoover, the ranking federal official in charge of broadcast regulation during the Coolidge Administration, supported a tax on radios to the production of radio programming, giving the United States a 'public option' in broadcasting, similar to the UK's British Broadcasting Corporation.[6] On the political left, opposition to radio advertising was based on a desire to resist corporate control of a medium that was likely to have its most profound impacts on those with little education or access to culture. All objections, right and left, were ignored by Congress. By the time Hoover was inaugurated as president in 1928, commercial radio had made itself a fact in the air. In what may qualify as the first blush of American neo-conservatism, the interests of retailers to pursue markets (i.e., consumerism) had trumped the interests of both traditional conservatives and progressives. A milestone was reached in equating consumerism with the public interest.

The 1927 launch of the National Broadcasting Company, the first commercial radio network, assured advertising its primary role as the business of American broadcasting. Even so, many in the advertising establishment were slow to embrace radio. It was only in the past half-century that advertising had evolved into a respectable profession from an artisan trade known for producing hand bills, painted signs and sandwich boards. The rise of mass-circulation periodicals redefined the advertising business, giving it a literary pedigree. No longer a business for printers and sign painters, the emerging profession attracted Ivy Leaguers who saw themselves as educated people of refined taste whose defining professional talent was an ability to apply the scientific principles of psychology in the interests of their clients. The effectiveness of magazine advertising was spectacular and, along with wealth, it brought an unexpected degree of cultural power to the profession.

Long-held customs and taboos were undermined by ad campaigns. Women in large numbers were convinced to smoke cigarettes in public by sophisticated magazines. Men were discouraged from maintaining facial hair by ads for shaving products. By the turn of the twentieth century, it became apparent that advertising could be used to sell personal problems as well as products to alleviate them. In *Dirt on Clean: An Unsanitized History*, Katherine Ashenberg offers an instructive example. An ad for Odorono [pronounced, 'odor; oh, no'], one of the first deodorant soaps, appeared in a 1919 edition of *The Ladies Home Journal*, depicting a woman in short sleeves extending her arm in front of a man's nose, confident that Odorono is protecting her from the possibility of 'a certain odour.' Considered pornographic by Victorian standards in its frank reference to a body function, the ad led hundreds of readers to cancel subscriptions to the *Journal*. Even so, sales of Odorono rose by 112 per cent within a year of the ad's appearance (Ashenberg. 247–8). The founders of the industry achieved profits, status and power through the magazine publishing industry.

John Young and Raymond Rubicam, young colleagues at a Philadelphia agency, were among the first to understand the potential of radio advertising. They quit their jobs and opened Young & Rubicam (Y&R) in New York, making broadcasting the house specialty. Y&R billings jumped from $6 million in 1927 to $37 million during a ten-year period that otherwise included the shank of the Great Depression. Well prepared to take advantage of the television boom after the Second World War, Y&R saw billings surpass $100 million in 1951, even though only the largest metropolitan areas had television service at this point.[7] In the 1960s, Y&R was first to produce colour commercials. Meanwhile, blue-chip 'full-service' agencies, such as J. Walter Thompson (named after its founder, the 'father of magazine advertising') and BBD&O, were large enough to take advantage of the broadcasting bonanza without soiling any of the old hands in the executive suite. They used their considerable resources to produce fully sponsored network programmes for their clients, and signed the most popular stars of vaudeville and the movies as hosts and spokespersons.

Sterling Cooper, as we learn in the early episodes of *Mad Men*, is neither an innovator nor a blue-chip house. Its middling status is best revealed in frenzied efforts to land big-time clients in the hopes of inflating its billings and reputation. In 'Flight 1' (2:15), for example, Duck Phillips (Mark Moses), an accounts manager whose personal life is in disarray, floats the idea that American Airlines is looking for a new agency to remake its image after a plane crash. Sterling Cooper jumps the gun and drops a loyal client, Mohawk Airlines (a regional carrier based in upstate New York), to pursue what turns out to be Duck's pipe dream. Second-tier agencies of this type lacked the resources to produce fully sponsored shows for their clients and so clung to the gentility of their print orientation as consolation. By the late 1950s, television was moving away from full sponsorship in favour of spot ads, allowing a mid-size agency to offer integrated campaigns that included radio and TV commercials. This explains why Sterling Cooper does not have a television department until 1960 – years after the medium has become ubiquitous – and why Harry Crane (Rich Sommer), one of the agency's lowest paid, least well-regarded media buyers, is picked to head it. Despite the billings television is beginning to produce for them, Bert Cooper (Robert Morse) and Roger Sterling (John Slattery) treat it as a necessary evil. The TV department is not the kind of place where a rising star such as Don Draper (Jon Hamm) would want to find himself.[8]

Makeovers

Don, as we learn from scattered flashbacks throughout the series, was born Dick Whitman, the result of a prostitute-john transaction. His biological mother dies in childbirth and the attending midwife carries him to the doorstep of his father, a farmer who accepts responsibility and raises him. Boyhood memories suggest hard times on the prairie and then something much worse after Dick's father dies. We see Dick fleeing with his stepbrother from the home marked by abuse and neglect. Nonetheless, Dick grows into a young man of striking possibilities. Through the eye of his memory, he is depicted as an idyllic, athletic youth in tee-shirt and jeans, living in a world of car engines and spontaneity. Except for his grim expression, he seems a kind of twentieth-century update of Walt Whitman's vision of American masculinity, as articulated in *Leaves of Grass.*[9]

From this blurry chronology of events, a definitive act emerges. Dick sees an opportunity to shed the consequences of his past and seizes it. The last American G.I. standing on a Korean War battlefield, he rips the dog tags from the throat of Don Draper, a dead officer, and steals his identity. Attempts to obliterate the past by reinventing the self occur frequently in American literature. F. Scott Fitzgerald's Jay Gatsby, who does it to win the love of a woman, circa the First World War, is probably the most celebrated example. But Don Draper appears closer in spirit to William Faulkner's Thomas Sutpen, who attempts to overcome the indignities of his hillbilly origins by rebuilding himself into the slave-owning patron of a Mississippi cotton plantation (Faulkner). Young Dick, who suggests Whitman's 'divine *literatus*', a natural American poet unencumbered by the past, becomes Don, who like Faulkner's white-trash slavemaster, is unable to appreciate the virtue of his own innocence when he is mistreated. Hoping to cleanse himself of shame, Dick trades down the divine gift of language for a knack at producing manipulative slogans in service to Mammon, and so, as Don, gets the job and the wife and the house and the presumption of pedigree, and what else? Something is missing, but he doesn't know what. Fulfilment is difficult for him to envision, perhaps impossible to achieve, because the life he has made is an unending series of seductions: clients, mistresses, neighbours and, of course, the buying public. Dick Whitman-as-Don Draper is a life as an advertising campaign: a child spawned in the lost America of love drapes himself in the trappings of a gentleman to sell himself to the world.

The American nature of Dick-as-Don is emphasized by the parallel character of Lane Pryce (Jared Harris), the British financial officer sent by Sterling Cooper's new owners in season two to control costs and keep an eye on the bottom line. Although Pryce knows nothing about Don, per se, a brief time in New York convinces him that secret identity is an American birthright. 'In America, work gives them the chance to succeed without needing to build upon the trappings of family connection, school, social status, etc.', he tells his wife Rebecca (Embeth Davidtz), an unamused Londoner who bristles to return to civilization. 'I've been here six months and nobody has asked me what school I attended', he says ('The Gypsy and the Hobo', 3:37). Although the Americans think of him as a too-proper British gentleman, Pryce is only a cusp-class bureaucrat at Putnam, Powell and Lowe. He loyally serves his unappreciative socially superior bosses, who think nothing of reassigning him from New York to Bombay, without regard for his feelings or future. Pryce envies the Americans their freedom, but as an Englishman, seems incapable of attempting an escape from destiny (à la Don). In the last episode of season three ('Shut the Door. Have a Seat'), he revolts. Screwed once too often by London, Pryce becomes an American, joining Don, Roger and Bert in their plan to defy Putnam's sale of Sterling Cooper by stealing back their own clients and breaking off to form a new agency.

Don's escape from destiny lands him in a thoughtfully placed house in the New York suburbs. Aiming higher than a plot in Levittown, he buys in Ossining, on the eastern shore of the Hudson River in the long, narrow strip of New York State that is geographically and temperamentally tied to New England, but in matters of power – politics, and trade – serves as an outpost of New York City. It was here that John D. Rockefeller came to wash himself clean of Ohio oil and West Virginia coal to become a genteel philanthropist, and where Franklin D. Roosevelt was born to save capitalism from the impractical consequences of its own excess. In 1963, just as Don and Betty (January Jones) are experiencing serious marital problems, Timothy Leary leaves Harvard for a house in Millbrook, 45 minutes north, because, as he wrote in his diary, he no longer cared to 'drink martinis' or otherwise look, think or act like 'several million liberal middle-class intellectual robots'.[10] Ossining is linked to the seat of power in Manhattan by a railroad built at grade along the Hudson by Commodore Vanderbilt, and for those in the motoring mood, by the Taconic State Parkway, which allows no truck to sully its ornately landscaped right of way. (The diesel-belching New York State Thruway, completed just in time for *Mad Men* in 1960, sits miles beyond the west bank of the river, where passenger trains gave up the ghost to busses long ago.) Don may feel especially at home in a town that has a secret identity of its own. Incorporated as Sing Sing in 1825, the village changed names in 1901 to escape association with its famous penitentiary, whose electric chair, beloved 'Old Sparky', began executing prisoners in 1891 and was still in use when the Drapers came to town.

Don buries his head in the *Times* until the train has made its way past Harlem and descended into the Park Avenue tunnels. Living in an eternal shadow of the past, he hides the facts of his life from the people closest to him. When his long-lost stepbrother somehow manages to find him, Don sends him way, offering a check instead of accepting the gift of an intimate capable of sharing his greatest burdens. Don does not kill Dick, but carefully suppresses – locks him in a drawer – so he can conjure an objective correlative when writing effective ad copy. Similarly, Don holds on to his protégé, Peggy (Elisabeth Moss), although her working-class mousiness, pounded into her on the subway, reminds him of everything he has worked so hard to leave behind. He needs her to explain the mysteries of femininity that elude a motherless child. Don demands sexual independence – the privileges of a stud – but hedges his bets by holding on to his wife for as long as he can. Her main line blondness and effortless skill at horseback riding make him believe in his claim to gentility. Don takes pleasure in actions he believes are free of consequence. He smokes and drinks, day and night, seeing no consequence for his mind or body. He has sex with clients, prostitutes and his daughter's teacher, seeing no consequence for his marriage. He has gone so far as to become another person, seeing no consequence for himself.

Don's personal drama will only end when *Mad Men* is cancelled or a sweet movie deal pulls Jon Hamm from the series. Otherwise, with the mythic part of the Sixties still to come, Dick Whitman may yet reclaim Don's body and move it to Ojai, the East Village or Nepal. The seeds of beatnik marijuana have already been planted in the storyline, and many hands will be forced as a hundred flowers bloom. Ken Cosgrove (Aaron Staton) will have to choose between writing fiction and telling lies. Joan Holloway (Christina Hendricks) will decide whether she wants to be valued for her rare organizational abilities or rare bust size. The black power movement will likely send Paul Kinsey (Michael Gladis) to a twelve-step programme. Stonewall awaits Sal (Bryan Batt). Until those forks in the road, *Mad Men* offers viewers an opportunity to reconsider a variety of contemporary behaviours that have not yet gained the political baggage of social, medical or legal consequence: smoking as a personal choice without social consequence and drinking as a personal inclination rather than a disease with genetic overtones. Men bully women with their sexual fantasies on *Mad Men* because it is in their gregarious nature to do so. Parents slug bad kids and reward good ones with plastic bags at play time. This is a drama that makes good use of the willing suspension of disbelief.

Smoking and alcoholism, perhaps because they persist among cultural crimes as desperate problems, are singled out for extreme treatment. On *Mad Men*, characters do not merely smoke at business meetings and in restaurants, they light up in crowded elevators and blow smoke rings. When Don is brought in by a cop on a DUI, he rolls his eyes during the officer's lecture in the style of a wealthy teenager on *Law & Order* who has just run over a homeless person with his father's Escalade. In 'The Gold Violin' (2:20), the Draper family end a Sunday outing by pulling the picnic blanket out from under the garbage, magician-style, before piling into the (sub-10mpg) Caddy to head home.

In seeking the inner life of a guild that stands guard over American consciousness, Weiner has crafted a humane comedy of manners, leaving the viewer room to negotiate personal space between self-congratulatory spikes of moral superiority and giddy escapes into antisocial fantasy. He has done for sexism, racism, anti-green behaviour and other varieties of post-modern selfishness what Andy Warhol did for the Campbell's Soup can, the Brillo box, Marilyn Monroe and Mao Zedong. *Mad Men* disrupts the seamlessness of ubiquity, re-presenting what is common anew to the imagination, the one realm where aesthetic qualities may enjoy a relaxed relationship to social and moral consequence. If such terms as 'imagination' and 'realm' conjure the spectre of Rod Serling, do not attempt to adjust your set. *Mad Men* is cut from the same stone as *The Twilight Zone* (CBS, 1959–64). Its sense of foreboding – the certainty that everything is normal and about to go nuts – pulls the spirit of Serling into every episode of *Mad Man*. The office scenes at Sterling Cooper, in particular, suggest *Patterns*, a 1955 Serling teleplay that warns of a workaholic nightmare tucked behind the Diner's Club card in the corporate lifestyle wallet. *Mad Men* shines a spotlight on the crucial moment in history when art is having its identity stolen by communication, and the sanest people in America are beginning to suspect they are standing in brown fields waiting for cancer. Some of them may yet escape by dropping out.

'The objective of advertising', Marshall McLuhan wrote in 1951 'is the manipulation, exploitation, and control of the individual' (McLuhan, 21). Yet somehow the sensitive souls of Madison Avenue did not return that malice. They called him down from Toronto to ply him with hefty honoraria and multiple martini lunches, taking much too much pleasure in the fact that a bona fide intellectual with a Ph.D. in literature from Cambridge University had looked at their work and called it an art form.[11] In an industry staffed with a surfeit of well-paid operatives skilled at writing, drawing, making films, mixing sound and doing just about anything else that appears to be 'art', but fails to qualify because critics reject it, this recognition was taken as no small pat on the back. If McLuhan had the power to make the advertising industry's production workers into artists, by implication advertising executives were impresarios. They were not destroying teeth by selling hundreds of tons of new sugar or committing murder on the roads by selling cars that did not need to be safe to be sold, or planting the cells of tumors in the lungs of cigarette smokers. They were just putting on a show. *Mad Men* takes up where McLuhan left off by examining, through drama, the personal consequences of believing that the creative act can be devoid of moral consequence.

Works Cited

Ashenberg, Katherine. *The Dirt on Clean,* Toronto: Alfred A. Knopf Canada, 2007.
Faulkner, William. *Absalom, Absalom!* New York: Random House, 1936.
McLuhan, Marshall. *The Mechanical Bride* (1951) rpt. Eric McLuhan and Frank Zingrone (ed.), *The Essential McLuhan.* New York: Basic Books, 1995.

Notes

1 A 'police procedural' is a subgenre of detective fiction in which plot chronology follows the steps of an official police investigation. It is worth noting that the original *Law & Order* television series was structured so that the first half-hour was a police procedural and the second half-hour a courtroom drama. The police procedural proved so much more popular than the courtroom segment that the latter was reduced to an incidental feature in the *Law & Order* spin-offs (*Special Victims Unit*, NBC, 1999-present; and *Criminal Intent*, NBC, 2001–07; USA Network, 2007-present), and is not included at all in some episodes.

2 For an example of the exposition problems faced by occult television series, see the explanation (in writing) of why the character Lorne (Andy Hallett) in *Angel*, a green-skinned nightclub manager with horns on his head is a caring, loving person rather than an evil demon at http://en.wikipedia.org/wiki/Lorne_(Angel).

3 Sitcoms were at the cutting edge of television content during the 1970s, spurring public dialogue on such subjects as ethnic diversity, homosexuality and gender politics. For example, *Maude* (CBS, 1972–78),

a top-rated sitcom produced by Norman Lear, included a two-part episode, seen by an audience numbering in the tens of millions, in which the title character chooses to have an abortion. As odd as it may seem to contemporary viewers, Maude is neither struck by lightning for killing her baby nor awarded the Nobel Peace Prize for acting responsibly. As late as 1992, Vice President Dan Quayle publically criticized the sitcom *Murphy Brown* (CBS, 1988–98) for allowing the title character to give birth to a child out of wedlock without negative consequence.

4 Trivia alert: *Bosom Buddies* (ABC, 1980–82) and *thirtysomething* (ABC, 1987–91) were set at advertising agencies, but neither was set during the 1960s and the latter took place in Philadelphia.

5 This reading of *Mad Men* weighs heavily on two books: Kenneth Burke, *The Philosophy of Literary Form*, 1941 Third Edition (Berkeley: University of California Press, 1978), in which the author argues that the public rhetoric of a democratic society is driven and shaped by private conversations; and James Davison Hunter, *Culture Wars: The Struggle to Define America* (New York: Basic Books, 1991), in which the author catalogues and (accurately) predicts a long-range realignment of American politics based on social and cultural issues that were brought into public rhetoric during the 1960s and found political form in the Reagan presidency.

6 The British Broadcasting Corporation (BBC) was founded as a private corporation in 1922 and came under state control in 1927.

7 Reference for Business, Company History Index at http://www .referenceforbusiness.com/history2/57/Young-Rubicam-Inc.html.

8 See *A Face in the Crowd*, dir. Elia Kazan (1957) DVD, Warner Home Video, 2005, for an evocative portrayal of the dislocation experienced by print-era advertising executives in the television age. A case in point is the character Macey (Paul McGrath), an articulate Princeton graduate. He is repeatedly ridiculed for defending 'dignity' and suffers a heart attack.

9 I refer here to the 1855 edition (the so-called 'sexy' edition). See Malcolm Cowley (ed.), *Walt Whitman's Leaves of Grass*, (New York: Viking Press, 1959).

10 Timothy Leary, (1995). *High Priest* (Berkeley, California: Ronin Publishing), pp. 42–3. From a manuscript written by Leary in 1968.

11 'Advertising is the greatest art form of the twentieth century'. A search performed on this exact quotation will yield more than one hundred websites, many of them scholarly reference sites that attribute it to Marshall McLuhan. Not a single one of them, however, offers a source for the quotation. I agree with William Knowles, a McLuhan scholar

and emeritus professor at the University of Montana, that it sounds more like something McLuhan said than something he wrote, but none of the websites offers an electronic recording to verify that. It is also quite possible that McLuhan neither wrote nor said it, but that the one-liner was made up by an advertising executive and attributed to McLuhan.

Creative Team and Cast List

Creator, Executive Producer, Showrunner, Head Writer and Director:
Matthew Weiner
Co-Executive Producer/Director: Scott Hornbacher
Co-Executive Producer/Writer: Tom Palmer
Supervising Producers: Lisa Albert, Andre Jacquemetton and
Maria Jacquemetton
Co-Producer and Writer: Dahvi Waller
Producers: Dwayne Shattuck, Blake McCormick and Todd London
Executive Story Editors: Cathryn Humphris and Robin Veith
Script Supervisor: Jennifer Getzinger
Staff Writers: Kater Gordon, Bridget Bedard, Chris Provenzano,
Rick Cleveland, Andrew Colville and Brett Johnson
Directors: Alan Taylor, Ed Bianchi, Tim Hunter, Lesli Linka Glatter,
Andrew Bernstein, Phil Abraham, Paul Feig, Jennifer Getzinger,
Michael Uppendahl, Daisy von Scherler Mayer and Barbet Schroeder
Production Designer: Dan Bishop
Art Director: Christopher Brown
Set Designers: Camille Bratkowski and Mark Haber
Directors of Photography: Chris Manley, Phil Abraham, Frank G.
DeMarco, Bill Roe and Steve Mason
Costume Designer: Katherine Jane Bryant
Supervising Editor: Malcolm Jamieson
Editors: Chris Nelson, Tom Wilson, Cindy Mollo, Conrad Smart,
Malcolm Jamieson, David Seigel and Leo Trombetta
Composer: David Carbonara
Music Supervisor: Alex Patsavas
Music Editor: Jenny Barak
Set Decorator: Amy Wells

Sound Mixer: Peter Bentley
Special Effects: Tom Bellissimo

Cast List

Don Draper: Jon Hamm
Betty Draper: January Jones
Roger Sterling: John Slattery
Joan Holloway Harris: Christina Hendricks
Peggy Olson: Elisabeth Moss
Pete Campbell: Vincent Kartheiser
Bertram Cooper: Robert Morse
Paul Kinsey: Michael Gladis
Ken Cosgrove: Aaron Staton
Harry Crane: Rich Sommer
Salvatore Romano: Bryan Batt
Herman 'Duck' Phillips: Mark Moses
Lane Pryce: Jared Harris
Freddy Rumsen: Joel Murray
Trudy Campbell: Alison Brie
Francine Hanson: Anne Dudek
Sally Draper: Kiernan Shipka
Bobby Draper: Jared Gilmore
Gene Hofstadt: Ryan Cutrona
William Hofstadt: Eric Laden
Conrad 'Connie' Hilton: Chelcie Ross
Rachel Menken: Maggie Siff
Midge Daniels: Rosemarie DeWitt
Bobby Barrett: Melinda McGraw
Jimmy Barrett: Patrick Fischler
Miss Farrell: Abigail Spencer
Henry Francis: Christopher Stanley
Mona Sterling: Talia Balsam
Margaret Sterling: Elizabeth Rice
Jane Siegel Sterling: Peyton List
Greg Harris: Sam Page
Father John Gill: Colin Hanks
Lois Sadler: Crista Flanagan
Kurt: Edin Gali
Lee Garner, Jr.: Darren Pettie

Episode Guide

Season One

1:1 'Smoke Gets in Your Eyes'
Original Airdate: 19 July 2007
Written by: Matthew Weiner
Directed by: Alan Taylor

1:2 'Ladies Room'
Original Airdate: 26 July 2007
Written by: Matthew Weiner
Directed by: Alan Taylor

1:3 'Marriage of Figaro'
Original Airdate: 2 August 2007
Written by: Tom Palmer
Directed by: Ed Bianchi

1:4 'New Amsterdam'
Original Airdate: 9 August 2007
Written by: Lisa Albert
Directed by: Tim Hunter

1:5 '5G'
Original Airdate: 16 August 2007
Written by: Matthew Weiner
Directed by: Lesli Linka Glatter

1:6 'Babylon'
Original Airdate: 23 August 2007
Written by: Andre Jacquemetton and Maria Jacquemetton
Directed by: Andrew Bernstein

1:7 'Red in the Face'
Original Airdate: 30 August 2007
Written by: Bridget Bedard
Directed by: Tim Hunter

1:8 'The Hobo Code'
Original Airdate: 6 September 2007
Written by: Chris Provenzano
Directed by: Phil Abraham

1:9 'Shoot'
Original Airdate: 13 September 2007
Written by: Chris Provenzano and Matthew Weiner
Directed by: Paul Feig

1:10 'Long Weekend'
Original Airdate: 27 September 2007
Written by: Bridget Bedard, Andre Jacquemetton,
    Maria Jacquemetton and Matthew Weiner
Directed by: Tim Hunter

1:11 'Indian Summer'
Original Airdate: 4 October 2007
Written by: Tom Palmer and Matthew Weiner
Directed by: Tim Hunter

1:12 'Nixon vs. Kennedy'
Original Airdate: 11 October 2007
Written by: Lisa Albert, Andre Jacquemetton
    and Maria Jacquemetton
Directed by: Alan Taylor

1:13 'The Wheel'
Original Airdate: 18 October 2007
Written by: Matthew Weiner and Robin Veith
Directed by: Matthew Weiner

Season Two

2:14 'For Those Who Think Young'
Original Airdate: 27 July 2008
Written by: Matthew Weiner
Directed by: Tim Hunter

2:15 'Flight 1'
Original Airdate: 3 August 2008
Written by: Lisa Albert and Matthew Weiner
Directed by: Andrew Bernstein

2:16 'The Benefactor'
Original Airdate: 10 August 2008
Written by: Matthew Weiner and Rick Cleveland
Directed by: Lesli Linka Glatter

2:17 'Three Sundays'
Original Airdate: 17 August 2008
Written by: Andre Jacquemetton and Maria Jacquemetton
Directed by: Tim Hunter

2:18 'The New Girl'
Original Airdate: 24 August 2008
Written by: Robin Veith
Directed by: Jennifer Getzinger

2:19 'Maidenform'
Original Airdate: 31 August 2008
Written by: Matthew Weiner
Directed by: Phil Abraham

2:20 'The Gold Violin'
Original Airdate: 7 September 2008
Written by: Jane Anderson, Andre Jacquemetton and
    Maria Jacquemetton
Directed by: Andrew Bernstein

2:21 'A Night to Remember'
Original Airdate: 14 September 2008
Written by: Robin Veith and Matthew Weiner
Directed by: Lesli Linka Glatter

2:22 'Six Month Leave'
Original Airdate: 28 September 2008
Written by: Andre Jacquemetton, Maria Jacquemetton
    and Matthew Weiner
Directed by: Michael Uppendahl

2:23 'The Inheritance'
Original Airdate: 5 October 2008
Written by: Lisa Albert, Marti Noxon and Matthew Weiner
Directed by: Andrew Bernstein

2:24 'The Jet Set'
Original Airdate: 12 October 2008
Written by: Matthew Weiner
Directed by: Phil Abraham

2:25 'The Mountain King'
Original Airdate: 19 October 2008
Written by: Matthew Weiner and Robin Veith
Directed by: Alan Taylor

2:26 'Meditations in an Emergency'
Original Airdate: 26 October 2008
Written by: Matthew Weiner and Kater Gordon
Directed by: Matthew Weiner

Season Three

3:27 'Out of Town'
Original Airdate: 16 August 2009
Written by: Matthew Weiner
Directed by: Phil Abraham

3:28 'Love Among the Ruins'
Original Airdate: 23 August 2009
Written by: Cathryn Humphris and Matthew Weiner
Directed by: Lesli Linka Glatter

3:29 'My Old Kentucky Home'
Original Airdate: 30 August 2009
Written by: Dahvi Waller and Matthew Weiner
Directed by: Jennifer Getzinger

3:30 'The Arrangements'
Original Airdate: 6 September 2009
Written by: Andrew Colville and Matthew Weiner
Directed by: Michael Uppendahl

3:31 'The Fog'
Original Airdate: 13 September 2009
Written by: Kater Gordon
Directed by: Phil Abraham

3:32 'Guy Walks into an Advertising Agency'
Original Airdate: 20 September 2009
Written by: Robin Veith and Matthew Weiner
Directed by: Lesli Linka Glatter

3:33 'Seven Twenty Three'
Original Airdate: 27 September 2009
Written by: Andre Jacquemetton, Maria Jacquemetton
    and Matthew Weiner
Directed by: Daisy von Scherler Mayer

3:34 'Souvenir'
Original Airdate: 4 October 2009
Written by: Lisa Albert and Matthew Weiner
Directed by: Phil Abraham

3:35 'Wee Small Hours'
Original Airdate: 11 October 2009
Written by: Dahvi Waller and Matthew Weiner
Directed by: Scott Hornbacher

3:36 'The Color Blue'
Original Airdate: 18 October 2009
Written by: Kater Gordon and Matthew Weiner
Directed by: Michael Uppendahl

3:37 'The Gypsy and the Hobo'
Original Airdate: 25 October 2009
Written by: Marti Noxon, Cathryn Humphris
    and Matthew Weiner
Directed by: Jennifer Getzinger

3:38 'The Grown-Ups'
Original Airdate: 1 November 2009
Written by: Brett Johnson and Matthew Weiner
Directed by: Barbet Schroeder

3:39 'Shut the Door. Have a Seat'
Original Airdate: 8 November 2009
Written by: Matthew Weiner and Erin Levy
Directed by: Matthew Weiner

Season Four

4:40 'Public Relations'
Original Airdate: 28 July 2010
Written by: Matthew Weiner
Directed by: Phil Abraham

4:41 'Christmas Comes But Once a Year'
Original Airdate: 1 August 2010
Written by: Tracy McMillan and Matthew Weiner
Directed by: Michael Uppendahl

4:42 'The Good News'
Original Airdate: 8 August 2010
Written by: Jonathan Abrahams and Matthew Weiner
Directed by: Jennifer Getzinger

4:43 'The Rejected'
Original Airdate: 15 August 2010
Written by: Keith Huff and Matthew Weiner
Directed by: John Slattery

4:44 'The Chrysanthemum and the Sword'
Original Airdate: 22 August 2010
Written by: Erin Levy
Directed by: Lesli Linka Glatter

4:45 'Waldorf Stories'
Original Airdate: 29 August 2010
Written by: Brett Johnson, and Matthew Weiner
Directed by: Scott Hornbacher

4:46 'The Suitcase'
Original Airdate: 5 September 2010
Written by: Matthew Weiner
Directed by: Jennifer Getzinger

4:47 'The Summer Man'
Original Airdate: 12 September 2010
Written by: Lisa Albert, Janet Leahy, and Matthew Weiner
Directed by: Phil Abraham

4:48 'The Beautiful Girls'
Original Airdate: 19 September 2010
Written by: Dahvi Waller and Matthew Weiner
Directed by: Michael Uppendahl

4:49 'Hands and Knees'
Original Airdate: 26 September 2010
Written by: Jonathan Abrahams and Matthew Weiner
Directed by: Lynn Shelton

4:50 'Chinese Wall'
Original Airdate: 3 October 2010
Written by: Erin Levy
Directed by: Phil Abraham

4:51 'Blowing Smoke'
Original Airdate: 10 October 2010
Written by: Andre Jacquemetton and Maria Jacquemetton
Directed by: John Slattery

4:52 'Tomorrowland'
Original Airdate: 17 October 2010
Written by: Jonathan Igla and Matthew Weiner
Directed by: Matthew Weiner

General Index

For titles of television programmes and individual television episodes, see *Television Series Index*

Television Series Index

N.b.: Television programme titles are italicized. Individual episode titles (all of which are from *Mad Men* unless otherwise noted) are enclosed in quotation marks with the season number and episode number provided in parentheses.